# Merchants of Fear

## An Investigation of Canada's Insurance Industry

# James Fleming

VIKING

VIKING

Penguin Books Canada Limited, 2801 John Street, Markham, Ontario, Canada
L3R 1B4
Penguin Books, Harmondsworth, Middlesex, England
Viking Penguin Inc., 40 West 23rd Street, New York, New York 10010 U.S.A.
Penguin Books Australia Ltd., Ringwood, Victoria, Australia
Penguin Books (N.Z.) Ltd., Private Bag, Takapuna, Auckland 9, New Zealand

First published by Penguin Books Canada Limited, 1986

Printed and bound in the United States of America


**Canadian Cataloguing in Publication Data**

Fleming, James MacLean, 1951-
    Merchants of fear

ISBN 0-670-80759-1

1. Insurance — Canada.  2. Insurance Companies — Canada.
3. Insurance — Canada — Finance.  I. Title.

HG8550.F54 1986        368'.971        C86-094373-9

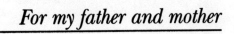

*For my father and mother*

# Acknowledgements

Samuel Johnson, the eighteenth-century English poet, critic and essayist, once said of the act of writing: "Nothing is ended with honour which does not conclude better than it began." I am heavily indebted to numerous people who, over the course of two years, helped me turn some rather inchoate ideas into a completed manuscript.

My original motivation to write the book arose out of the recognition that there was a great need for a systematic analysis of the past record as well as the current strengths and weaknesses of Canada's life insurance industry; a book that would not only profile important people and companies but also search for patterns of behaviour, good and bad, that have characterized the industry over the decades, and make concrete proposals for change. The project could not have been brought to fruition without the assistance of certain key individuals.

Thanks to my agent, David Colbert, who proposed that I write the book in the first place and thereafter served as my confidant and guide through a new and labyrinthine world of contracts and deadlines. I am indebted to the people at Penguin Books, whose confidence in my abilities often surpassed my own and who never failed to provide words of encouragement and support when they were most needed. Publisher Morty Mint, whose energy pervades the whole company, recognized from the start that insurance is a subject that can variously outrage and intrigue readers, and his enthusiasm for the book never flagged. Senior editor David Kilgour served as an uncompromising arbiter of the manuscript's content and style. His suggestions for revisions and additions were always insightful, and his ability to coax more out of a tired writer through gentle persuasion and heartening words was remarkable. Copy editor Kathryn Dean displayed unsurpassed diligence as she scrutinized each word and line of the manuscript, improving sentence structure, clarifying confusing passages and fixing errors and repetitive phrases. Thanks also to Bob Scott, a freelance researcher, who tracked down missing facts for me in his usual thorough manner. These people saved me from embarrassing shortcomings in the book's style and content; any that remain are solely my responsibility.

No first-time author should be without the wise counsel of an individual who has already travelled the alternately exhilarating and exhausting road of book writing. In my case that individual was Peter Cook, editor of the *Report on Business Magazine*. Thanks to him for his advice, as well as for the patience he and my other colleagues at the magazine showed for my sometimes itinerant ways.

I also extend my gratitude to several librarians who selflessly gave of their time to help me track down a multitude of articles, books and annual reports. The efforts of Celia Donnelly and Mary-Jane Wilson of *The Globe and Mail* business library were tireless. So, too, was the assistance of Theresa Butcher, chief librarian of the Maclean-Hunter library. Other helpful librarians working at newspapers and insurance companies across the country are too numerous to mention. I thank them all.

I am most indebted to Christine, my wife. She carried the twin responsibilities of working at a full-time job and running a household while the book was in gestation. Thanks also to my two children, Sarah, 8, and Iain, 3, who for the better part of two years knew their father as that man working in the study with the door closed. Perhaps they will become part of a new generation of consumers who are better informed about an industry whose activities affect everyone.

James Fleming
Toronto, July 1986

# Contents

# Merchants
of Fear

# Introduction

The chauffeur-driven Cadillac Sedan de Villes, sleek Jaguar Sovereigns and Mercedes sedans began arriving at the hideaway at about four in the afternoon. Winding down a country road near Lake Simcoe amid the drizzle and fog of an early April day, they turned into a secluded, tree-lined laneway that led them to their destination—an elegant stone manor on the sprawling grounds of The Briars, a 200-acre luxury resort about an hour's drive north of Toronto. The Briars is an oasis of refinement and grandeur amid the farmland and rustic villages of southern Ontario's cottage country. For weary members of the monied class, the manor itself offers the comforts of fine living: its elegant dining rooms, original oils and thick carpets have more in common with a private men's club than a holiday resort.[1] But on this spring day, The Briars had become the exclusive preserve of the men who climb out of the luxury automobiles at the manor's front door. For the next three days

---

[1] Named after an estate on the island of St Helena which once provided refuge for Napoleon, The Briars estate was originally carved out of the southern Ontario wilderness in about 1820 by a British navy captain, William Bourchier. A veteran of the Napoleonic War, Captain Bourchier received the land as a grant from the Crown in 1819. In subsequent decades, a succession of well-heeled owners steadily expanded its perimeter with outbuildings and lawns. In 1977, it was reincarnated as a commercial resort.

1

they will be discussing issues that affect Canadians from Vancouver to Halifax and millions of foreign citizens as well.

They are the senior executives of Canada's $70-billion life insurance industry, a collection of 169 large and small companies that do business with the roughly 13 million Canadians who hold individual life insurance policies and another 25 million people around the world who are covered by group plans through their employers. In total, Canadians have $679 billion worth of life insurance; that ranks them among the most security-conscious people in the world. On a per capita basis, Canadians, with an average $26,900 of insurance each, are surpassed only by the Japanese, who own an average of $35,400 (Cdn) and the Americans, with $30,710.[2] With more than $16 billion in assets, Manufacturers Life Insurance Co. of Toronto is the largest of Canada's life insurance companies and ranks among the 15 largest insurers in North America. But it is dwarfed by the likes of the Prudential Insurance Company of America, the largest U.S. insurer, with assets of $91.7 billion (U.S.) Still, Canada's insurers have a strong international presence. More than 2 million people in 20 countries around the world own life insurance policies worth $228 billion from Canadian companies. The biggest foreign market for Canada's insurers is in the United States, where residents buy 80 per cent of the insurance Canadian companies sell abroad each year; residents of the United Kingdom buy 16 per cent; Caribbean and Latin American clients buy about 2 per cent; and inhabitants of Asia buy another 2 per cent.

The gathering of life insurance chief executives at The Briars is a rather remarkable event in Canadian business. Every year, they repair to some suitably secluded spot for a top-secret parlay. Lesser souls like chief operating officers, vice-presidents or aides of any sort are strictly excluded. The industry body

[2]These figures are for the end of 1984 and are the latest comparative statistics compiled by the Canadian Life and Health Insurance Association (CLHIA).

which organizes the event, the Canadian Life and Health Insurance Association (CLHIA), calls it, rather innocuously, a seminar. In fact, it is a conclave, unparalleled in the rest of Canadian business, which allows the captains of life insurance to compare notes on a host of troubling common concerns while they sip gin, play pool or relax in a jacuzzi. No written record of the heart-to-heart chats is even provided to the companies the executives represent, let alone to the general public. Indeed, the existence of the annual get-togethers is little known outside insurance circles. CLHIA representatives are quick to point out that the talks never relate to such unseemly topics as price fixing, which would break federal anti-combines laws. But it is surely consoling to the chief executives to be able to hob-nob with their counterparts in other companies, to thrash out shared problems and to chat about the future of the industry. The get-togethers are like glorified T-groups for uptight executives.

At the April 1986 meeting, the sense of camaraderie begins the moment the men walk in the door. After checking in at a reception desk where a pleasant clerk hands out room keys, the guests stroll into a nearby lounge where earlier arrivals are already milling about. Competitors in the business world, they are colleagues in this refuge of serenity. In one corner near the bar, Earl Orser, the chubby, energetic chairman of London Life Insurance holds forth on the latest industry developments to a circle of listeners, including John Acheson, the soon-to-retire chairman of Dominion Life. Just yesterday, the House of Commons Committee on Finance took the unprecedented step of summonsing a number of executives from London Life's corporate parent, Trilon Financial Corp., to testify about the dangers of self-dealing (carrying out transactions between subsidiaries or between subsidiaries and their parents) in corporate conglomerates. Orser seems variously shocked and intrigued by this unusual event. Elsewhere, lesser lights in the insurance world are renewing old ties. Down the bar, a couple of reinsurance company heads talk about the hard times in their business, which specializes in sharing part of the risk on life insurance policies in return for a cut of the premiums. Many of the executives have already gone to their rooms to freshen up for dinner in the Explorers' Room.

The dinner, held after more drinks at a well-stocked bar at the rear of the dining room, is a very relaxed affair. There are the senior statesmen of Canadian companies, like Orser, and Jack Masterman, the CEO of Mutual Life; the czars of foreign interlopers, like Gordon Farquhar of Aetna Canada and Charles (Skip) Armstrong of Metropolitan Life; and the fringe players from smaller companies. The class distinctions dissolve in an atmosphere of male companionship as jokes are exchanged and the dinner proceeds.

But there is an unmistakable undercurrent of anxiety beneath the conviviality in the group. The executives know that in discussion groups over the next two days, they will have to deal with some very contentious issues, including plans for the creation of an industry-administered policy-holder compensation fund, which would cover policyholder losses in the event of a company failure. The idea has been forced on the industry. Most of the executives think the plan is unnecessary but they know if they don't do it, the federal government will do it for them. Then, too, there will be free time to discuss the slew of controversies that has enveloped the industry, from the misdeeds and low image of agents, to consumer paranoia about the growth of financial conglomerates and the associated issues of concentration of power, self-dealing and conflicts of interest. Many of the executives regard these unsettling issues as they would a bad case of indigestion that, hopefully, with the help of a Rolaid, will just go away and let them continue the comfortable existence they have enjoyed for decades. An alert minority knows differently.

## *Silent Partners*

For most of their existence, insurance companies have operated in a comfortable and carefully nurtured anonymity as far as the public is concerned. That is a remarkable fact, considering their pervasive role in the lives of Canadians and their hefty contribution to Canada's economic well-being. The life companies comprise the largest, most important sector of Canada's insurance industry. They employ more than 60,000 people, of which about 35,000 are engaged in administrative work and another 24,000 in sales. As a group, life insurers annually pump billions of dollars into the economic system by investing more than $60 billion worth of assets in government bonds, corporate stocks, mortgages on homes and businesses, and real estate. Life insurance is sold by mutual companies, which have no shareholders and are theoretically owned by their policyholders, and by stock companies, which are owned by shareholders. (A tiny proportion of life policies is also sold by an odd assortment of 41 fraternal benefit societies, such as the Grand Orange Lodge, the Canadian Woodmen, and the Order of Italo-Canadians, which provide coverage for their members.)

Life insurance companies offer a variety of products to the public, including a range of life policies, registered retirement savings plans (RRSPs) and annuities. The majority of life insurers also offer health insurance. More than 22 million Canadians are covered by disability insurance (which protects against loss of income if the insured becomes disabled), extended health care plans (which pay medical bills not covered by provincial plans) and dental plans.

But consumers who want to insure their home or car must obtain coverage from property and casualty (P & C) insurance companies, otherwise known as general insurers. These companies also offer coverage to businesses that want to insure their buildings, equipment or goods; to professionals who want coverage against lawsuits from dissatisfied clients; and to organizations, ranging from day-care centres to governments, that need liability insurance to protect them from lawsuits brought, for instance, by victims of accidents on their premises. The Insurance Bureau of Canada (IBC), the general industry's public relations body, estimates that 114,000 people work in the private general industry in Canada. Thousands more are employed by government-run automobile insurance organizations in British Columbia, Saskatchewan, Manitoba and Quebec. General insurance companies have more than $18 billion in assets; their investments range from bonds and stocks to oil rigs. General insurance is the lubricant that keeps the engine of the economy turning over.

The arcane reaches of the insurance world are inhabited by a low-profile group of foreign-owned companies: the reinsurers. A total of 45 reinsurance companies operate through branches or subsidiaries in Canada, most of them specializing in sharing the risk on policies sold to the public by property and casualty companies. Typically, a general insurer signs a treaty with a reinsurer in which the reinsurer agrees to share 50 per cent of the risk on the policies the general insurer sells. In return, the general insurer pays the reinsurer 50 per cent of the premiums collected from policyholders. If a claim occurs, each company pays 50 per cent of the amount. This spreads the risk around to prevent unexpected claims from bankrupting the general insurer. Sometimes, the reinsurer goes one step further and spreads the risk it has undertaken to several other reinsurers. It can be an almost endless chain of risk sharing, with every company along the way taking a share of the profits from premiums. The same system can also apply to a single, large policy. In yet another variation, called excess loss insurance, the reinsurer agrees to pay claims in excess of an agreed amount—for instance, anything over $1 million.

In 1985 alone, reinsurance companies raked in $1 billion in premiums by reinsuring general insurance policies. A smaller

group of 16 federally registered reinsurance companies specializes in offering reinsurance on life policies. But most life reinsurance (80 per cent) is handled by the major life insurance companies themselves. If a consumer happens to have a
$1 million life insurance policy, the odds are that his company
has ceded (passed on) 50 per cent of the risk to another life
insurer or to a reinsurance company.

## Sins of Omission and Commission

Canada's insurance industry has enough skeletons in its closet
to keep a team of osteologists busy for a year. The men who
have presided over life insurance companies in past decades
(women are only now reaching the outer fringes of power)
have done so in sublime indifference to many of their industry's shortcomings. That is not to say that insurance executive
suites have been inhabited by brigands or swindlers—though
the industry has had its share of rogues. If all the industry's
chief executives and company directors, past and present, were
gathered together at a grand convention (a favourite pastime
of insurance world denizens), they would look like a pretty
respectable lot. Men of money and influence all: financiers,
lawyers, actuaries, a healthy smattering of politicians and even
a few prime ministers. At the bar, you might see Sir John A.
Macdonald (the first president of Manufacturers Life) chatting
about business with Sir Charles Tupper (the first president of
Crown Life) or George Gooderham, a distiller and financier
who was a founding director of Manufacturers. Then, too,
there would be many once-prominent faces now seen only in
the grainy photographs of company history books, from which
the executives peer severely in their morning coats and wing-
back collars.

Despite their pedigree, some of the industry's earliest leaders misused the money policyholders entrusted to them, investing it in ill-fated ventures in which they had large personal

interests. Other company owners treated the insurance business as just another way—the easiest way, in fact—to add to
their personal fortunes. Over the decades, the majority of insurance executives have treated their responsibilities as overseers
of policyholders' funds with the utmost seriousness. They have
thought it a happy coincidence that their diligent handling of
vast pools of cash has also enabled them and their companies
to prosper. But it is not a happy coincidence. As much as the
executives hate to admit it, the interests of common men and
women have generally taken a back seat to building up profits
and making their companies so stable that they are now more
like mausoleums than modern corporations.

By the 1950s the ossification process was so far gone that the
industry didn't seem to notice as the rest of the world of commerce passed it by. While other industries experimented with
new management techniques, getting rid of old paternalistic
approaches and promoting people on the basis of merit, not
longevity, the insurance fraternity lived a Rip Van Winkle existence. As other capitalists were cooking up new approaches to
meet the changing needs and desires of consumers, insurance
companies offered up the same old gruel: decades-old policies
that offered little variety and paltry rates of return to policyholders, who were given to believe that they had purchased
both a clever savings vehicle and an insurance contract. These
are the industry's collective sins of omission.

But there have also been sins of commission. Down the hall
from the gathering of executives at the fictitious convention,
there is a loud, much larger gathering of life insurance agents.
(The two groups have never liked each other much.) Standing
in gaggles, the agents are a bumptious lot: the talk is loud and
the jokes are funny as each one attempts to draw attention to
himself. (There are few females in attendance; women are
newcomers to the business and currently make up only about
15 per cent of life insurance agents in Canada.) Some recount
earnest stories of how they saved widows and children from

destitution. Others tell funny tales about how they scared the pants off clients and clinched a sale with fabrications about the hardship encountered by people who didn't buy insurance. This tactic is called "backing the hearse to the door," and most of the nattily dressed group admit that they have resorted to it at one time or another.

Exploiting clients' fear of calamity: it has worked well for the life industry as a whole over the years. A line in a London Life agent's manual from the late 1800s is typical of the time-tested approach. Composed by a head office bureaucrat to inspire the troops, it read: "It's an awful thing for a man on his death-bed to consider, that, ere his corpse grows cold his widow may be haggling with the undertaker for the price of a coffin." Some companies still go through comparable routines in employee training programs. An agent in a major Toronto-based company recalls that when she was being trained along with a group of other recruits they were all shown a film that was designed to impress upon them the importance of life insurance. The film depicted a happy mother and father walking through a park with two children. Suddenly, the father disappeared, leaving only a dotted-line silhouette of where he once stood. The agent says she walked out of the session in disgust.

In a room within earshot of the boisterous group of the life agents, a smaller group of more subdued insurance people is talking quietly about fire prevention and the alarming increase in property thefts over the years. All of the men in this hall are wearing galoshes in case it rains. They are the executives, adjusters and assorted clerks of the property and casualty indus-try who spent their lives in the practical business of insuring homes, cars, ships and boilers. (They are all together because they usually saw eye to eye in life; they shared a common mission of fending off fraudulent claims by customers.) Most of them have foreign accents—British, Swiss and German—and all are busily complaining about how they had to spend most of their careers in that God-forsaken place, Canada. Some of them, notably those from companies that have failed, chat about how vicious the business cycles are in general insurance; the reinsurance company staff mingling among them nod their heads in agreement. Others talk about how easy it was to sell general insurance compared to life insurance, since customers usually came to them to buy it, rather than the other way around. But a few confide that they, too, resorted to scare tactics in their advertising, to lure clients to their door.

Exploiting fear has always worked well for agents haggling over a kitchen table with a prospective customer and, on a wider scale, for companies trying to attract business through publicity. Insurers have always told prospective customers that their products offer security and protection from life's set-backs. There is an ill-defined line between stressing protection and exploiting fear, however, and some of the earliest advertise-ments trod dangerously close to that line. In 1923, Imperial Life startled its more conservative competitors by using posters showing a large umbrella. The text below the picture read: "Is this all you have put away for a rainy day?" But the heyday of scare campaigns began in the 1940s. Life insurers set the pace. Take, for example, a chilling newspaper ad of 1940s vintage put out by Confederation Life. It shows the sombre face of a young executive. Half of the face is blacked out. The caption below reads: "Jim was only half insured," and the text goes on to say, "...he didn't realize it until a friend died and his widow asked him for advice. Then the inadequacy of his friend's life insurance started Jim thinking about his own."

More morbid messages poured out of the offices of the property and casualty insurers. One noteworthy example from the same era is an ad put out jointly by the companies writ-ing automobile insurance in Ontario. It depicts a terrible crash scene with smoke and flames rising from two cars. In one corner a group of people is standing over a casualty; in another, a survivor is talking to a police officer. Large letters scrawled across the picture proclaim: "The truth about car insurance."

In succeeding years, insurers mixed the message of fear with lines that pulled at the heart strings of potential buyers. A 1955 London Life ad depicts a young executive shaking hands with a new boss. The message below says: "His father would have been both proud and happy, if he had lived to see this day. He did not live—but the life insurance he provided for his family enabled this boy to complete his education in preparation for the career of his choosing." A 1956 plug for Mutual Life shows a lovely home with the warning: "It could be protected by mortgage insurance—so that if anything should happen to the owner, his family could go on living in it and be spared the heartbreak and trouble of moving into less comfortable living quarters." Metropolitan Life ended a 1966 ad for life insurance with the line: "There's no obligation—except to those you love." A 1968 shocker by the Canadian Surety Company mixed fright with a public service message promoting driver education courses. It showed the silhouette of a paraplegic man sitting in a wheelchair. The message reads: "Remember lucky Bill. He's 42 now. Lucky Bill hasn't walked in 22 years. His home is a wheelchair. His world is a hospital ward. He's completely paralyzed. One moment...ONE SECOND...cost him a lifetime."

In recent years, most insurance companies have toned down their attempts to scare consumers into buying their product. The themes of responsibility to loved ones and preparing for a secure retirement are now dominant. Many companies, conscious of the aging of the population and the growing demand for retirement products, stress planning for the future. For example, London Life's ads stress: "Life is for the Living." But fear tactics are alive and well in the agents' bag of sales tricks and they keep creeping back into advertising campaigns, if in a less offensive way. Blue Cross, a company that offers group medical and dental plans to employees of 40,295 Canadian companies, has a television advertising campaign that appeals directly to the worries of travellers. The scene shows a married man in his mid-thirties in a hospital ward. He's talking anxiously on the phone, obviously to a relative back home, and saying: "She'll be in hospital for at least a week." Then a male voice-over warns: "Outside Canada, emergency hospital bills may have to be paid up front and you may not have the money." Metropolitan Life launched a multimedia advertising blitz in 1986 featuring the cast of characters from the Peanuts cartoon strip. Some are plain funny, others mix humour with fear of life's pitfalls. One shows Linus sucking his thumb and clutching a blanket. The caption reads: "Happiness is a Metropolitan security blanket." Another shows Snoopy skipping along, and then tripping. The message: "Unless you have the reflexes of a mongoose, get Met; it pays."

### The Origins of Insurance

Insurance is a business like no other. It is not something tangible that a buyer can consume, drive or show off to the neighbours. It exists for one major reason: human fear of calamity. There is nothing inherently wrong with that. Peace of mind is a worthwhile objective for anyone. Insurance becomes a problem only when the industry exploits consumer fears unduly. For country singer Dolly Parton, security means insuring her breasts for $3 million. Actress Betty Grable insured her legs for $1 million. Canadian-born master magician Doug Henning has a $3-million policy on his hands. Ambitious human endeavours, from the exploration of North America to the launching of space satellites, would never have happened without insurance. Strength in numbers: that is the essential idea behind insurance in all its forms. Insurance policies spread the risk of death or accidents from the policyholder to the insurance company. The company, in turn, often spreads the risk further still, to reinsurance companies. That way no one is left destitute or bankrupt if a loss occurs.

Insurance may not be the world's oldest profession, but it certainly has been around for a long time. Thirty-seven centuries ago, in Babylon, when Hammurabi's code was the law of the day, travellers were insured against muggings, farmers against crop failure and merchants against loss of cargo. From there the insurance idea was developed by the Rhodians, the Phoenicians and the Greeks, who developed marine insurance in its earliest form. Roman *collegia* (burial societies) defrayed the cost of funerals for paid-up members. In mediaeval Europe, trade guilds offered fire and health insurance to members of a common occupation. But modern-day insurance emerged in England during the seventeenth century, and, strangely enough, owes its existence to the introduction of coffee to England.

Popular history has it that the Archbishop of Canterbury, William Laud, introduced the drink to English society in the mid-1600s. The Archbishop learned of its pleasing taste from a Cretan *emigré*, a scholar he had brought home to study at Oxford. Coffee was not about to supplant beer or tea as an English favourite, but its introduction did spawn the creation of coffee houses, where merchants gathered to talk business and to trade gossip. One such coffee house was opened by Edward Lloyd some time shortly before 1687 on Tower Street in London. In 1691, Lloyd moved his shop to more spacious quarters on Lombard Street, and within years it became the chief commercial sales room in England, where ships, wine, and brandy, among other items, were sold at auction. Eventually, Lloyd's customers also got into the business of marine insurance. They set up informal groups (later called syndicates), whose members collected premiums from shipowners, and in return, literally wrote their names at the end of a document (thus the term underwriters) that held them liable to a portion of the loss if a ship sank. Today Lloyd's is the largest and best-known market for insurance in the world. Lloyd's is not a company; it is a $5 billion market where brokers meet to place business with about 23,000 underwriting members who accept risks from all over the world. Profits for members can be high, but there have been rough patches over the years, too. The 1906 San Francisco earthquake cost Lloyd's members $100 million. Losses from the sinking of the Titanic in 1912 totalled a more manageable, but still substantial, $5 million. At present, its members are struggling under the weight of undetermined losses piling up over asbestos-related lawsuits in the United States. Thus far, the few thousand claims settled have cost them $1 billion. But a 1981 scandal involving crooked underwriting managers who misappropriated more than $50 million in investors' funds has done even more damage to the market by besmirching its once impeccable reputation.

Compared to insurance in England, which has existed for 300 years, the North American version is only middle-aged. The first American insurance company was founded in Charles Town (later Charleston), South Carolina, in 1735. Called the Friendly Society for the Mutual Insurance of Houses Against Fire, it was a shortlived venture. In 1740, half the city burned to the ground and the fledgling company went broke. Another early company was founded by Benjamin Franklin a few years later. It was called the Philadelphia Contributorship for the Insurance of Houses from Loss by Fire. Later, its name was changed to Hand-in-Hand, and it is still in existence. Mutual Life Insurance Co. of New York—the first modern life insurance company in the United States—set up shop in 1843 on what is now Wall Street.

In Canada, general insurance companies have been operating since 1804, when Phoenix of London set up an office in Montreal. In 1809 the first Canadian insurance company, The Fire Association of Halifax (later known as the Halifax

Insurance Company) was founded. Both companies are still operating today. Life insurance appeared on the scene much later. The first life company to set up shop was the U.K.-based Standard Life, which opened in Quebec City in 1833. Slightly more than a decade later, in 1847, the first Canadian life company, Canada Life, was founded. It was Hugh Baker, a Hamilton, Ontario, bank manager who launched the venture after he got fed up with having to make a 1,000-mile trip to New York by horseback, stagecoach and steamboat to buy a life insurance policy.

### An Industry in Turmoil

The life insurance executives who gathered at The Briars in 1986 had more troubling issues to consider than the industry has ever faced before. In the past, life insurance companies had much in common with the church in the public's mind—both were required for certain rites of passage in life. In much the same way that many people call on a parson or priest only when they get married or die, some have thought that insurance companies are useful only at times of great or sudden change: when they get married, need protection from calamity, retire and need an annuity, or die. But that is all changing.

Since the mid-seventies insurance companies have faced unprecedented threats to their ossified, cash-rich existence. The first wave of change came as consumers belatedly clued in to just how bad a bargain most life policies were and moved their cash in a torrent to high-return investments. Rising interest rates were the main catalyst behind the exodus of consumer savings away from the insurers to better-yielding instruments. Life insurers have lost a great deal of ground to banks and trust companies recently: their share of the total assets of Canadian financial institutions is shrinking. In 1967, the life companies held a 19.1 per cent share, compared with 37.3 per cent held by the banks and 10.5 per cent by trust and loan companies. At the end of 1984, the life insurers' portion had fallen to 12 per cent; the banks had increased their part to 40.5 per cent; and trust and loan companies had matched the life insurers at 12 per cent. The remainder of the asset pie was split up between other financial institutions like investment dealers, co-operatives and pension funds. To help staunch the outflow of funds from insurance investments, the industry has scrambled to update its product lines.

The next wave of change will expose life insurance companies to public scrutiny more than ever. The regulatory framework in which life insurers have operated for more than 50 years is changing. For the first time since 1932, the federal laws that govern the operations of most life insurers (149 companies are federally registered; the remainder are provincially registered) are undergoing an overhaul. Quebec's Insurance Act of 1984 has set the pace for change by freeing life insurers registered in the province to do a host of things they always hankered after. For the first time, Quebec-based insurers were given the green light to diversify through financial holding companies into an expanded range of businesses, from selling stocks and administering trust funds to taking deposits and managing real estate. The policyholder-owned mutual companies were given the same rights as their shareholder-owned counterparts, the stock companies, to issue preferred shares in order to shore up their capital base.

No one is expecting the changes in federal legislation to go that far. But they should go a long way in freeing the nation's life insurers from the regulatory shackles that have confined them. In all probability, they will be able to acquire control of other financial service institutions like trust companies for the first time. One report by the federal Finance Department on financial regulation, the so-called Green Paper of April 1985, even suggested that insurers should be allowed to get into banking. A November 1985 report on the Green Paper by the House of Commons Committee on Finance, Trade and

Economic Affairs was more generous. It recommended that insurers be freed to set up subsidiaries in any lawful line of business.

The scene is set for life insurance companies to step out of the dim recesses of the financial world to centre stage, where they will be subjected to much more public scrutiny. The change will be most dramatic for the mutual insurers. In many ways they have been insulated from the normal vicissitudes of commerce. Since the time most of them converted to mutual companies from stock companies in the 1950s and early '60s amid a wave of paranoia about foreign takeovers, their executives have been content to watch as premiums rolled in and profits swelled. Life was leisurely. After all, there are no real shareholders to report to in mutual companies. As a result, members of stock companies regard their mutual cousins with disdain. Barry Francis, vice-president of corporate affairs at Crown Life, a stock company, has worked in both types of operation. "The bottom line is seldom mentioned in mutual companies," he says. "Things are done in a much more lavish fashion in terms of executive perks and office decoration. It's a big daisy chain for executives."

Stock companies are more worried about the bottom line— they have shareholders to report to—and as a result, they have generally been faster to react to changing consumer needs and have led the way in the modernization of management techniques. Such shareholder-owned companies as Great-West Life Assurance and London Life provide good examples of this.

There are signs, however, that the mutual companies are playing catch-up as fast as they can. It's hard, after all, for a hulking ocean liner to change course in mid-voyage. A minority of the larger mutuals have shucked off old attitudes to product design and marketing, and are updating their management methods. Several are also trying to position themselves to take advantage of the wider powers of diversification they expect to receive from Ottawa. Mutual Life Assurance Company of

Waterloo has acquired a stake in the trust industry through an indirect holding in a small Toronto-based company called Mutual Trust. Manufacturers Life tried to do the same by acquiring a 30 per cent stake in Canada Trust (the limit permitted by law), but it subsequently lost that interest in a takeover battle to Genstar Corp. of Vancouver. Sun Life executives say they are scouting the Canadian terrain for a trust company or a mutual fund company to buy. All this presages a burst of takeover activity by the large mutuals that will be financed by the bulging pool of profits (called surplus, in industry jargon) they have to throw around. Sun Life alone has a surplus of more than $1.8 billion at its disposal. Says Terry Shaunessy, an analyst with Merrill Lynch Canada: "In Sun Life's case, what may happen is that it just might end up buying a Trilon or a Power Financial. Neither would be a big acquisition for Sun Life." Shaunessy sees the life insurers as the emerging players in financial services. "They've become more performance oriented," he says. "They have started to realize the power they have—they've got capital and loads of it." Insurance companies, he concludes, "are the wild cards in the evolution of financial services because they represent just gigantic pools of capital." Trilon Financial and Power Financial are not bit players in the drama, however. They symbolize another trend in financial services that the regulators are trying to take into account with legislation. Trilon is a financial conglomerate, controlled by Brascan, which has its fingers in life insurance (London Life), property and casualty insurance (Wellington), as well as the trust (Royal) and real estate (Royal LePage) businesses. Power Financial, a subsidiary of Power Corp. has a similar array of subsidiaries, including Great-West Life and Montreal Trust.

The ambitious intentions of the large mutuals, as well as the expanding orbits of the financial conglomerates, raise a plethora of public issues, from concern over concentration of power in the financial industry to worries about conflicts of interest and self-dealing.

The property and casualty companies face an entirely different future. If anything, the only role they will play in the corporate concentration sweepstakes will be as takeover targets for the life insurers and the conglomerates. Being much smaller in size, the general insurers make easy prey for acquisitive life insurers. But lately, the property and casualty business hasn't been an attractive field to expand into. The industry's business practices have already been thrust into the public spotlight by the 1985–86 worldwide liability crisis, which attracted headlines about the sudden inability of everything from amateur sportts organizations to municipalities to obtain coverage.

Blaming the law courts for high awards in liability cases, the general insurers jacked up their premium rates by multiples of three to eight. The reinsurers, who also had a hand in creating the crisis, suddenly stopped writing certain kinds of high-risk business. Then both groups confidently predicted that the crisis would pass. It is passing, largely because of the premium increases on insurance for autos, professional malpractice, product liability and third-party liability. Having set a public furor in motion, the general insurers began to hope that it would subside before it prompted governments to step in with drastic action like public insurance, but neither they nor the reinsurers should be allowed to escape so easily. It is time for a close examination of the way they do business, the way they are regulated and how both can be improved.

### A Time for Reappraisal

Over the last century, the insurance industry in Canada has rarely had to undergo a close scrutiny of its affairs by either government-appointed bodies or journalists. The first and only federal royal commission into the affairs of life insurance companies was undertaken in 1906, after a similar investigation in New York State revealed a pattern of misdeeds and shoddy practices by American insurers. The findings of the Canadian probe were less dramatic, but certain companies were singled out for allowing excessive management expenses and questionable investments. Observed the commission: "…insurance companies tend to become powerful aggregations of money with financial rather than insurance aims. The power to engineer these aggregations becomes a thing to be desired."

Another ambitious probe into the operations and conduct of both the life and general insurance industries was undertaken in the mid-seventies by the Select Committee on Company Law of the Ontario Legislature. The feisty chairman of the committee, D. H. Carruthers, came to some conclusions that the insurers didn't like at all. Among other things, Carruthers criticized the life insurers for a front-end-loaded commission system under which "salesmen tend to neglect non-selling activities such as ongoing policy advice and may fail to give objective advice." He also took aim at the industry's high policy lapse rates—the number of policies that are cancelled within 13 months of issue—arguing that consumers suffer when policies lapse because they lose any premiums they have paid and also because the administrative costs to the company of lapsed policies are passed on to other clients. Carruthers also excoriated the life industry for, among other things, making it difficult for consumers to understand complicated life insurance products and failing to provide proper information to help eliminate that confusion. The name Carruthers is now a dirty word in life insurance circles.

The general insurance industry also came under some heavy fire from Carruthers. In regard to auto insurance, he criticized the hodge-podge of rating criteria used by different companies across Canada. The criteria used, such as the area where a policyholder lives, and the age and sex of the operator, are sometimes not reliable. Said the Carruthers report: "Some companies may be applying rating factors on which there may not be sufficient or accurate loss experience data. As a result rates may be arbitrary and not adequately objective." It also noted: "Many factors (used in rating vehicle owners and drivers) discriminate against certain groups of the driving public." Young male drivers would certainly agree. Property insurers in general were also criticized for inadequate disclosure to the buying public of exactly what accidents or events are covered by policies, what is not covered and how the insured's loss claims are to be calculated and verified.

Apart from making some overdue efforts to simplify policy wordings, the insurance industry hasn't come far since Carruthers unleashed his bolts.

This book is a modest attempt to take the reader on a journey through Canada's insurance industry, to see its workings and to rattle skeletons that life and general insurers have tucked away in their closets in the hope that they won't be noticed. For two years, starting in 1984, the author criss-crossed the country from Halifax to Vancouver, travelling more than 15,000 miles in total and conducting more than 300 interviews with players in, and informed observers of, the insurance business. In the course of his travels, he dined sumptuously with executives in private dining rooms atop office towers and in their homes; talked with unscrupulous agents in dimly lit bars and met with their honest counterparts in trophy-filled offices; grilled federal and provincial regulators and their investigators; polled the views of academics; and finally, strained the patience of numerous librarians.

In the following pages, the failings of life insurers will come under close scrutiny, including the products they offer to the public and the way they market them. I will also appraise the operating practices of property and casualty insurers and reinsurers. But this survey of the industry is more than an effort to criticize insurers for their faults. The hopes, fears and failings of the people who make up the insurance industry, from executives to agents, are laid bare. Companies have personalities, too. This book takes a close look at the inner workings of insurers that have broken out of the somnambulent pack; the companies that have undergone sweeping, often painful, changes to bring their operations up to date. Some—notably, small foreign-controlled companies—are on the leading edge of change in terms of policy innovation and management practice. All are noteworthy because of their expansive designs. They are truly the wild cards in the unfolding financial services scenario. Finally, this book surveys what the future might hold for Canada's insurance industry and makes a series of recommendations on how its glaring shortcomings can be corrected, and how consumers, whose fears fuel the industry, may be better served. I hope this volume will be useful to readers who want to be better informed about the workings of an industry that affects their lives every day and who want to be able to buy insurance wisely. At the very least, it should provide some food for thought for the insurance czars when they gather at their next conclave.

James Fleming
Toronto
July 1986

# PART I

*Uneasy Adversaries:*
*The Battle between Company and Consumer*

# CHAPTER 1

## *The Company First:*
## *Policies at a Premium*

THE OFFICES OF THE Financial Life Assurance Company oc-
cupy the fifth floor of a nondescript brick office building in
Etobicoke, Ontario. A rickety elevator delivers the visitor to a
cramped waiting room economically furnished in basic brown.
Rather inexpensive oil paintings of bucolic scenes line the
wall. The spartan theme extends to the executive suite of Hugh
Haney, president of the firm. Plain by insurance industry standards, his office furniture looks as if it has been hastily rented
from an office equipment company. On first appearance, the
headquarters suggests that Financial Life sits in some back-
water of the industry.

Haney, a wiry man with an Abe-Lincoln-style beard, is clearly
a stranger to the soft life of executive dining suites, limousines
and private clubs enjoyed by his counterparts at the old-line
insurers. He spends his spare time hiking, canoeing and camp-
ing: to which the photos that hang on his wall attest. One
framed poster stands out from the montage. It features a signed
picture of mountain-climber Sir Edmund Hillary below rows
of stylized blue mountain peaks. Gazing admiringly at the

picture, Haney pays his friend Hillary what must be the insurance executive's highest form of praise. Hillary, he says, "lives on the leading edge of adventure." Hillary might understand Haney's own uphill struggle in life: to introduce innovation—and a better deal for consumers—into the life insurance industry. Says Haney: "I'm not well-liked by many in the industry."

Nearly 15 kilometres away, in the financial heart of Toronto, the twin $100-million-apiece glass towers of the Sun Life Assurance Company, Canada's second-largest insurer, straddle University Avenue. It is a windswept thoroughfare, home to a host of other insurance companies and, judging from the usual paucity of pedestrians, little other activity. The executive suites of Sun Life are situated on the sixth floor of the eastern tower. In the waiting room, separated from the inner sanctums by locked glass doors, an exquisite hand-painted Chinese tapestry worth several hundred thousand dollars covers one wall.

The suite of Donald Gauer, chief financial officer of the company, occupies a decidedly roomy corner of the floor. Thick carpeting and lustrous rosewood walls create a subdued, elegant air. Gauer, a quiet-spoken man with a gentle disposition, sits languidly in his office, explaining how life insurance companies design policies and set premiums using conservative, time-tested methods that are necessary to ensure the firms' financial integrity. He makes it all seem uncontroversial, logical and above reproach.

Haney and Gauer represent two drastically different mind-sets in the life insurance business. Irreverent and disparaging of the old-line companies, Haney thinks many of their policies are simply bad buys for consumers, particularly the long-time mainstay of their individual business, whole life. Says Haney: "If I had any I'd cash it all in." He adds, "If those policies were fully explained and the true costs were fully disclosed, no one would ever buy it."

By contrast, Gauer swears by whole life—he personally owns several policies. His main complaint with the policy-designing process at Sun Life is that he constantly has to remind its actuaries not to price insurance products too cheaply. Says Gauer: "I have to keep reminding some of our actuaries from time to time that they cannot sell a product at an inadequate price." Actuaries, being human, he says, "get terribly concerned about being competitive—having a price just slightly better than not just the other guy but *all* the other guys."

### Old Habits Die Hard

The rift between Haney and Gauer over whether whole life insurance is a bad buy is only one of a host of controversies about the products sold by both life and general insurance companies. Critics within and without the industry are challenging the quality of its most widely sold products on the basis of their price and the benefits they provide to consumers. But to understand what makes an insurance policy good or bad, it is first necessary to understand how insurance companies design and price their products. How does a company decide the premiums a policyholder should pay for different types of coverage? What factors make insurance more expensive for one person than for another? How does the company make its profits? The answers to these questions determine the attractiveness of an insurance policy from the consumer's point of view.

Insurance is based on a relatively straightforward principle. It is simply a means of spreading the risk of death, sickness or property loss of one individual over a wider group of people. If everyone pays enough money into a central fund so that a single large claim or a series of claims doesn't bankrupt it, then every member can rest assured that he or his family will be able to collect from the fund if he dies or his property suffers damage. Insurance companies are the arbiters in the process by which funds are collected and claims are paid out. In between, however, they also take some profit for themselves.

In the case of life insurance, the price of policies is determined by actuaries, who have prepared for the job with years of university training in mathematics and actuarial science. They are the gurus of the life insurance world. In deciding how much to charge for, say, each $1,000 of insurance in a whole life policy, they start by calculating how many policyholders are likely to die and collect on their policies each year. This is called the mortality rate. Second, they determine how much the company has to pay each year for expenses like salaries, offices and marketing. Third, they add in another cost: the interest rate that the company will pay each year to policyholders on the so-called cash value of their policies. The cash value is the savings feature of a life insurance policy. Each year the company puts a portion of a policyholder's premium into this fund and pays a fixed, low-interest rate on the total. The cash value, of course, only accumulates on paper. The policyholder doesn't ever collect it unless he cancels his policy. If he simply dies, the money stays in the company's coffers. Nevertheless, the actuary calculates how much the company will have to pay in interest on the cash value of policies and estimates how much the company will have to pay each year because of cancelled policies.

*Voilà.* By combining these cost factors, the actuary gets an idea of how much the company will have to pay out in total for each $1,000-worth of whole life policies it sells. The next step is simple. The actuary only has to set the premiums charged to clients high enough to make sure that the company's income from premiums surpasses the money it pays out in claims and expenses—and allows the company to cream off a profit. Life insurers also add to their profits, or surplus, by investing policyholder premiums and past profits. Insurers, of course, don't operate on a strictly year-to-year basis. Rather, they funnel money into another pool, called a reserve, which is kept large enough to meet all future policy claims and then some.

But being conservative chaps, actuaries also devised another scheme to make sure that their companies stay financially healthy. They created so-called "participating life insurance policies." With these, the customer supposedly participates in the company's profits. But that is not what really happens. The policyholder pays higher premiums for this type of policy and if the company does well financially each year, it pays the policyholder so-called "dividends," which is money the person can either pocket or use to increase the coverage of the policy. The company is under no obligation to pay these dividends, even though the client must pay the higher premiums. Policies without the dividend feature are called nonparticipating policies. They are cheaper.

Actuaries use the same principles to price most types of life insurance. The major exception is term insurance, which is less costly for the consumer because it doesn't have any cash value feature. Term insurance is just what it sounds like. For a fixed period of time, usually five or ten years, the policyholder pays a set premium for a fixed amount of insurance.

Insurance in all its forms, whether property and casualty, liability or health, is priced using similar calculations. General insurers, for instance, keep tallies of how many claims they have had to pay out in past years for houses that burned down, property that was stolen or cars that were damaged in accidents. Their experience has allowed them to single out certain types of property or clients as being high-risk; that is, more liable to make claims. Homeowners pay more for home and contents insurance if they are frequent travellers, live in an area more prone to vandalism or arson (such as luxury or slum areas) or dwell in remote locations not easily accessible to fire-fighting services. Auto owners are classified by another set of criteria. They pay more for insurance if they have a bad driving record, if they are young, male or live in an urban area, where the rate of accidents is highest. Only Manitoba, Saskatchewan and British Columbia, where auto insurance is sold by government corporations, have eliminated age, sex and marital status as a basis for determining car insurance rates.

Like life insurers, general insurance companies try to set their rates so they surpass claims in any given year. They are supposed to set aside part of their premium income in reserves to meet future claims, but the rest they take as profits. In recent years, general insurers have paid out more in claims than they have collected in premiums. This is called an underwriting loss. Fortunately, however, most companies have made more than enough profit on their investments to make up for the shortfall, and this keeps their operations in the black. As a back-up to protect themselves from high or unexpected claims, life and general insurers also pass some of the risk of the policies they write (sell) to reinsurance companies. The agreements between the two insurers is called a reinsurance treaty. They entitle the reinsurance company to a share of the premiums the policyholder pays but they also oblige the reinsurer to pay an agreed portion of any subsequent claim.

That, in a nutshell, is how insurance policies work. If the basic principles for their design and pricing were followed in good faith, there would be little reason to question the industry's integrity but, unfortunately, abuses have crept into the system. In recent years, the products and prices of insurance companies have been subjected to a torrent of criticism. In insurance, more than any other business, old, questionable habits die hard.

### The Trouble with Life

Don Gauer typifies the conservative style of most of the actuaries who run Canada's life insurance industry. To them, caution is synonymous with financial responsibility, price cutting with foolhardiness. Actuaries dominate the upper ranks of the business. For decades a degree in actuarial science has been a key credential for the chairman's seat. Presiding over their

domains with an equanimity born of financial comfort, actuaries have displayed a resistance to change that would have
proved the undoing of any executive in normal commercial
enterprises subject to the usual ups and downs of the business
cycle.

Since the mid-nineteenth century, actuaries have carried
out their cryptic calculations with everything from quill pens
to main-frame computers. But all their ciphering has shared
one remarkably constant characteristic. In the end, when they
have put mortality rates, company expenses and interest-rate
projections into an equation to calculate premium levels, the
policyholder has been overcharged. Many companies have
used either mortality tables that were outdated and therefore
did not take into account increases in the general population's
longevity; interest rates that were far too low; company expenses that were too high—or a combination of all three. The
company, in short, has come first.

Until the last several years, many firms were using mortality
tables calculated in 1958, when Canadians had much shorter
lifespans. (Mortality rates have been improving by 2 to 3 per
cent a year in recent decades due to medical advances.) At the
same time, companies paid very low interest rates on the cash
value of policies, usually about 2 or 3 per cent until a few years
ago. That practice attracted heated criticism beginning in the
late 1970s, a decade in which inflation averaged more than
7 per cent annually, making life insurance quite an unattractive investment.

Gauer rejects the criticisms. He concedes that "in the old
days we used to keep our guaranteed [interest] rate underlying
the premium at 2 1/2 per cent. But regularly within Sun Life's
existence, he adds, rates have fallen below that level in the
economy. "Now," he says, "with interest rates having gone up,
we can go to a guaranteed rate much higher—4, 5, 6 per
cent—knowing that the difference between the current rate
then gets paid out as dividend." Concludes Gauer: "It is true

that you build in low interest rates, low guaranteed rates which you think will be the minimum experience over the next 90 years. So you have every right—more than that, you have a responsibility to keep that rate low." Helen Anderson, former co-chairman of the Economic Policy Committee of the Consumers' Association of Canada, does not agree: "Life insurers' claims each year are half of what they take in through premiums. Now if you always took in twice as much money as you paid out every year you can imagine how wealthy you'd be. That's what they're doing and they've been doing it for ever."

Over the past five years, consumers have grown justifiably baffled, concerned and outraged by the way insurance companies design many of their policies. Most complaints have been directed at whole life insurance, alternately called ordinary life, straight life or permanent insurance, and marketed under a profusion of brand names. For decades the industry has been selling whole life as a combination forced savings and insurance plan. The policyholder pays a level premium for the life of the policy, which means that the higher cost of death protection in later years (when the risk of death increases) is moved forward to the early years of the policy. This leads to young policyholders in their thirties or forties paying much more for their insurance protection than is warranted during those years and at a time when their living costs and other financial responsibilities are heaviest. The burden is even greater for those who have policies that can be "paid up" over a set number of years (say, 30), rather than the type that allows premiums to be paid over a person's lifespan.

Most whole life policies are also of the "participating" variety. Critics point out that in participating policies, the buyer is overcharged on premiums on the pretext that if the company earns a better rate of return on its investments than anticipated, it might, if it chooses, return part of the proceeds to the policyholder in the form of "dividends." These can either be taken as cash, left on reserve at the company to earn very low interest or used to buy more insurance. In short, the policy-holder is assuming a greater portion of the insurance firm's risk, with no assurance that he will be compensated for doing so. It is simply impossible to imagine a similar system existing anywhere else in the financial world. In response to consumer dissatisfaction about problems like these, the design and selling of whole life have undergone some modifications in the past decade. As Gauer points out, firms have built higher guaranteed interest rates into policies. And agents, conscious of the fact that consumers are becoming better informed, now downplay the savings features (cash values) of the policies they sell and emphasize their insurance value. But most firms do not offer nonparticipating policies because they are a much less lucrative product for the agent, who receives commissions calculated as a percentage of premium payments, and they are less profitable for the company.

## A History of Neglect

The staying power of participating whole life policies in Canada is symptomatic of the industry's resistance to change. In the 1800s, the first century of their existence in North America, insurance companies lived in a relatively cloistered world, thriving on the naivety of consumers and giving them a better buy only under duress. Even in the 1850s, however, insurance companies did have to cope with some "meddling," reform-minded regulators. At that time, a number of critics became concerned that whole life policies accumulated no cash reserves for the policyholder. The premium payments piling up in the companies' coffers only entitled the buyer to death benefits. Examining the industry's history in the 1800s, a 1980 study for the Ontario legislature noted: "Both in Canada and the United States, it became apparent that many insurance companies were profiting handsomely from the premiums they held for long periods. Except in the case of a few companies, these premiums were 'forfeited' or lost to insureds who lapsed or cancelled their whole life policies."[1]

The first breakthrough came in 1867, when Elizur Wright, then commissioner of insurance in Massachusetts, and a crusading industry reformer, successfully campaigned to obtain a non-forfeiture law providing policyholders with single-premium extended term insurance if the buyer cancelled his whole life policy—that is, he could take the cash value of the whole life policy and buy term. Then, in a landmark decision in 1876 (*New York Life Company* v. *Statham*), the U.S. Supreme Court ruled that a policyholder has an "equitable right" to the premiums held in reserve, "subject to a deduction for the value of the assurance enjoyed by him whilst the policy was in existence." And eventually, through further regulation in the United States and the force of competition in Canada, all insurance companies offered cash values to whole life policyholders. Unfortunately, however, a policyholder can only collect these cash values by cancelling the policy—hardly a wise form of savings. Furthermore, cash values build up rapidly only after a policy has been in force for about ten years. (This is to discourage clients from cashing in their policies too often.) Before that time, the policyholder loses money by cashing in the policy because the policyholder has paid more in premiums than the cash value is worth.

## The Return of Term

Since the mid-1970s the comfortable, profitable world of the life insurance firms has been subjected to unprecedented tumult. The first wave of assault came, ironically, from term insurance. The earliest and purest form of insurance, term had been supplanted by whole life beginning in the eighteenth

[1] The Select Committee on Company Law, *Fourth Report on Life Insurance*, 1980.

century in England. But term has had a second coming. It was introduced to Canada by Occidental Life (now Transamerica Life) in the 1930s, causing great upset in the conservative industry, which saw it as a threat to profits. Term slowly increased in popularity among consumers until it enjoyed a hey-day in the 1970s. With it, a buyer pays strictly for insurance payable on his death; there are no cash values or other bells and whistles attached. Typically, a buyer can get four or five times as much term insurance as whole life insurance with the same premium payments. Most term policies only last five or ten years, although commendably, the vast majority are renewable, meaning that the buyer can renew the policy without new evidence of insurability. Term premiums present a major disadvantage, however: they increase with the age of the policyholder, and they become prohibitively high in later life. Still, they are the best buy for young couples with dependants and a mortgage to worry about. A term policy with a death benefit of, say, $100,000 can be bought by a 30- to 40-year-old at about the same cost as a much smaller, and completely inadequate, amount of whole life. Canny consumers can end up better off financially in their later years through investing the money they have saved by buying term instead of whole life. That way, the savings—in anything from registered retirement savings plan accounts to guaranteed investment certificates or government bonds—will be theirs when they want it. By contrast, they can't get at the cash value savings in their life insurance unless they cash in the policy.

In the seventies, term insurance increased from 29 per cent of the total amount of individual life insurance purchased in Canada in 1970, to 50 per cent in 1980. By 1983, term policies had fallen back to 36 per cent of policies sold, but for good reason. Beginning in 1974, consumers were offered several new varieties of life insurance which answered some of their criticisms about the old-type policies.

## The Shock of the New

The next wave of change began in Halifax, a city far from the cosy society in which the major Toronto, Montreal and New York companies operate. In 1974 a team of product development actuaries at Maritime Life Assurance Co., led by Ted Moffatt, a plain-talking, burly actuary born in Amherst, Nova Scotia, broke ranks with the insurance fraternity by introducing the first "new money" policy to North America. ("New money" is a term for policies in which the company pays interest rates similar to those prevailing in the economy on the cash value of the policy.) Called an Adjustable Single Premium Whole Life (ASPWL) contract, it was a whole life policy with some special twists. The consumer paid a single premium up front to buy it and, unlike the case in traditional policies, the company paid the buyer current interest rates on the policy's cash value. Maritime Life—and later the North West Life Assurance Company of Vancouver, which followed suit with a similar policy—paid an 8 per cent rate of return compared with the 3 to 4 per cent returns offered by other firms. Consumers could cash in their old policies with another company and then use the cash value to buy a much larger amount of insurance from Maritime Life. If interest rates in the economy dropped after a given period of time, Maritime could call on the policyholder to pay more premiums so that the company could be assured of meeting its obligations. Conversely, if interest rates rose, then the company could increase the amount of insurance without calling on the policyholder to pay more premiums.

The rest of the industry panicked at the thought of the new-style policy spreading, since they thought it would lead to a rash of cancellations by their policyholders eager to get a better deal. In fact, the Life Underwriters Association of Canada (LUAC), an association representing most of the industry's agents, made representations to the federal Department of

Insurance seeking to put an end to the new policies. In a bulletin issued to members, LUAC complained that the policy ran against "the principle of equity among policyholders"—essentially because some would have cheaper insurance than others.

Maritime executives note that federal regulatory authorities were not swayed by the industry's protests. Nevertheless, the product's sales collapsed after the federal government's November 1981 budget, which made policy cash values over a certain level subject to income tax. The cash values in Maritime's policy, large in the early years because of the single, up-front premium payment, did not meet the government's yardstick for avoiding tax. Nevertheless, consumers who bought Maritime's policy in the mid-seventies benefitted handsomely.[2]

With the sale of new single premium policies scuttled by the budget change, Maritime went back to the drawing boards and developed another new money policy without the large, up-front premium feature. Called LifeTerm, its benefits also change with interest-rate experience. When interest rates in the economy go up, the company makes a better return on its investments. Therefore, it can afford to give the client more coverage for the same cost. When rates go down the client must pay more for less insurance. Here is an illustration of how interest-rate fluctuations would affect a $100,000 Life-Term policy bought by a 40-year-old male nonsmoker in July 1985 with an initial annual premium of $726. The company guarantees the initial premium for a five-year period. At the

[2] Here is an example. On July 1, 1974, a male, age 35, could buy a $100,000 Adjustable Single Premium Whole Life policy for a single premium of $9,823. Under the terms of the contract, the buyer was entitled to a guaranteed cash surrender value of $13,443, by 1984 and $15,768 by 1989. Those values were projected on the basis of the level of interest rates in 1974. As years passed and interest rates in the economy rose, Maritime was able to enhance the policy's coverage and cash value projections. In 1979, after a five-year period, the company made a contract adjustment that raised the face value of the policy to $116,500 from $100,000 for the next five years. Likewise, the guaranteed cash value was raised to a projected $14,816 in 1984 and to a projected $17,378 in 1989. In 1984, another upward revision was made in the benefits.

beginning of each five-year period, benefits are determined for the next five years. If interest rates in the economy have increased by, say, 2 per cent, the annual premium for the renewed policy remains at $726. But the coverage increases to $121,030. By contrast, if interest rates in the economy have decreased by 2 per cent, the annual premium increases to $910.56. The coverage decreases to $80,908. Of course, if interest rates have decreased, the policyholder also has the option of maintaining a lesser amount of insurance with no change in premium.

But new money policies, which are now offered by numerous firms, are only one form of innovative products that have been introduced to the industry by maverick firms over the protests of the old-line institutions.

### Giving Nonsmokers Their Due

The advent of nonsmoker policies in the early 1980s evoked similar consternation in conservative circles. When Haney was chairman of Laurier Life, he introduced non-smoker policies that offered discounts of up to 50 per cent below standard whole life policies. (Laurier was the second company in Canada to offer these policies. The first was Seaboard Life Insurance Company of Vancouver, now amalgamated with Fidelity Life.) The industry reacted with dismay to the introduction of nonsmoker policies. Explains Haney: "When we can out with nonsmoker policies, the people who sold all their business on a blended rate [which included good and bad risks] suffered. The nonsmokers left them and came to us, leaving them with just the smokers. So they got upset. Eventually," he says, "the old-line companies came out with their own nonsmoker policies. But they didn't want to." After leaving Laurier in 1984 and taking over as president of Financial Life, Haney further upset the industry by introducing a never-smoked policy, offering even greater discounts.

Compared with another type of policy that was introduced to the industry, however, new money and nonsmoker policies only mildly disturbed the equanimity of the long-established firms.

### Universal Life: The Emperor Has No Clothes

*"No longer will the insurance company be able to hide conservative mortality assumptions, large expense charges and low interest rates within a combination whole life policy. Now all aspects of calculations will be laid bare to the scrutiny of the sophisticated consumer."*
Robert Brown, consulting actuary and assistant professor of actuarial science, University of Waterloo

With those words, Brown summed up the main impact of so-called "universal life insurance" policies that have become increasingly popular in North America. A cousin of policies in existence in Great Britain since the 1960s, universal life made its debut in North America in 1979 when E. F. Hutton, a New York-based financial conglomerate, began marketing a version of the plan for Life of California. Universal is like earlier new money policies in that it offers current market rates of return to policyholders. But the similarity stops there. Universal life, which is marketed under a variety of brand names, is a transparent insurance policy. The premium paid by the policyholder is unbundled, which allows the purchaser to see how much goes for the death benefit and how much to cash value. The premiums are placed in a separate account—called a side fund—which is invested in short-term securities yielding far more than the old bonds in the company's general account. Each month, the company deducts an amount from the policyholder's side-fund which is equal to the premium payable on a yearly, renewable term policy for the coverage the buyer has chosen. The funds left in the policyholder's account (minus various expense charges) are the cash value of the policy, on which the company pays interest each month. Not only can the buyer see how the payments are being used, but she also has the flexibility to choose the amount of coverage she wants, and to specify her monthly payment and the length of time that she wants to pay those premiums. Essentially, universal life combines the features of whole life and term insurance. Says Brown: "Isn't it ironic that after decades of vehemently arguing against the advice 'buy term and invest the difference,' the life insurance industry is now applauding a product whose design is based exactly on that philosophy?" He adds: "Where we used to design and sell what was good for the company, we will now be forced to design and sell what is good for the policyholder."

There is some debate, however, over just how good a deal universal life is for the consumer. Writing in *Canadian Consumer* (August 1985), economist Monica Townson points out: "Although you seem to be getting a whole life policy at term insurance rates, it's actually not so. The premiums you pay will be clearly higher than those you pay for an ordinary term insurance policy. In other words, there's still an amount of 'forced savings' in this policy."

Other criticisms go further. Although companies may advertise their universal life product as offering, say, a 10 per cent return on savings, in actuality the return is much lower after policy fees and other charges are taken into account. The policy might have no net earnings for the first several years and not reach the advertised rate of return until after its twentieth year. In 1984, Brown analysed the universal life product of a major Canadian company and found that the charges and fees consisted of these components: the interest earnings above 4 per cent on the first $500 of the buyer's side-fund; 7.5 per cent of annual premiums and a first-year fee that fluctuates with the age and size of the policy. Examining a policy sold by a major U.S. firm that promised an 11 per cent return, William Scheel, professor of insurance at the University of Connecticut, discovered that after fees were deducted, the policy did not break even until after the fourth year and by the tenth year had reached only an 8 per cent return.

Even critics in the industry say that universal life is a flawed product. Says Irwin W. Goldberg, a senior consultant with the U.S-based Life Insurance Marketing and Research Association (LIMRA): "Universal life is another attempt by the industry to continue to satisfy both protection needs and savings in one product." But in doing that, he adds: "You don't end up either with the most competitive insurance coverage or the most competitive savings vehicle."

### Variable Life: Sharing the Risk

A host of other new policy types has come onto the market in recent years, all with slightly different features to allure—and often confuse—the consumer. They include variable life, introduced by the U.S.-based Equitable Life Insurance Company. This type of policy also features unbundled premiums and separate-account investing—this time through a wider range of assets, primarily common stocks. Variable life policies have cash values that increase or decrease daily, depending on investment results. The death benefit increases or decreases annually, but it will not fall below a guaranteed amount.

### Adjustable Life: A Product for the Fickle

If that is too challenging for a consumer, an adjustable life policy can be purchased instead. Under this plan, the face amount and the premium can be changed by the buyer at will, although evidence of insurability is required when the policyholder decides he would like to increase his coverage.

This plan, therefore, offers more flexibility than traditional whole life plans with fixed face values and fixed premiums.

All the new plans, introduced by the industry as more competition creeps into it, have shaken insurance companies out of a decades-old complacency. Having gained a foothold after their introduction by innovative companies, the plans spread as reluctant, conservative firms, fearing a massive flight of policyholders to competitors, brought out their own versions of the new products. While the latest products are an advance over older policies, they remain chronically flawed: all have that impossible combination of protection as well as a forced savings element. And industry iconoclasts say there are other, more fundamental problems that make many products unnecessarily expensive. Says Haney: "The absolute, primary problem that the life insurance industry has is that it is saddled with an extremely expensive and inefficient distribution system." One difficulty, he says, is that most companies use a career agency system, selling through company agents in branch offices, rather than through independent brokers. "All the big companies have career sales forces where it's a tied agent operating out of a branch office with a manager and all the infrastructure," he complains. The cost of operating these branches and hiring and training agents is immense, he says, especially when the high turnover rates are agents is taken into account.

Another problem according to Haney, is the very high commissions paid to agents in the first year of a policy: commissions that range from 100 to 200 per cent of the first year's premiums. That causes a problem because many policies lapse during the first year, leaving the company with a loss that must be recovered by increasing the costs of policies. Haney puts it this way: "When people lapse the policy a year later, that company has lost money on that and don't think they are philanthropic and pick it all up—it's passed into average premium rates in the future."

## The Consumer's Dilemma

Unfortunately, despite the drawbacks of most policies, life insurance remains a necessity for most consumers (children and young, single workers excluded). But what type of policy should be chosen? The field is wide open, and there is no shortage of come-ons to increase the insurance companies' business. Television and print commercials portray the secure good-life that can be enjoyed if a family puts its fate, and its money, into the hands of the advertised firm. Credit card companies beckon consumers to buy travel insurance in direct-mail campaigns. A number of firms in Canada offer mail-order life insurance, for which the consumer simply fills in an application that comes through the mail-slot. Surprisingly, however, mail-order policies are no cheaper than other policies, despite their low distribution costs.

The major firms spend millions each year building their image in the public eye. Advertising agencies scramble eagerly to win the right to handle the accounts of the insurance giants. Crown Life Assurance's account, for example, is estimated to be worth between $1.5 million and $2 million annually. But there is a paucity of hard information in the blitz about the companies' products and pricing. Part of the reason is that outdated laws in Canada prohibit insurance companies from doing comparative advertising, a holdover from an era in which inducing consumers to switch policies— called "twisting" in the industry—was considered unethical.

For the average young wage-earner, with a spouse and dependents, term insurance is a priority. It can be obtained through an employer's group plan, which might offer insurance worth one, two or three times the employee's annual salary, or by selecting an individual policy. If the buyer is confident that he can take the money saved by buying term instead of whole life and invest it wisely, then term is the type to buy. However, some consumers have neither the time nor the inclination to manage investments. Only about 10 per cent of individual Canadians, for example, invest in the stock market.

A good solution for the investment-wary consumer is to buy a small amount of whole life, say, a $25,000 policy, with a term rider for a much larger amount. Later in life, when term premiums become too expensive and insurance needs diminish, the term can be stopped, leaving the buyer with the whole life contract only. Several companies offer such a policy at competitive rates. Alternatively, if the consumer is willing to gamble on the fluctuation of interest rates, he should buy a new money or universal policy and keep his fingers crossed.

Some specific kinds of insurance should be avoided. One is endowment insurance. It is a generally disparaged product with high premium payments and low benefits that is paid up after 10 or 20 years. Self-serving agents (whose commissions would be high on the early-paid premiums) used to market it as a great savings vehicle for "the children's education." Any agent who tries to sell the product should be promptly shown the door. The so-called "term-to-100" policies is another trap to be avoided. It is marketed as a term product that lasts your lifetime. In fact, it is really a whole life product in disguise.

Female consumers can expect to enjoy lower insurance costs than men. Women now live, on average, seven years longer than men and this lower mortality rate, say the companies, justifies a certain degree of price discrimination. Most companies charge a woman about the same rate as a male two to five years younger. In 1985, Sun Life, for example, charged a 35-year-old male nonsmoker $14.69 per $1,000 of whole life insurance each year. By contrast, a female in the same category paid $13.91 per $1,000, a little more than a 33-year-old male would pay. However, it remains to be seen how much longer insurance companies will be permitted by law to continue this practice. It may last only until a disgruntled male consumer fights the system in court using the equality provisions of Canada's Charter of Rights.

### Sharing the Nest Egg: The Great Annuity Debate

Senior citizens must make difficult choices about what to do with their life savings. At age 71, consumers have to roll their RRSPs into an annuity if they want to avoid paying tax in one crushing blow on their retirement nest egg, and life insurance firms are the only financial institutions permitted to sell annuities. It seems unjust that after a lifetime of saving, a pensioner, perhaps struggling to make ends meet, must give an insurance company a hefty cut of his funds in order to minimize the tax burden. But that is exactly what happens. By the end of the year in which he reaches age 71, he must choose the annuity that offers the best deal. In return for his life savings, the insurance company will pay him a monthly income, after taking a cut for expenses and deducting a charge for insurance based on the age, health and sex of the individual—women are given lower monthly payments since they are expected to live longer than men.[3] An annuity will pay the individual a monthly payment for as long as he lives. But if the buyer dies a day after taking out the annuity, the insurance company keeps the money; that is, unless it is a joint and last survivor annuity. This type will go on paying monthly benefits after the first spouse dies, until the death of the second spouse. But as might be expected, the insurance company slices off an even greater share of the funds in return for the feature.

[3]Discrimination on the basis of sex may soon become a thing of the past in annuities. A special study group on pensions reported to the federal government in May 1985 that women should receive equal treatment when it comes to pension payments, a recommendation that could have impact on the annuities. About 250,000 Canadians belong to money-purchase company pension plans

Insurance firms offer other variations on annuities. The consumer can elect to receive payments for a guaranteed period of time, say 15 years, after which payments cease. Or the consumer can choose a term-certain annuity which will make payments up to a defined age, say 90. But once again, the company's cut is larger with this kind of annuity.

Yet another option exists. The consumer can also buy a Registered Retirement Income Fund (RRIF), which is a similar product offered by trust companies. Like annuities, RRIFs provide payments designed to end at age 90. The point of an RRIF is that while the buyer receives a monthly, quarterly or semi-annual payment every year, the balance of the funds continues to earn interest. Since payments increase every year, these plans offer some protection against inflation. In contrast, an annuity provides a fixed monthly payment that may be worth less as time goes on, because of inflation. Still, the

under which the employer and the employees make monthly contributions to the plan. Whatever money builds up in the plan over the years is used to buy an annuity when the employee retires. The study group concluded that the monthly payments women receive from these annuities should be equal to the higher monthly payments received by men, but they could not agree on how this could be achieved. Some members favoured the use of unisex mortality tables, under which the monthly payments to men would be decreased and the payments to women increased. The other members though equality could be better achieved by asking employers to make contributions that were from 10 to 20 per cent higher for female employees than male employees. That way, the amounts that women have to invest in an annuity when they retire would be greater, allowing a life insurance company to give them monthly annuity payments that would be equal to men's, even though women live longer. Subsequent to the study group's report, the federal government's May 1985 budget did declare that men and women should receive equal pensions. In mid-1986 life insurers and major employers were still wrestling with how this would be achieved. No one wanted to pick up the tab.

Some senior citizens also resent the fact that they are forced to roll their RRSP funds into an annuity at age 71 in order to protect the money from income tax. However, an attempt in 1985 by 71-year-old Alexander Gerol of Mississauga, Ontario, to take this provision out of the federal Income Tax Act failed. Gerol argued before the Ontario Supreme Court that the provision violated the Charter of Rights and Freedoms. But Mr Justice Alvin Rosenberg threw out the case, saying that it is up to Parliament, not the courts, to decide whether the provision should be eliminated.

disadvantage of RRIFs is that the payments may be too small to begin with in the early years. It may take about ten years before the gradually increasing payments of an RRIF exceed the monthly payout from an annuity. Either way, in old age, it is difficult to avoid sharing your savings with an insurance firm.

Whichever life or annuity policy a consumer selects, some comparative shopping is necessary. Admittedly, this is a difficult task. As a select committee of the Ontario legislature stated in a report on insurance in 1980: "It is evident that the lack of meaningful price information presents at least an obstacle to competition and an obstacle to proper choice by consumers. It appears unrealistic to the Committee to allow consumers to purchase a product as important as life insurance without some means of defining the cost of that product and comparing the cost among competitive products. In fact, such a situation with respect to insurance products, to the extent that it occurs, appears to be a strange anomaly in an otherwise price conscious society."

### The Replacement Crisis

*"Most policies which have been in effect for ten years or more could probably be changed to the benefit of the policyholder."*
Conclusion of the Joint CLHIA/LUAC Committee on Replacements (March 1982)

This statement, taken from a confidential industry task force report obtained by the author, sums up a conundrum faced by insurance companies. As the public becomes more knowledgeable about insurance, increasing numbers of consumers are replacing old policies—which were developed using outdated mortality rates and low interest-rate assumptions—with better policies. For the consumer, the benefits are usually indisputable; for the industry, the costs are immense. When old policies are allowed to lapse or are cancelled, the bread and butter of the companies' balance sheets—investments made with the premium payments from old policies—is lost. And it cannot be readily replaced by new business, which is less lucrative for the company, and does not even make money for the firm in its early years because of administration and commission costs.

According to another confidential report by the Committee on Replacements, which was approved at the CLHIA annual meeting on May 28, 1985, replacements are rising at an alarming rate. It noted that all policy surrenders (cancellations), as a percentage of individual insurance premiums, rose from 17.6 per cent in 1975 to 24.9 per cent in 1980 to 33.6 per cent in 1981. In its report, the committee noted the example of a major Canadian company which examined its books for the first eight months of 1982, during which time it sold almost 13,000 individual life policies. The company found that in the same period, almost 11,000 policies were surrendered, and 8,000 lapsed, for a net loss of between 5,000 and 6,000 policies.

In the report, the committee made some observations about the causes of the replacement problem which industry spokesmen are generally reticent to admit publicly. The committee, made up of insurance executives, warned that such factors as changing risk-classification systems (like preferred rates for nonsmokers); rising inflation and interest rates; more cost-conscious consumers; and the eagerness of agents to replace customers' policies in order to earn new commissions have all given the trend momentum.

The consumer often wins by replacing old policies that have high costs and low benefits. Said one chief executive officer in response to a survey by the industry committee: "If a company does not keep up with the competition in products and pricing, or maintain its agents' service to the policyholder, that company should not be surprised if some agent of another company does such servicing, to the detriment of the original company." But as the committee observed in its report, from the company's point of view, replacements are almost always "bad." "Only the healthier policyholders replace, leaving companies with poorer than expected mortality on remaining policyholders; and new acquisition expenses take long periods to recover..." It is difficult, however, to feel a great deal of sympathy for the life insurance companies. After decades of neglecting the needs of consumers, they are finally, belatedly, feeling the effects of competition. More upheaval is necessary before the odds are stacked less in the life insurers' favour and more in favour of the consumer.

### The Pitfalls of General Insurance Policies

Consumers can be thankful that they have been better served by the policies offered by general insurance companies. There is, after all, less room for abuse in establishing insurance coverage on a car or home than in determining life insurance amounts, where companies can manipulate cash values and dividends to increase profits at the expense of the policyholder. Still, the products offered by property and casualty insurers are not immune to criticism.

The Consumers' Association of Canada has been chastising the general insurers for some time over the lack of choice offered to a consumer who wants to insure his home and its contents. "The problem with homeowner polices," says Helen Anderson of the CAC, "is that they are big undigestible lumps." Anderson explains that the policies sold by most companies include fire, theft and liability insurance whether the buyer wants all three or not. For example, she says, a homeowner might have a swimming pool on his property but not want the coverage provided by liability insurance to protect himself against someone who sues him after being injured while swimming. But he has no choice in the matter. The policy will charge him for liability insurance. Another, smaller anomaly in homeowner policies that bothers Anderson is a provision allowing 5 per cent of the home's total coverage for outbuildings. Most homes don't even have outbuildings. A garage is not an outbuilding, but a woodshed or toolshed is. Nevertheless, the policyholder pays, whether he has an outbuilding or not.

Other problems abound. Good luck to a consumer who wants to buy only fire insurance on his home. Some companies have fire insurance policies but they certainly don't push them—better to sell the client an all-embracing, more expensive policy, which includes fire insurance. Then, too, homeowners with a high-ratio mortgage could find themselves in real difficulty when they try to buy insurance. Mortgage lenders insist that a borrower have fire insurance on his home equal to the value of the mortgage. That means, says Anderson, that the coverage in his homeowner's policy could be "so high that it covers the land, which can't possibly burn down."

General insurers have been turning a deaf ear to the complaints of the CAC for years, and they continue to do so. But they are extremely concerned about another challenge to the way they do business. A groundswell of opposition has arisen across the country to their practice of discriminating against certain drivers on the basis of sex, age and marital status in determining rates for auto insurance. In all the provinces except Manitoba, Saskatchewan and British Columbia, where government corporations run automobile insurance, male, unmarried drivers under 25 still pay more than anyone else for insurance. The fact is that these drivers, as a group, do cause more accidents. Male drivers under 25 comprise 11 per cent of all licensed drivers in Canada, yet they are involved in 26 per cent of accidents. But the industry's habit of charging them more than older or female drivers is being challenged as unfair discrimination. In August 1985, when Michael Bates, a 22-year-old from Etobicoke, Ontario, made that argu-

ment before a board of inquiry set up by the Labour Ministry
of the Ontario government, he won his case. Bates complained that in 1983 Zurich Insurance quoted him a yearly
rate of $1,002 to insure a 1976 Chevrolet Camaro while a
woman pretending to be his sister, with the same driving
record, was quoted a rate of $522. In agreeing that the rate
was discriminatory, Frederick Zemans, the chairman of the
board of inquiry, concluded that Zurich had not proved that
its classification of drivers by age, sex and marital status was
essential for its economic efficiency and was not "reasonable"
discrimination as permitted under the Ontario Human Rights
Code.

Zurich, backed by the entire general insurance industry, is
appealing the decision in court. The insurance companies
are arguing that the Human Rights Code permits rate discrimination on the basis of sex and age because it is reasonable
on economic grounds. If Zurich loses it appeal of the decision, insurers have warned that the premiums of other drivers will have to be raised by as much as 12 per cent. That is
not necessarily so. If insurance companies kept better track of
the driving records of individual drivers, rates could be geared
to the number of accidents and speeding convictions a driver
has rather than the insured's age or sex. Drivers often switch
companies without giving accurate information on previous
accidents and claims, and so the new insurance company, in
turn, usually tries to get in touch with the former to check
the applicant's driving record. But some companies neither
initiate nor respond to these inquiries because they feel it is
too time consuming. Currently, the automobile insurance companies in Ontario are trying to create a central, computerized
pool for claims records. It is a good idea. With such information readily available, insurers will be in a position to throw
out the old discriminatory rating system and replace it with
one based on an individual's personal driving record. Not all
young, male drivers, after all, are reckless joyriders.

More than ever before, the policies sold by life insurers and their cousins in the property and casualty field are being examined closely by wary consumers. Many of the policies do not stand up well to scrutiny. For decades, consumers have been too bewildered by the twists, turns and complicated jargon of policies to know whether or not they were being rooked. Increasingly, as consumers become better informed, the initial confusion over insurance-company bafflegab is turning into condemnation.

# CHAPTER 2

## *Easy Targets:*
## *The Company as Victim*

*"Man's Life is a warfare against the malice of men."*
Gracián, a seventeenth-century Spanish philosopher
and priest

INSURANCE COMPANY LAWYERS or claims adjusters writing a
philosophic treatise on human nature would almost certainly
come up with an opinion of man resembling Gracián's pre-
Enlightenment view. In those days before faith in reason and
human progress gained prominence, human beings were universally regarded as wallowing in a state of sin, as backsliders
naturally disposed to deceit and treachery. One can't really
blame insurance company types if they have taken on the
attitudes that mediaeval monks held toward the mass of common men. They are regularly confronted with cases of fraud
or petty larceny by policyholders. People who would shudder
at the thought of robbing a bank find it much easier to make
a phony claim to relieve the huge, faceless insurance company of a few hundred thousand dollars or more.

Hardened by their experiences with clear-cut cases of fraud, adjusters look closely for suspicious signs in all claims. Did the man who disappeared hiking in the bush die, or did he take off to start a new life? Was the car accident victim driving while he was in a drunken stupor, thus voiding the policy? Did the claimant who died of cancer a few months after taking out a large policy really not know of the illness when she filled in her policy application? Did the businessman burn down his store to collect on insurance? In the 1944 suspense movie, *Double Indemnity*, Edward G. Robinson, playing a life insurance adjuster, sums up the requirements of the job in a nutshell. Trying to convince a reluctant salesman, Fred MacMurray, to become an adjuster, Robinson says: "A claims man is a bloodhound and a doctor, a judge and jury, and a father confessor all in one."

After a company's shrewd team of claims specialists have determined that a claim is fishy, the company refuses to pay up. Often, life insurers hand the case over to private investigation companies like Equifax Services or Intertel, which do a bustling business tracking down perpetrators of insurance fraud around the world. It is a myth, propagated by television, that private investigators spend their time catching unfaithful husbands or wives in the act. Insurance companies keep them too busy to bother with the nickel-and-dime stuff. General insurance companies can either call on the services of private adjusters, who often style themselves after Columbo, the television detective, or refer suspicious claims to the Insurance Crime Prevention Bureau (ICPB), an industry-funded group whose investigators co-operate with police in sniffing out phonies. There is plenty to keep all these sleuths busy because fraud is a growing problem in the life insurance industry. Says Bruce McDonald, chief counsel and vice-president of Manufacturers Life: "The number of fraudulent claims is increasing." It is no less a problem for general insurers. The ICPB alone handles 4,000 investigations of suspected fraud each year. ICPB vice-president Murray Swift estimates that a minimum of 15 per cent of the total claims made against general insurers in Canada each year are fraudulent. Some in the industry put the figure at 40 per cent.

Popular myth has it that insurance companies will invariably find a way of avoiding paying claims, often by pointing to a loophole in the policy to justify their action. An article entitled "The Origins of Life Insurance" in *Punch* magazine gives a satirical illustration of how the public sees insurance companies. States the article:

> The Modern Era, or Golden Age, of insurance can be said to have been ushered in by the birth, in 1623, of Josiah Smallprint. Son of a Lincolnshire pharmacist, young Josiah spent his early years amusing himself among his father's alembics and phials. It was thus, on November 18, 1641, that he stumbled upon an ink which could be put onto paper by type, but which remained invisible until the paper was put at the back of a drawer. Upon removing the paper from the drawer and examining it again, the owner found it to carry all sorts of information hitherto unnoticed.
>
> The first example of Josiah's handiwork to be used commercially was the phrase "…always provided that a pig flew past at the time the accident occurred."
>
> There is a statue to Josiah, 1st Baron Smallprint, in the foyer of Policymonger's Hall.

Anyone who has lost jewellery, for instance, and later discovered that the small print in the insurance contract limited the company's liability to a fraction of the jewellery's value, or anyone who has been crippled by an accident and found that the insurance company doesn't define him as disabled since he can still move his left arm and right leg, will find *Punch*'s viewpoint bitterly amusing. But it is only partly true. In fact, insurance companies often prove to be easy targets for fraud.

### Missing at Sea

The water of the Gulf of California was calm as the 25-foot sailboat motored away from its moorings at the small harbour in Marina Del Ray. The three men on board seemed to be in high spirits, talking loudly and drinking in the warm spring sun as they pushed off at about noon hour. Only one of them knew anything about sailing. Bruce Ross, a 33-year-old electrical contractor, had leased the boat from Marina Sailing, ostensibly to give his two friends, Paul Hopp and Joel Feigenheimer, a sailing lesson.

Both Hopp and Feigenheimer later told police that tragedy struck the trio that March afternoon in 1983 when the weather in the Gulf turned nasty. After the men had spent hours drinking heavily and lolling about in the sun, they said, the wind had picked up and turned cold, forcing them to put on their shirts and windbreakers. As the spray from five-foot waves lashed over the boat's railings, Ross and Hopp had their hands full keeping the vessel under control. Feigenheimer went below to sleep. Repeatedly, said Hopp, Ross went to the bow to fix faulty guy wires on the front sail, leaving Hopp alone at the wheel in the stern. But, according to Hopp, Ross went forward to check the guy wires one last time and did not return. Manning the wheel, Hopp could not see the bow over the cabin in front of him. Alarmed, he scampered forward to look for Ross as the boat careened out of control. There was no sign of Ross; he had fallen overboard and disappeared.

It was a sad case. A young man in his early thirties, Ross had a wife and two small children. At 10:30 that night when the Ventura County police arrived at the home of Mrs Ross in nearby Thousand Oaks, she took the news very badly. Luckily, however, her husband was heavily insured. He had two policies worth a total of $550,000 from two U.S. life insurers, Old Republic Life Insurance Company of Chicago, and American United Life Insurance Company of Indianapolis. Ross also had a smaller policy, worth $50,000, from a major Canadian insurer (which agreed to reveal its embarrassing involvement in the Ross case on the condition that it remain anonymous). In the company's downtown Toronto headquarters, claims specialists studied the Ross file, found the tale convincing and dispatched $50,000 to the bereaved Mrs Ross.

The two American insurers were not so ready to part with their money. They hired a firm of private investigators, California International Investigators Inc. of San Francisco, to conduct a probe into the alleged drowning. The investigators worked very much like police, looking into the background of the three men, questioning anyone who saw the three that day and interrogating Hopp and Feigenheimer. It was more than the two men, unaccustomed to breaking the law, could take. They cracked and, after being granted immunity from prosecution, told their story to a Superior Court judge in Los Angeles, where the two insurance companies were contesting Mrs Ross's death claim.

The bizarre scheme Ross and his associates dreamed up sounded like the plot from a poor episode of *Hawaii Five-O*. In fact, the three hadn't even got out of the bay where the marina was located before they let Ross off on the shore. While still on board the boat, Ross had hurriedly shaved off his dark-brown beard, pulled on a silly-looking, shoulder-length wig with bangs over his short curly hair, and changed his clothes. No one was going to recognize him. But it was all to no avail. Ross was apprehended by police and subsequently sentenced to five years in jail. In mid-1986 the Toronto insurer was trying to get its money back.

## The Man Who Never Was

The rookie life insurance agent at Manufacturers Life Insurance Co. was delighted when he got the phone call out of the blue from Samuel Otomroh. Otomroh was calling for his nephew, who wanted to take out a $100,000 life insurance policy. The problem was, said Otomroh, that his nephew, Albert Okon, was kept very busy in his job as a manager of a Toronto firm which sold household products, and was seldom at home. Could the agent please drop the policy application off for Okon to sign? Eager for business, the agent agreed. A short time later, the signed application, with a premium payment, was mailed to the agent's office. Breaking company rules, the agent signed the application as having witnessed Okon's signature. The beneficiary of the policy was Otomroh.

The policy was approved by the company, and issued on May 4, 1981. The agent was worried about overlooking company rules, but he was reassured when he delivered the policy and finally met a man identifying himself as Okon, whom the policy showed as a 21-year-old born in Nigeria.

Months later, Manufacturers was notified that, sadly, Okon had died of pneumonia in Kumasi, Ghana. The documentation was convincing. It included a medical certificate of death, signed by the attending physician at the Kumasi hospital where Okon had passed away, and a letter authenticating the death, signed by a local medical offical. Otomroh filed a claim to collect his $100,000.

The sharp claims specialists at Manufacturers, however, found the case altogether too suspicious. First, they served Otomroh notice through his lawyer that the claim was being denied. Then they called in Intertel to conduct an investigation into the mysterious Albert Okon. It did not take long for Intertel's sleuths to discover gaps in the alleged life history of Okon. For one thing, Canadian immigration authorities had no record that Okon ever entered, lived in or left Canada. More troubling still, a four-month investigation in Ghana by an Intertel agent based in Abidjan, in the Ivory Coast, revealed that Okon had never been admitted to the hospital he supposedly died in and the doctor who signed his death certificate had not worked there for several years. The agent even travelled to the village where Okon was allegedly born and learned from the local chief that no one under that name had lived or died in the village. An Intertel report to Manufacturers in 1982 concluded that "beneficiary Samuel Otomroh has attempted to defraud Manufacturers Life of the $100,000 claim in that the person of Albert Okon is fictitious." Police never got a chance to lay fraud charges against Otomroh because he disappeared and has not been heard from since.

### Acting on Instinct

In *Double Indemnity*, Edward G. Robinson uncovers a scheme in which Fred MacMurray, the salesman, and Barbara Stanwyck, his icy mistress, murdered her husband to collect on a $100,000 insurance policy. Robinson, a veteran of 26 years in the business, sniffs out the plot by instinct; he talks about a little man inside him who acts up when a claim is false. "I've been living with this little man for 26 years," Robinson tells MacMurray, "and he's never been wrong." In real life, too, claims specialists rely on gut instincts as much as hard facts to discover false claims.

George Tingey couldn't sleep. The director of consumer service at London Life Insurance Co. tossed and turned as he thought about a huge life insurance claim for $506,443.84 sitting on on his desk at the office. After 38 years' experience in claims and counterclaims, Tingey had developed a sixth sense when it came to phony ones. "It's too neat, too perfect," he thought to himself.

The claim involved Parnpreet Singh Chhina, 27, who came to Canada from India in 1980 looking for a better life. Chhina had every reason to believe he would prosper in his new country. He had a bachelor of science degree from a university in his native India and a master's degree in English literature. He also took a banking and real estate course in Toronto. But the only job he could find was as a parking attendant.

In March of 1982, his wife, Surrinder, applied for and received a $500,000, ten-year term policy on her life; her husband was listed as the beneficiary. Company officials had the impression that Surrinder came from a wealthy family in India and wanted the large policy for reasons of prestige.

Just seven months later, on October 5, Chhina called the insurance company's office to say that his wife had died in an accident while on vacation in Suranussi, India. She had been riding in a jeep on a rough road when it overturned. By chance, a doctor had been following in another vehicle and pronounced her dead on the spot. In making the claim, Chhina produced all the necessary documentation in a package—the death certificate, the police report, the doctor's statement and even a cremation certificate.

Payment was approved on the claim by London Life executives on October 27, 1982. It included the $500,000 face amount, plus $6,443.84 in interest accumulated since the supposed date of death.

Still, Tingey couldn't get the claim out of his mind. The day after Tingey had approved the claim and put it in his mail basket, he went into the office and told his secretary: "Get that policy back." Then he hired an investigation service, Philadelphia-based ESIS International, and alerted the fraud squad of the Metropolitan Toronto Police of his suspicions. ESIS dispatched an agent to the Punjab. His findings were puzzling. The police report had been signed by Surrinder's father, the head of a local police college. The doctor who had signed the death certificate could not explain why the woman's body had not been sent to a hospital for a post mortem. But the breakthrough came in Toronto. Metro police staked out Chhina's Toronto apartment and one day caught Chhina entering the apartment with Surrinder on his arm. Tingey's sixth sense had paid off. Chhina was later sentenced to 15 months in jail for attempted fraud.

## Watchdogs in the Claims Department

Before a claim ends up in court, insurance companies do everything in their power to avoid being duped out of their money. They employ well-trained experts to detect fraud or even innocent misrepresentation by policyholders. Bruce McDonald, chief claims counsel of Manufacturers Life, and the nine lawyers in his department are the last line of defence Manufacturers has to ward off policyholders who make what are considered to be unjustifiable claims. "We're not looking for reasons not to pay," says McDonald. "But if something doesn't look right, we investigate further." If a claim seems suspicious, life insurers have the right to investigate the claimant's hospital and medical records. (A clause in the claim form permits them to do so.) Sometimes their probe reveals that the patient had a history of illness that wasn't revealed in the health questions on the insurance application form. "It is not uncommon," says McDonald, "to discover that a claimant was diagnosed as having cancer only a few months before applying for a policy and neglected to mention it in the application form." The pressure is on life insurers to discover such oversights by the policyholder within the first two years of issuing the policy. The law provides that within the two-year period, the insurance company can void the policy or raise premiums if it discovers such mistakes. After the two years are up, the policy is incontestable and the company must prove that the customer *intentionally* misled the insurer in the application for insurance. "It has to be something quite blatant," says Bruce McDonald.

Manufacturers has learned the hard way how difficult it is to refuse a claim after the two-year period has elapsed. In 1982, it received a $500,000 death claim after the policyholder, a married woman in British Columbia, died of accidental drowning. The policy had been in force for more than two years. When Manufacturers investigated the case, it found that before she had taken out the insurance, the woman had been in and out of detoxification centres for alcoholism. This fact was not revealed in two life insurance policies she bought from the company in the late 1970s shortly after her last drying-out session. Manufacturers, alleging that she intentionally misled the company about her state of health, refused to pay the claim. In 1984, the woman's husband, her beneficiary, sued Manufacturers in the British Columbia Supreme Court. The court ruled in the beneficiary's favour, concluding that Manufacturers failed to prove that the woman intentionally misrepresented her condition on her policy applications. Said the judge: "A question asking about 'illness' would not necessarily have brought to mind her problems with alcohol. Thus the incontestability provision operated." A subsequent appeal by Manufacturers in 1985 was dismissed. Concludes McDonald: "You won't find too many companies trying to void policies after the two-year period. It's very difficult to prove civil fraud."

Life insurance companies have had a hard time refusing claims on policies more than two years old since 1880, when the world's first so-called "unconditional" policy was sold by Sun Life. Sun introduced the policy after it lost a bitter court battle over its refusal to pay a claim on the death of a Mr Wright, who had committed suicide. In those days, policies carried the condition that if an insured committed suicide at any time the policy was void. There was also an interminable list of other activities, occupations and even dwelling places, such as the "unhealthy" southern latitudes of the United States, which were forbidden in the pages of small print attached to policies. To the outrage of Robertson Macaulay, Sun's managing director at the time, the jury that heard the case completely ignored evidence that Wright had committed suicide and, obviously showing little sympathy for the rich insurance company, ordered it to pay the claim.

Macaulay was appalled by the court decision, since it meant that all the conditions then attached to policies were essentially meaningless in the eyes of the law. As a result, he introduced the unconditional policy, which had three sentences on its front page:

• The assured may reside in any part of the world without extra premium.
• The assured may engage in any occupation without extra premium.
• This policy will be indisputable on any ground whatever after it has been in force for two full years.

Sun's novel policy proved to be a hot seller because clients liked its relative simplicity. Other companies soon followed suit and eventually the "unconditional" policy became part of insurance law.

Occasionally, of course, life insurance companies don't prove to be easy targets at all for claimants who think they should be paid. One of the first cases of attempted fraud against an insurer occurred in 1894. In that year, Manufacturers Life received a $2,000 claim after the death of a policyholder, Antoine Pettigrew of Rivière-du-Loup Station in Quebec. The beneficiary making the claim was a local hotel owner, J. N. Anctil, whom Pettigrew had described in his policy application as "My protector." An investigation showed that Anctil was anything but Pettigrew's protector. Manufacturers discovered that the deceased was not a "farmer" as he had stated but had no occupation or means at all. In fact, he lived at Anctil's hotel where he performed menial tasks and was given ready access to plenty of liquor, which evidently hastened his death. When Anctil's claim was refused in a well-publicized court hearing, the ruling was seen as a death blow to so-called wagering policies, in which the beneficiary pays the premiums, hoping the policyholder will die.

Equally controversial cases have been sensationalized by the press in more recent times. One legal action in 1983 involved no subterfuge or attempted fraud by the claimant, but it ranks as one of the stranger cases in insurance law. It involved wealthy Mississauga developer Peter Demeter, who sued Dominion Life Assurance Co. and two other companies[1] for a total of $3 million on the grounds that he was the beneficiary of his dead wife, Christine, who had taken out insurance with the companies. The Hungarian-born businessman made the claim even though, in a sensational trial in 1974, he had been convicted of second-degree murder in the death of Christine, a beautiful, blond model who had been beaten to death by unknown assailants in the couple's garage.

Demeter's action against the companies was not as nonsensical as it might appear. At the trial, his lawyers argued that his earlier conviction for the murder of Christine was based on fabricated evidence given by several witnesses and that fresh evidence important to the case had been discovered. Since Demeter had already lost an appeal of the criminal conviction, his suit against the companies was an attempt to reopen the whole case in a civil proceeding. As Demeter testified: "I am not here for the money, I am here to reopen my case." Supreme Court of Ontario Justice John Osler was not impressed by Demeter's arguments. In September 1983, Osler dismissed the lawsuit saying, "It would be an affront to one's sense of justice and would be regarded as an outrage by the reasonable layman to let these actions go forward."[2]

[1] The other companies were the Transamerica Occidental Life Insurance Company of California and the British Life Insurance Co.
[2] In another bizarre twist involving the Demeter murder, the daughter of Peter and Christine took the same companies to court in 1981 in an attempt to collect a total of $412,524 in insurance on her mother. Although she was not named as a beneficiary in the policies concerned, the daughter argued she was the next of kin of Christine Demeter and it would be equitable for her to receive the proceeds. The action was dismissed.

## *Duelling with the Adjuster*

In the ranks of insurance people, no one can surpass the claims adjusters employed by general insurers as masters in detecting false or exaggerated claims. They emerge from special courses on "negotiational techniques" as capable as bloodhounds. If a claimant doesn't have a mountain of information on how much an item cost, where it was bought and how it was lost, he is in for a rough time. With pride, Edward Chick, vice-president of claims for Royal Insurance of Canada, describes the interrogation techniques used by the company's 420 claims adjusters. The emphasis, he says, is on using a combination of courtesy and firmness, which is developed in role-playing sessions. He demonstrates how an adjuster might question a claimant in a phone conversation over the loss of a $15,000 piece of jewelery:

"First of all, where did you buy it?"

"Oh, you don't know."

"Can I have the receipt?"

"You don't have a receipt."

"Can you tell me when you bought it?"

"Can you tell me the month and year?"

"Well, if you are so specific as to when you bought it, why can't you tell me which store you purchased it in?"

"Oh, you can't."

"Now, $15,000 is a pretty substantial item. Did you buy it near where you live in Toronto?"

"You don't know where you lost it. Are you sure you lost it?"

And so the grilling goes, with the adjuster asking a series of ever-more-detailed questions designed to confuse or intimidate dishonest claimants. Finally, the adjuster usually asks the person to take just one more look to see if the jewellery was simply misplaced. "You may never hear from that person again," says Chick.

Insurance adjusters have to be tough. According to Chick, false or misleading statements by policyholders are commonplace among the roughly 200,000 claims Royal handles each year. Often, the client innocently exaggerates the claim. Says Chick: "That's where an experienced adjuster has to sit down with the insured and say, 'Well that seems a little bit out of line. Can we help you retrace some of these things?'"

Some of the most difficult claims to deal with involve medical injuries—in particular, back problems. "There are some injury claims involving lingering pain," says Chick, "where we investigate the record of the claimant and discover that he has a history of injury claims with different insurers for the same pain." Royal sends such cases on to the Insurance Crime Prevention Bureau (ICPB), which keeps records of past claims in order to be able to detect repeat claimants. Says Chick: "If I have a reply from ICPB that the person has had six claims, one after the other, I think at the very least that it calls for a further inquiry of that person."

General insurance companies have their hands full trying to detect dishonest claims. But fraud affects them in other ways, too. To client companies they offer bond coverage, which insures the client firm against fraud or theft by employees. Sometimes that involves a junior employee picking a handful of bills out of a till. At other times the crimes are more serious. Chick recalls one case that involved a senior executive of a major Toronto-based real estate development company. "The man, who was in a very, very responsible position," says Chick, "not only got a salary increase, but he altered the figures to give himself a bigger raise and made it retroactive." Not a bad trick if you can get away with it.

A handful of small, financially shaky general insurance companies take their reluctance to pay claims a little too far. Some are notorious for dragging out the payment process for more than a year on relatively straightforward, uncontested claims. The company's intention, of course, is to hang on to the cash a little longer and earn interest or investment income on it. Meanwhile, the consumer is left in a state of anxiety and financial hardship. The practice is too common in Canada and should be monitored more stringently by regulators. At Royal, Chick tries to make sure that sort of thing never happens. Each claims adjuster is given a written copy of the company's principles. They include "a commitment to settle legitimate and reasonable claims promptly and fairly within the policy conditions; and the making of arrangements for appraisals and repairs without unnecessary delays." To its credit, Royal has a program called the Royal-Aide Program which helps resolve seemingly intractable differences between the company and claimants before they end up in court. The unsatisfied client is offered the opportunity to select an expert representative—a lawyer, for instance—who will meet with a representative from Royal. The two arbitrate the dispute and decide on a reasonable settlement. Royal pays for the process, including the costs of the client's spokesperson. The only condition is that the client must sign a document in which he agrees that the decision of the two arbitrators will be final. There aren't too many people who take advantage of the service, according to Chick, who suggests that one reason might be that the clients are sometimes bluffing in the first place.

### Restaurant Flambé

It was already midnight on November 2, 1977, and Lisle Smith had had a long day. He had spent the evening with representatives from the Federal Business Development Bank (FBDB) and other creditors negotiating a further loan to keep his struggling French restaurant in Camrose, Alberta, afloat. Apparently happy with the result of the session, Smith busied himself closing up the restaurant for the night. His daughter and an employee did the usual checks to ensure that the restaurant was vacant and securely locked. After driving home, Smith hadn't been in bed long when he received a phone call from the City of Camrose police informing him that the restaurant was on fire. He hurriedly woke up his daughter and drove to the scene. Despite the efforts of the fire department, the restaurant was effectively destroyed by the blaze. But when Smith later filed a claim to Royal Insurance to collect on a $100,000 policy covering the restaurant's stock and equipment, the claim was refused. Smith sued.

In court, there was never any dispute that the fire was caused by arson; but exactly who set the fire was more difficult to determine. At the trial in July 1981, Royal defended its refusal to pay the claim on the grounds that Smith himself was the arsonist. The nub of the company's case was that Smith alone had a motive to set the fire and the opportunity to do it.

The court heard that in September 1977, Smith had opened the dining establishment with high hopes. At first, there was a surge in business which seemed to ensure the restaurant's success, but that soon tapered off. What is more, Smith, who set up a holding company to own and operate the restaurant, had spent much more than he expected to set up the business. He had estimated start-up costs of $115,000; the actual cost was closer to $182,000. The Federal Business Development Bank had granted him a line of credit for $75,000 to get the enterprise off the ground. Smith himself had put in $40,000 he had borrowed from a bank. Now the restaurant could not pay for its operating costs and Smith needed more money.

The entrepreneur's session with his creditors that November evening had been rewarding. The man from the FBDB had agreed to recommend to his superiors that Smith's line of credit be increased to $104,000, provided that Smith personally chipped in another $14,000 and that his other creditors agreed to hold off on the majority of their claims until the restaurant had the earnings to pay them. The creditors agreed.

Despite the fact that Smith had received his financial life preserver, the trial judge, S. V. Legg, was much more impressed by evidence that he felt implicated Smith in the crime. The judge noted that there were only four keys to the restaurant, three of which were in the hands of employees. But only Smith, he concluded, had a motive to set the fire, since he was considerably in debt. Justice Legg concluded that "the balance of probabilities" suggested that Smith was the arsonist. Smith's claim against Royal was dismissed.

Undeterred, Smith took his case to the Alberta Court of Appeals in 1983 and won. The appeal judges disagreed with many of Justice Legg's conclusions. In a written judgement, they stated that Smith, in fact, stood to go further in debt as a result of the fire, since the $100,000 policy was far below the actual worth of the equipment at the restaurant. In addition, the restaurant itself was estimated to be worth more than $200,000. Smith could have gained more by selling the restaurant than by burning it down and collecting the insurance. More important, the appeal court set a precedent by ruling that simply establishing motive and opportunity was not enough to prove guilt in cases of alleged arson. Smith collected his insurance money. William Turnbull, a Royal claims specialist, in no way suggests that Smith should have been found guilty, but he points out that the ruling makes it harder to prove arson. "The decision has made it much tougher for a company to succeed," he says.

Fire losses are one of the biggest drains on the general insurance industry's coffers. According to the most recent statistics compiled by the Fire Commissioner of Canada, losses from fires totalled $816 million in 1983. The most vexing aspect of the fire loss figures from the industry's point of view is that about 13 per cent of the fires were known or believed to have been the result of arson. Measured in dollars, arson accounted for at least $150 million in damage during the year. The figures show that most arsonists reside in Quebec, which had 2,656 known or suspected cases of arson in 1983. Ontario came a close second with 1,982 and British Columbia placed third with 1,185 cases. The tallies for other provinces were considerably lower, ranging from 706 in Alberta to none in Prince Edward Island.[3]

In most instances of arson, charges are never laid. Although there were 7,948 cases of intentionally set fires in Canada in 1983, only 1,643 charges were laid in connection with the crimes. Arsonists, whether they are pyromaniacs, revenge-seekers or financially strapped entrepreneurs trying to cash in on an insurance policy, tend to carry out their crimes in the stillness of night. The chances that the criminal will be spotted by a passer-by at 3:00 A.M. are rather remote. Usually, there are no witnesses, and the odds are that the fire will destroy any evidence the criminal leaves behind. Insurance companies, of course, have the right to deny payment on claims which they believe involve a client intentionally burning down a home or business to get out of debt. Murray Swift of the Insurance Crime Prevention Bureau estimates that about 15 per cent of arson-caused fires are set by the owners of the property. But insurers have a very difficult time proving arson in court. As the appeal judges in Lisle Smith's case pointed out, the fact that the alleged arsonist had a motive for the crime and an excellent opportunity to carry it out is not enough to lead to a conviction. Arson is a crime with many known victims—39 people died in intentionally set blazes in 1983—but few known perpretrators.

## More Headaches

Automobile thefts are another costly problem for general insurers. The latest figures compiled by the ICPB show that there were 75,252 motor vehicles (cars and trucks) stolen in 1984. Of those, 19,417 were never recovered. According to the ICPB, a minimum of one-third of the unrecovered vehicles were driven

[3]The totals for the other provinces were: Manitoba, 406; New Brunswick, 279; Newfoundland, 129; Nova Scotia, 290; Saskatchewan, 259; the Yukon and N.W.T., 32.

off bridges, hidden in dense bush or otherwise disposed of by their owners in order to collect insurance money.

Fraud causes financial setbacks for all insurers. Life insurers pay out millions of dollars (no accurate figures are kept) to claimants who fill out policies and fail to mention potentially terminal health problems or to con-artists who fake death. Says Bruce McDonald: "A decade ago there were hardly any court cases involving fraud. Now we see several a year." For general insurers, the greatest toll is not taken by fraudulent fire or stolen-vehicle claims, but by the claims of thousands of average citizens who fake a myriad of smaller losses on everything from jewellery to bicycles. The cost of all these minor cases of larceny, according to Jack Lyndon, president of the Insurance Bureau of Canada, "is far the higher than losses from fire or anything else." General insurers paid out $1.2 billion more in claims during 1985 than they earned from premiums. Yet Murray Swift estimates that payments on fraudulent claims totalled more than $1.2 billion. Without them, the underwriting loss would have been wiped out.

In light of the prevalence of fraud, it is understandable if insurers resort to elaborate countermeasures that sometimes make even completely honest claimants feel like felons. Yet, if the system is to function at all, there has to be an element of trust between the public and the industry. Otherwise, the system would collapse under the costs of continual lawsuits launched by disgruntled policyholders or suspicious companies. Says Ed Chick of the Royal: "I still happen to believe that the industry is governed by good faith, but there is always a percentage of people that are going to try to beat the system."

# CHAPTER 3

## *Saints and Sinners:*
## *The Agents*

*"Selling life insurance is a job very close to the ministry."*
John Acheson, chairman of the Canadian Life and
Health Insurance Association, 1985–86

*"The insurance business is vicious, dirty and nasty. If some-
one hurts someone else, they think up a scheme to get them
back."*
a Toronto life insurance agent

THE MEN AND WOMEN who moil for gold in the insurance
industry have an image problem. They haven't been entirely
trusted by the public since the seventeenth century, when
insurance was the sport of speculators who would bet on the
longevity of a public figure, and then have him murdered by a
band of brigands. In the 1600s, when the first modern insurance firms were being formed in England, insuring goods,
ships and chattels had some respectability; selling life insurance did not. Daniel Defoe, a failed British merchant and the
prolific writer of such novels as *Robinson Crusoe*, expressed a
popular view of life insurance in that era. "Insuring of life I

cannot admire. I shall say nothing of it, but that in Italy, where stabbing and poisoning is so much in vogue, something may be said for it."

In the 1800s, when the first life insurance firms took root in Canada and the United States, one of the greatest problems they had to face was the apathy and outright hostility of the general population. The public viewed insurance agents as something akin to snake-oil salesmen. Besides, the whole idea of insurance seemed a contradiction of the Biblical exhortation to trust God in all things. Since that time, however, insurance companies have made great inroads into consumer pocketbooks. Canadians have flocked to life insurance in droves. Although Canada was one of the most insured nations in the world in 1984, Canadians are ambivalent about insurance agents. Surveys show that consumers rate agents as a group slightly below used car salesmen in terms of trustworthiness. Yet most those same respondents rate their own agent highly and consider him or her to be an exception to the popular opinion that agents are a money-grubbing lot.

Dishonesty among agents, of course, is not more prevalent in any particular racial group or ethnic minority. Yet most of the cases of insurance crime described in the following pages involve agents who have exploited their own kind. The cases have been selected because they rank among the most serious, not because they represent any general trend.

For the life insurance industry, its lack-lustre image could be a costly obstacle in the growing competition with other sectors of the financial services industry for consumer savings. To the dismay of the industry, a confidential, nationwide survey carried out by the Canadian Life and Health Insurance Association in 1985 revealed just how little faith consumers have in the financial stability of insurance companies and the expertise of their agents. In a phone survey of 1,000 Canadians that cost $40,000, the CLHIA asked consumers to answer a series of questions relating to so-called "Strategic Issues" facing the industry. A preface to the study remarked, "Since life insurance companies and salesmen were not rated highly by the consumer, CLHIA does not plan to make the consumer study public." The survey revealed that only 4 per cent of Canadians ranked life insurance companies as the most secure financial institutions, compared to 69 per cent for banks, 15 per cent for credit unions and 8 per cent for trust companies. (Stock brokerages placed last, with 2 per cent, behind even the life insurers.) A surprising 18 per cent of Canadians actually believed that life insurance companies were the least secure financial institutions, which is, of course, an extremely ill-informed point of view. No federally licensed life insurer has ever failed, although a few provincially registered companies have.

The survey also asked respondents to rate the financial capability of life insurance agents and other financial advisors on a scale of 1 to 10. Life insurance agents came last, with an average score of 4.6. Canadians were more likely to trust the advice of accountants (7.3), bank or trust company managers (6.8), credit union managers (6.2), lawyers (5.6) or stockbrokers (5.5). The study revealed in stark terms the dimensions of the life insurance industry's public relations problem. In reaction to the study, the industry launched a $1.6 million advertising blitz in late 1985 to help reverse its sagging reputation.

"It's a shame the public has the perception of the agent that it has," comments John Acheson, former chairman of the CLHIA. "The life insurance agent lifes in a negative world for 10 months out of 12 every year. Good agents must be dedicated, put the clients' interest uppermost." An agent must withstand the gruelling pace of the job, the night calls, the rejections, adds Acheson. "But the man or woman who is well suited to the calling of life insurance has the best job in the industry, perhaps in the country." In fact, the insurance industry probably has no more miscreants and swindlers than has any other trade or profession, even though there are so many ways to abuse the insurance system that larceny and fraud are actually made easy.

Most successful agents operate with a strong dose of self-motivation, a bottle of stress pills in their back pocket and enough sincerity to sell snowshoes to Africans. One successful agent recalls how he lacked confidence in himself when he was first considering becoming a life insurance salesman. "I was talking to an agency manager who was trying to recruit me," recalls the agent. "He knew I was reluctant, so he asked, 'How many women have you taken to bed?' I said, 'Quite a few.' So the manager said, 'There, you've sold everyone.'"

Life agents emerge as proselytes from company sales training programs that last from two to four months. To obtain a licence to sell, they must also spend a few hours a day for three to four weeks preparing for an examination administered by the provincial superintendent of insurance or by industry-appointed bodies in each jurisdiction. General insurance agents are also required to pass provincially administered examinations to obtain a licence. (In Ontario only, a self-regulatory body, the Registered Insurance Brokers of Ontario, administers the examination for licensing.) But the training and examinations only prepare the agents for the real test to come: the school of hard knocks. "The insurance business has its own natural selection process built right in," says James Roszak, president of Transamerica Life. "Only agents who can tough it out make it." Indeed, selling life insurance is a frenetic, high-pressure career in which only the most resilient survive. It is a high-speed treadmill that never ends. A typical agent spends most of his day on the phone drumming up new sales prospects; most evenings and weekends are spent on sales calls in territories that can range from 50 square miles for city-based agents, to 200 square miles and more for their small-town counterparts. It is a male-dominated business. Only about 15 per cent of the more than 24,000 life agents in Canada are female, even though women buy about 40 per cent of the life insurance policies sold in the country each year.

Selling general insurance is much easier. It doesn't have to be forced on people in the way that life insurance does. Whether they are agents working for a large company or independent brokers working out of their own offices, general salespeople can usually sit and wait for clients to call them, not vice versa. The general insurance business does not collect industry-wide statistics on the number of female agents or brokers, but industry spokespeople agree that general insurance, like life, is sold mainly by men.

The best salespeople in either type of insurance see their jobs as fulfilling an important public need, and in many cases this is true; the worst see their work as a way to make fast money from uninformed and gullible consumers. Many of them use a trump card in their deck when it comes to clinching a sale: the prospective client's fear of calamity.

General insurance salespeople like to remind the public of the costs of catastrophe in order to drum up business. On Bloor Street West in Toronto, there is a small, family-owned property-and-casualty brokerage that knows how to catch the attention of passersby. A large poster in the window prominently displays gruesome photographs of car wrecks, burnt houses and other accidents. The caption, in bold letters, reads: *Don't let it happen to you.*

Life insurance salespeople have to resort to the fear factor even more often than do general insurance agents. In confidence, even the agents with the most missionary zeal about the value of life insurance say that they regularly employ scare tactics. "You always have to assume the guy is buying," says one top-selling agent. "If the guy says he wants to put it off until later, I say, 'If you're not here, who will I talk to?'" Another super-salesman has a trusty, entirely *untrue* tale he likes to tell the minute he gets inside a prospective customer's door. He launches into a story about the super guy he met two months ago. When the agent tried to sell him a policy, his wife argued that the family needed a new refrigerator more than insurance. So the family put off buying insurance. "Well," says the agent, "wouldn't you know it. A few days later the guy got killed in a car accident on the expressway. Maybe you heard it on the radio? Anyway, the wife got the refrigerator, but the family was left destitute."

This is only one of a vast repertoire of stories commonly used by agents. Another top salesman is lucky enough to have an office overlooking a cemetery. Often, when a client comes in to talk about insurance, the agent walks over to the window, admires the view and, with a sweep of his arm toward the tombstones, says, "That is not a dress rehearsal." The ploy usually works. Concludes another salesman who, for several years in a row, has been a member of the industry's prestigious Million-Dollar Round Table for top-selling agents: "You've got to back the hearse right up to the door."

## The Underside of Life

The mood in the beverage room of the New Windsor House in Toronto is warm and consoling. Everyone in the place, from the Donegal girl tending the bar to the jovial patrons sipping pints of dark-brown Guinness stout, seems to be Irish. Much of the talk in the darkened room is of news from "back home." In one corner, a couple of old men banter in a lilting brogue as they play their daily game of darts. A large green shamrock is displayed proudly on the wall.

The life insurance broker slips quietly into the room and joins the interviewer at a small table. He has come to talk about the seamy side of the life insurance business—on condition that he remain anonymous. Over the past decade, Mickey (not his real name) has worked for about eight major life insurance companies in Canada, and he says he has seen every trick in the book. His angular features, bushy moustache and balding head ringed by a thatch of longish brown hair give him a distinctly weasel-like appearance. The air of cunning is reinforced as he speaks, Guinness in hand, about selling life insurance. "To close a deal you have got to have killer instincts, whether the policy is good for the client or not," he says, the gleam in his eyes clearly showing that he's got what it takes.

Mickey blames many of the industry's woes on the companies, not the agents or brokers.[1] The biggest problem, he says, is that most companies pay salesmen lucrative commissions and bonuses totalling from 150 to 200 per cent of the first-year premiums on new policies. That means that if a customer buys a life insurance policy with first-year premium payments of $1,200, the agent can immediately collect a commission of up to $2,400. The system therefore subjects agents to a temptation that only the honest can ignore. It is a relatively simple matter for agents to peddle large insurance policies to people who cannot afford them. Using an illegal method called rebating, the agent simply offers free or discounted insurance to the customer, paying all or part of the premium out of his own pocket, then collects a handsome commission from the company that issued the policy. Before the victimized company catches on to the scam, the agent moves on to another firm. In some cases, the company will demand partial or full repayment of the commission only if the policy lapses or is cancelled within 13 months of issue. To avoid having to give up the commission, the broker simply

---

[1]In life insurance, there are both brokers and agents in most provinces. Brokers shop around for a customer, looking for the insurance company that offers the best rate. By contrast, an agent works exclusively for his sponsoring company; that is, the company that sponsored his licence. Brokers are not legally recognized in Ontario and Newfoundland, although both provinces allow an agent to engage in brokering if he has the written permission of his sponsoring company. In Ontario, agents effectively operating as brokers suffered a setback in 1985 when the Ministry of Consumer and Commercial Relations reversed a 1982 ruling allowing agents to operate as brokers if they received a blanket waiver from their sponsoring company. The new edict stated that the agent henceforth had to obtain written permission from his sponsoring company *every time* he wanted to sell a policy from another company.

gives the client enough money to cover 13 months of premium payments and laughs all the way to the bank. Mickey says he knows one man who wrote a policy on a supposed customer who was, in fact, already dead. "He did it for the commission," he says. "The company paid him 150 per cent commission within a week. It's the company's fault," he mutters. But in the next breath, he concedes that companies that have tried to reduce commission rates have failed because of broker outrage. "The brokers simply take their business elsewhere."

Another problem, says Mickey, is that companies will usually pay a higher commission rate to brokers if they bring in a certain level of business each year. A broker who sells policies with total annual premiums worth, say, $50,000, might get a commission rate of 120 per cent. But if he brings in $300,000-worth of premiums for the company, his commission rate plus incentive bonuses could rise to 200 per cent of first-year premiums. That puts pressure on brokers to make it to the $300,000 level. Often, a broker will find himself just several thousand dollars short of the magic number, says Mickey, "so he goes out to four or five friends and loans them the money to take out enough policies to push him over the top."

But the best way to make money as a broker, according to Mickey, involves one broker setting up a pyramid of brokers below him. The broker at the top goes to a life insurance company and says, "Listen, I can sell policies that will bring you $500,000 in premium payments each year." Impressed and eager for the cash, the company agrees to pay him its highest commission rate, say 200 per cent on each policy. Then, the broker and his band of subordinates go out and sell the company's policies. But all the applications are sent to the insurance company under the first broker's name. That way, there is a bigger pie of commissions for the dozen or so brokers in the pyramid to split among them. Mickey operated such a network in 1984; he made $150,000 after expenses.

Agents have scores of opportunities to defraud the public. One insurance agency manager discovered that a life agent in his office was illicitly taking out policy loans on her customers' policies. (In most whole life policies the client is permitted to borrow money from the issuing company up to the level of the cash surrender value of the policy.) She forged the necessary documents and pocketed the money, intending to repay it before the unwitting customers caught on. It's a handy way of getting a large, short-term loan. But it is also larcenous, as the crooked agent found out when the company, Mutual Life Assurance, discovered her scheme.

### Let's Do the Twist: The Dance That Lives On

Another illegal practice, calling twisting, is endemic in the industry, claims Mickey. Twisting occurs when a broker or agent entices a customer to cancel an old policy for a new one the salesman is peddling, without properly informing the customer of the pros and cons of each policy. Twisting is illegal because regulators fear that permitting it on a widespread basis would expose consumers to excessive manipulation by salesmen intent on selling new policies.[2] With a laugh, Mickey recalls the case in which an agency manager left one life insurance company to join another and took all the agents in his branch with him. Immediately, they went to their clients and got them to switch their old policies for new ones sold by the second company. When the first company cried foul, the agency manager paid a visit to their offices. He waved in the face of an executive a confidential memo which spelled out the company's practice of not hiring black sales

[2]In many jurisdictions, there is a legal loophole which permits the legal switching of policies. In Ontario, for instance, the salesman simply has the customer sign a government-designed form which lists in detail the advantages of the new policy over the old one.

staff.[3] "Do you want me to make a public stink about this?" he threatened. Chastened, his former employer bothered him no more.

With the cavalcade of new, improved life insurance products since 1980, twisting has become common in the ranks of most companies in the industry. One company even handed out a "Chubby Checker Award" to the agent who switched the most policies during a year. "Toronto is twist city," scoffs Mutual Life Assurance agent John Byrne.

But Toronto has no exclusive claim on the dance that has never gone out of fashion in the insurance industry. Earl McGill, superintendant of insurance for Manitoba, recalls a popular scam that sprang up in the Winnipeg area in 1984. Tired of using conventional methods to find new business prospects, a group of agents began conducting a phony telephone survey. An agent would phone up an unsuspecting consumer at home and say he was conducting a survey on behalf of the industry. Then he would ask a series of questions about the person's salary, number of dependents and overall financial situation. Finally, the agent asked how much insurance the individual had and which company he or she had bought it from. About six weeks later, another agent in the scheme would phone up the householder, subtly convey the impression that he represented the person's insurance company and ask to come over to talk about updating the existing policy. At the meeting the agent would suggest the client switch his policy to a cheaper policy with another company. Usually the ploy worked, since the new policies were for term insurance, the lowest-cost type of insurance. In some cases, the clients were probably better off with their new policies. But that did not eliminate the fact that unscrupulous agents were using deceit to achieve their ends. The agents involved lost their licences.

---

[3]In insurance circles, it is well known that several major companies discourage agency managers from hiring blacks or East Indians.

## *Picking the Company's Pocket*

The meeting was held in the utmost secrecy. Shortly before 10:00 A.M. on November 9, 1984, nearly two dozen chief executive officers, each flanked by a coterie of aides looking like pilot fish teeming around a cruising shark, began arriving at the Ontario Securities Commission (OSC) hearing room on the eighteenth floor of the Cadillac Fairview Building in Toronto. Just two weeks earlier, they had received a puzzling letter from the provincial Ministry of Consumer and Commercial Relations. The missive, which went out to 22 life insurance companies, had stated only that the ministry's staff was conducting an investigation and requested the executives' presence at the OSC that day. None of them knew the purpose of the meeting or, for that matter, who else was on the guest list. Tight security measures were in force. At the door of the hearing room the identity of each visitor was thoroughly checked.

Then, sitting quietly in rows of chairs in a venue normally devoted to meting out justice to backsliders and wrongdoers in the investment industry, the executives, their lawyers and administrative assistants waited with nervous anticipation to learn the reason for the extraordinary assemblage.

At 10:00 A.M. two investigators of the ministry's Financial Institutions Branch walked before them. The keynote speaker was Tom Turner, an intense 33-year-old with a quick mind and savvy that belies his age. His number two was Donna Murray, a cool, attractive 39-year-old who had previously worked for the Metropolitan Toronto Police fraud squad and, before that, the Criminal Investigation Bureau of the Peel Regional Police Force.

What Turner and Murray had to say made even the most jaded insurance men in the room shudder. With the help of a complex slide-show, the two revealed the findings of a probe they were conducting into the insurance industry. For

months, they said, more than 50 life agents had been operating in rings and systematically defrauding their employers.
So far, the results showed that at least 12,204 policies
worth $633 million had been sold by agents who were using
elaborate rebating and other illegal techniques. As Turner
explained it, agents in the rings were mostly exploiting un-
sophisticated members of their own ethnic communities. In
one variation of the scam, an agent would go to a prospective client and offer him or her a $100,000 whole life policy.
The annual premiums on such a policy might total $3,000,
far more than the client could afford, but that was no obstacle. The agent would just say, "Here's an application for
a policy. Don't worry—it's free." Then, using the same
method that "Mickey" described, the agent himself would mail
the company a cheque (drawn on his own account) to cover
the initial premium payment of $250. Within 10 to 15 days, the
company would mail the agent a commission cheque for
$4,500—representing 150 per cent of the first-year pre-
miums.

But the fraudsters used other devious methods as well.
Some companies do not require that the cheques for premium payments be signed by the policyholder; the agent's
signature will do. That opened up a situation in which an
agent could simply invent the name of a policyholder, give
the address of a friend and submit the policy with an initial
premium payment. Within two weeks the unscrupulous agent
would receive a fat commission cheque. The situation had
got so far out of hand that a computer check by the investigators revealed that two agents had sold 21 policies to a
handful of addresses; at one address alone, policies were
written to fictitious people with five different surnames used
in combination with eight different first names.

Several larger insurers, including Crown Life of Toronto,
Empire Life of Kingston and Standard Life of Montreal, had
been targeted by different rings. But the ministry had been

prompted to call the meeting of insurance executives by a particularly troubling scheme aimed mainly at the Norwich Union Life Insurance Society. It had been victimized by a ring beginning in June 1984. There was a "Godfather" in that particular scam, explained Tom Turner. He had a middle-man who set up agencies with a stable of crooked agents to carry out his scheme. A close relative served as a bagman, collecting the ring's profits. "The agents were targeting their own people," said Turner. "They were new Canadians—East Indians, Filipino, Guyanese." In one case, Turner pointed out, "an agent went to a client and got him to sign three or four applications for insurance policies from different com-panies at the same time. Then the agent mailed in the ap-plications in the names of other agents, who were in on the swindle. Next, the agent would set up a central bank account with enough money in it to cover initial premium payments on the policies." The agent paid out only $1,000 in initial premium payments from his bank account, but within weeks commissions totalling about $18,000 rolled in from the com-panies. Most of the agents who had targeted Norwich Union, however, used rebating techniques. The ill-gotten gains from 572 policies, sold in June and designed to collapse in Septem-ber, were split between the Godfather, the middleman and the agent who sold each policy.

When Turner and Murray had finished their presentation, their audience sat stunned by what they had heard. Alarmed by the dimensions of the corruption that had been outlined to them, many of the executives said that it was easy to under-stand how it had happened. Says Turner: "They acknowledged that it was their fault to some extent because of the commis-sion structures." If any of the insurance men doubted the seriousness of the rebating problem before the meeting they had no delusions when the session wound up at about noon hour. "They walked out of there true believers," observes Turner.

## Operation Lion

The investigation by Turner's team had been triggered several months earlier when the slippery and larcenous ways of one Kanwar D. Singh had come to the ministry's attention. Associates describe Singh as a well-educated man—he is said to have an M.A. in history from an American university—who has a well-balanced temperament and a penchant for philosophical musing. But an agent who witnessed Singh's scam first-hand is more blunt about his character. "He has no morals; he's ruthless. He showed up the insurance companies," says the agent, who at one point ran a pyramid of salesmen that included Singh and his band of thieves.

With the *sang-froid* of a snake charmer, Singh exploited the naivety of clients, deceived the companies that employed him and, for years, evaded the regulatory authorities. Since 1981—and possibly earlier—Singh had moved in the netherworld of life insurance, switching from one sponsoring company to another, looking for high commission rates that were susceptible to abuse by rebating techniques. But early in 1984, the 42-year-old Singh heard of an incredible policy that Crown Life was promoting. By selling the policy to insure the lives of infants, an agent could earn commission plus bonuses of up to 500 per cent of first-year premiums. Unable to pass up such a golden opportunity, Singh signed a contract with Crown to sell its policies in March 1984, then went to about six other agents and said, "Let's insure every Indian kid in the city."

In the next three to four months, Singh's ring, with the help of about 20 unlicensed operatives who lined up prospective clients, managed to peddle more than 250 policies. They simply went to unsuspecting members of the Indian community in Toronto and offered them one year's free life insurance. In most cases, Singh would ask the customer to write a cheque payable to Crown Life for a downpayment on the policy. Then Singh would hand the customer cash to cover the amount. In many homes where the applicant and his wife plus one or two children were insured, the total annual premium amounts were about $5,000 to $8,000 per year, far more than the family could ever afford. But, then, most of the policyholders had no idea of the face value of their policies, which ranged from $60,000 to $200,000, or of the premium payments required.

Singh's scheme began to unravel when a manager at Crown's head office noticed the incredible volume of policies the new hot-shot agent was selling. The name Singh rang a bell in the manager's head; years earlier, an agent with the same name had burned Crown using rebating techniques. Crown took a closer look at the policies and discovered a suspicious pattern: most policies were for amounts that didn't require credit checks; almost none of them required medicals. Alarmed, Crown cut off Singh's commission payments and called in the government investigators.

In the course of their investigation (called Operation Lion because Singh means "lion" in Hindi), Turner and his team of sleuths, Donna Murray, Charles Dimock and Wally Kowtun, managed to gather a bulging file of incriminating evidence against Singh. Distressingly, they also discovered that Crown was only one of several companies that Singh had conned since 1981. At a hearing on March 18, 1985, before the provincial superintendent of insurance, Murray Thompson, investigator Murray testified that Singh had submitted rebated business through Empire Life, Crown Life and Standard Life. "We suspect that 50 per cent of the business he submitted through Empire Life was rebated, paid for in whole or in part, and we further suspect that 70 to 80 per cent of the business he submitted through Crown Life and Standard Life involves the practice of rebating," said Murray. It was a lucrative scheme for Singh. The investigators found that in one nine-month period alone, Singh had submitted $350,000 worth of premium business to Standard Life. At the hearing, which Singh didn't show up for, chairman Thompson noted sarcastically: "I don't think such conduct should go rewarded only in remunerative ways." He then ordered that Singh be permanently banned from engaging in the business of selling life insurance.

Soon after discovering Singh's misdeeds, the Consumer and Commercial Relations investigators set up a computer program, called Sort, into which they entered information on suspicious agents, the types of policies they sold and the names of their customers. By March 1985, their time-consuming labours revealed a nefarious pattern of rebating and fraud against about 25 insurance companies. By February 1986, the investigators had lost count of the number of crooked agents their probe had uncovered. Their investigation had snowballed into a province-wide operation. "The agents started talking, consumers began to come forward," says Phil Yakubovich, deputy director of the Financial Services Investigation Branch at the provincial Ministry of Consumer and Commercial Relations. "The project was a probe into a few agents; now it has exploded. We've got them [cases of fraud and rebating] all over the province." Many of the agents have been called before ministry hearings where they have been stripped of their licences. Others are waiting to go before hearings. The anti-rackets unit of the Ontario Provincial Police has begun an investigation of the whole affair. By the fall of 1986, Yakubovich expects the OPP to lay fraud charges against many of the agents in one fell swoop.

Ontario has no corner on crooked life agents. The province has more agents operating within its borders than any other province—about 15,000 of the 24,000 agents in the country—and therefore the odds are that it will have more wrongdoers. But Yakubovich scoffs at the suggestion that the situation in Ontario is any worse than in other provinces. The reason insurance crime on a widespread scale has not been uncovered in other provinces, he argues, is that the governments haven't devoted enough resources to the job. "They don't have the people to find it," he says, pointing out that no other province has an investigation branch as large as Ontario's. "The more you dig, the more you find." David Holbrook, superintendent of insurance for British Columbia agrees. "We've been basically putting out brush fires," he concedes. "Most of our time is spent just checking the financial solvency of [provincially registered] companies." In 1986 the B.C. Ministry of Consumer and Corporate Affairs increased the number of investigators responsible for keeping an eye on 7,000 insurance agents and many more real estate agents and stockbrokers from 9 staff members to 12.

Since the discovery of widespread rebating in Ontario, the nationwide industry has taken some action to try to prevent the practice. In November 1984, the Canadian Life and Health Insurance Association, which represents most of the life insurance companies in Canada, established an eight-member task force to look into the problem. In April 1984, it recommended that companies not project commission based on early sales without evidence of bona fide customers; that commission payments be monitored to nab rebaters; and that privileged information on crooked agents should be shared between companies and regulators.

Yakubovich is a 53-year-old veteran who formerly worked as an investigator for the OSC and he has some well-informed opinions on what further steps the insurance industry should take to put its house in order. He stresses that an independent clearing house should be set up by the industry to keep track of policies. That, he says, "would prevent cases involving four different policies under the same name, each with a different birth date." Yakubovich also argues that the companies must take greater responsibility for the detection of bad agents. "Ask the companies what safeguards they have against agent fraud; what warning signs they have to prompt them to take a look at an agent's policies; what happens when a salesman has a banner year. Do they check his business?" Following the recommendations of the CLHIA task force, some companies have instituted better monitoring systems, but many do not have the time or the inclination to allocate substantial resources to catching bad agents.

It is clear that until companies agree to lower first-year commission rates so they are below 100 per cent of first-year premiums, the system will continue to be abused. Canadian provinces, which have jursidiction over insurance agents and the policies they sell, should pass laws similar to those already in force in New York State. There, commissions are limited by law to 55 per cent of first-year premiums. When special-performance bonuses and agent expenses are added in, each life insurer is not allowed to pay out more than 95 per cent of first-year premiums to any agent. As a result, rebating is not a problem in New York. But there is little likelihood that the Canadian industry will welcome such a law. Says Yakubovich: "The industry is very competitive. Everybody's struggling, trying to put out more perks for salesmen."

### Perfidy in Property and Casualty

Gord Cockburn's face tightens into a frown as he talks about his work. His silver-grey hair, neatly trimmed moustache and penetrating gaze give him the appearance of a spy-master in a John Le Carré novel. But Cockburn's sleuthing does not take place in the world of fiction. As an investigator for the Registered Insurance Brokers of Ontario (RIBO), Cockburn hunts down con-artists, crooks and incompetents working for Ontario's 3,500 general insurance brokerages, the companies that sell property and casualty insurance to home owners, car drivers and businesses, and market liability insurance to litigation-wary professional groups and organizations. Minor offenders in the brokers' ranks are dealt with by RIBO's discipline committee, where they can be fined or have their licences cancelled. More serious offenders are first dealt with by RIBO, then brought to the attention of the police and, in many cases, penalized by the criminal justice system.

Created by an Act of the Ontario legislature in 1981 to administer and regulate the provincial industry, RIBO is being watched closely by brokers and regulators in other Canadian provinces and in the United States because it is an experiment in self-regulation. Its success may spawn similar efforts in other jurisdictions, where supervision now rests in the hands of government departments that are undermanned and overworked. So far, RIBO has proven to be both rigorous and uncompromising in its supervision efforts. The dedication and track-record of Cockburn, fellow investigator Kevin Fitzgibbons and chief financial examiner Ingeborg Koch are impressive. They are a serious-minded group, spending their days rummaging through tell-tale financial documents of wayward companies or tracking down and confronting brokers suspected of improbity. The trio is kept very busy. RIBO's complaints committee, made up of brokers and well-qualified laypeople, received 790 complaints of broker misconduct in 1985 alone. Many of the complaints involved illegal financial legerdemain by the brokers, or the late filing of the financial forms that RIBO requires. Others, however, are cases of outright fraud. In the past, RIBO's staff has not divulged the details of its investigations to the press or public. However, with the approval of RIBO manager J. R. Coghill and consumer complaints officer Herbert Baker, the investigators opened up their files for the author.

## Man about Town

Andrew Stephen Tatar thought he had the system beat. Driving around Toronto in his baby-blue Cadillac, the 53-year-old lady's man was doing a thriving business selling general insurance policies to fellow Hungarian immigrants. When he was not selling insurance he liked to go to the Central YMCA in downtown Toronto to keep his chunky, heavily muscled body in tone. Unfortunately, Tatar was not that conscientious about his business habits. He often neglected to pass on the premiums he collected to the Kitchener-based brokerage he was working for. He simply pocketed them. "He was driving around selling policies out of his glove compartment and pocketing the premiums," says Cockburn with a scowl.

Most brokers are allowed to operate their own trust accounts into which they deposit premium payments from customers before sending the funds, minus commissions, on to the companies that issue the policies. The premiums are deposited in special trust accounts because the money does not belong to the broker, and it is illegal for him to use it for his own purposes. Tatar had run into trouble with the regulators once before. Even before the creation of RIBO in 1981, provincial government authorities had taken away Tatar's right to maintain a trust account and ruled that he could only sell insurance under the strict supervision of a sponsoring company. Tatar had a broker's licence, but it had severe restrictions on it. That didn't bother him much, though. When he started working for the brokerage in Kitchener he simply neglected to send the premiums on to the firm. But his sponsoring brokerage soon noticed that something was amiss. At first it was short about $40,000 in premium payments, then another $20,000. Soon the shortfall totalled about $130,000. RIBO was alerted.

Tatar was called in to the Toronto headquarters of RIBO where he was informed that since he was required to act under supervision, and the Kitchener brokerage company had disowned him, he was technically out of business. RIBO cancelled his registration as a broker. But Tatar ignored RIBO's orders and began selling insurance policies again, continuing to pocket the premiums. By this time, the fraud squad of the Metropolitan Toronto Police was on the case.

Sensing that his insurance misdeeds had attracted too much attention, Tatar went to ground. In a final attempt to crack down on him, RIBO used its powers of search and seizure, and in co-operation with the Metro police, staged a raid on his Toronto office early in April 1983. They were too late. Tatar had been there hours before and taken away any incriminating evidence. The only thing of note that the investigators found at the office, says Cockburn, were several spent pistol shells. In the following months, rumours of Tatar's whereabouts proliferated. Some informers reported seeing him in Europe; others said he was in the United States.

Finally, late in 1984, RIBO found its man by sheer chance. While in New York, a RIBO staffer, to his amazement, noticed Tatar's name in a newspaper advertisement. He was listed prominently as a broker acting for a major U.S. insurance company. RIBO immediately alerted the FBI and the U.S immigration authorities. Tatar was arrested on December 3 and delivered into the hands of police at the Canadian border. In court, he pleaded guilty to theft and defrauding the public of nearly $132,000. Early in 1985, he was sentenced to two years less a day in reformatory. Says Herb Baker: "He was a con-artist *par excellence*."

### A Land of Plenty

Pocketing premiums is a popular practice among many brokers looking for ways to make easy money. Baker recalls the case of Moshe Baba, a Christian Syrian who set up the Ninvah General Insurance Brokers, Inc. in Ottawa. Baba had worked for the United Nations in Ottawa but liked Canada so much that he left his U.N. job to begin a new life. The first sign that he was up to no good came from a public complaint in late 1982. Says Baker: "A customer called and said, 'I ordered insurance but when I had an accident, I was told there was no coverage.'" Baba's scam involved issuing pink liability slips to customers, indicating that they had bought insurance. But instead of sending the applications on to the insurance company, Baba simply took the premiums himself. RIBO revoked his licence, but the regulators at RIBO subsequently discovered that Baba was still selling policies and running an unlicensed company. In February 1984, he was found guilty in provincial court of "holding himself out as an insurance broker without a licence" and fined $2,000. His company was fined another $5,000, a figure that was later reduced, on appeal, to $2,000.

Much of RIBO's time is spent checking the financial statements of brokerages, looking for illegal financial manoeuvres. Herb Baker, the complaints officer, is a heavy-set man with a head of thick greying hair swept straight back from his forehead, giving him the appearance of a benevolent hedgehog. A former broker himself, he knows the kinds of tricks unscrupulous operators in the industry can get up to. In particular, he says, it is difficult to prevent brokers from illegally transferring money out of their premium trust accounts and using it for other purposes. "The sort of thing we're talking about," he says, "involves transferring trust funds for Vegas trips, moving funds in weird and wonderful ways." In a big firm, he points out, "there's a lot of room to move money around because there's a hell of a lot of money coming in. The trouble is, most firms don't have much current money to play with, so they withdraw it [illegally] from the trust side and this creates a trust shortfall." Some new brokerage companies illegally dip into their trust funds to cover the cost of starting up operations—buying cars, desks, computers and other supplies. To combat such abuse, RIBO requires companies to file financial reports regularly and does random spot checks. But, unfortunately, says Baker, "we are finding that an increasing number of misleading reports are being filed."

The only criticism that can be levelled at RIBO's investigators is that there are not enough of them. Three full-time sleuths are simply not enough to handle the volume of cases coming their way. But even with its limited resources, RIBO has established itself as an effective watchdog that should be copied by the life and general insurance industries of other provinces, where government regulators are run ragged trying to carry out their policing duties.

### The Million-Dollar Race-Horse Swindle

Roland "Rollie" Miljus and Michael Jasnich were leading members of the St Catharines, Ontario, business community. Since 1979 they had operated a prosperous general insurance brokerage, Young's-Graves Bloodstock Inc., at 60 James Street in the city. Their company specialized in selling insurance policies on the lives of thoroughbred and standardbred race-horses. For the most part, they sold policies issued by the Victoria Insurance Company, a large, Toronto-based insurance firm. The Bloodstock company (Jasnich was president and Miljus vice-president) had an arrangement beginning late in 1979 with Victoria, under which Bloodstock ceded to international reinsurers 100 per cent of the risk on each Victoria policy it sold. In other words, Victoria would issue the policy but it didn't stand to lose money: if the insured horse died, the reinsurers would pay off the claim. The entirely legal scheme is not unusual in the insurance business and should have kept everybody happy. Victoria, Bloodstock and the reinsurers would take a cut of the hefty premiums that each policy-holder paid.

Theoretically, after Bloodstock deducted a commission for selling a policy, the premium payments should have gone to Victoria; Victoria, in turn, was responsible for sending part of the funds to Somerset Broking Ltd. in Hamilton, Bermuda, which was authorized to act as an intermediary and pay the lead reinsurer, Aneco R.E.–Insurance of Bermuda and other reinsurers for their services.

But as Miljus and Jasnich discovered, the arrangement was open to abuse. For one thing, when Bloodstock sold a Victoria policy, all the premiums were initially paid directly to Bloodstock. Victoria was supposed to receive the funds at a later date. For another thing, Bloodstock was not required to send any policy documentation to Victoria; they simply sent a computerized summary of the policies sold and the alleged premiums paid each month to Victoria, Aneco and Somerset. The three companies had no way of knowing if their computerized statements were accurate. For their part, Victoria and Aneco were entirely unaware of the illegal scheme Jasnich and Miljus later devised.

By 1981, Miljus and Jasnich, two otherwise staid businessmen in their early forties, had got a taste of the big money to be made in livestock insurance and they wanted more. They approached John Harris, who ran the Somerset brokerage in Bermuda, and asked him to help them with a plan to funnel money down to Bermuda to avoid taxes. Harris agreed. He also helped Jasnich and Miljus to incorporate two Panamanian companies: one was Elizabethan Corp., owned by Jasnich; the other was Viscount Corp., owned by Miljus. Next, Miljus and Jasnich opened bank accounts in another tax haven, the Isle of Guernsey. The two Canadian insurance brokers had set up a circuitous route to launder money and they were ready to carry out their scam.

In February 1981, Miljus and Jasnich began skimming off part of the premiums paid by policyholders on large policies. It was easy. They charged racehorse owners a certain amount in premium payments, then reported a much lower amount in the monthly computer statements sent to Victoria, Aneco and Somerset. The difference was whizzed through so many international bank accounts and dummy companies and then back to Canada that it was almost impossible to trace. Sometimes the two men stole modest amounts of cash. On one policy with a face value of $550,000 and annual premium payments of

$100,750, they took only $13,000. Sometimes they got greedier. Then they wouldn't even report that a policy had been sold at all and pocket all the premiums, which in one case totalled $84,232.24.

The illicitly earned funds were denoted by a code #99 on Bloodstock's books, to help Jasnich and Miljus keep track of their income. On the instructions of the two men, the money was first deposited in the Toronto-Dominion Bank on Queen Street in St Catharines, which, of course, was unaware of the goings-on. Then the money was transferred to the account of Somerset Broking at the Bank of Butterfield in Hamilton, Bermuda; that bank was also an innocent party. On receipt of the funds at Somerset Broking, John Harris would receive instructions from the two Canadians about where to send it next. Sometimes he was told to send it directly back to accounts in Canada and the United States for retrieval by Jasnich and Miljus; sometimes he would send the money to the accounts maintained by Elizabethan Corp. and Viscount Corp. on the Isle of Guernsey.

Miljus and Jasnich soon found themselves enjoying a new standard of wealth. Between February 1981 and July 1982, they spirited away a total of $933,947.75 in premium payments that should have gone directly to Victoria Insurance. A more affluent lifestyle seemed to be in order. In 1981, Miljus and his common-law wife, Muriel Lynch, bought a nice parcel of property on Mount Forest Lane in Niagara Falls, built a luxurious house and stocked it with furniture, for a total price tag of $350,000. The money, of course, was all hot, but Lynch was unaware of the fact. Her husband told her that business was going well. Jasnich picked up a comfortable condominium in Florida for himself and his wife, Kathryn. She, too, was unaware of the source of her husband's new-found affluence.

But the comfortable world of the two couples suddenly began to sour in 1983. In January of that year, Kenneth Elliot, a new partner Jasnich and Miljus had taken on at Bloodstock, became suspicious about the blizzard of fund transfers the company was making. He took his concerns to the police.

On March 17, 1983, Elliot walked into the Toronto office of detective-sergeant Stuart Moore, a member of the Ontario Provincial Police's anti-rackets squad. Sitting at his desk in a converted basement storeroom that passes for an office, Moore listened to Elliot's tale of intrigue with interest. The two men agreed that Elliot would continue working at the firm and secret away documents that would give Moore a hard and fast case.

But Elliot did not keep his secret deal with the police. On March 24, he told his story to executives at the Victoria Insurance Company who reacted immediately. The vice-president of operations, Roy Lever, descended on Bloodstock's office with several Victoria staff-members and seized whatever documents he could get. Next, an interim manager, Graham Goodchild, was sent in to do a complete audit of Bloodstock's operations. For a year, Goodchild and Moore worked closely together, sifting through the maze of papers and records at Bloodstock that contained evidence of fraud. Their task was made less difficult by the fact that Miljus and Jasnich admitted their guilt from the start and co-operated completely with the investigation. On April 18, 1984, the police laid a charge of fraud jointly against the two insurance brokers. On October 31, 1985, they were found guilty and sentenced to two years in penitentiary.

As Moore recalls the case, his wizened face shows little emotion. After 34 years as a policeman and eight years in the anti-rackets squad there is little that can shock him. But he frowns as he talks about the sad circumstances of Kathryn Jasnich and Muriel Lynch. Mrs Jasnich now lives in the United States, he says, and Muriel Lynch still lives in St Catharines, but not in her luxury home, of course. Both guilty men gave up their personal assets to help make restitution to Victoria Insurance. "The women didn't know it was dirty money," says Moore. "They've lost everything."

### Selling with a Smile and a Conscience

Luckily for Canadian consumers, slippery operators like Singh, Tatar, Miljus and Jasnich are the exception, not the rule, in the ranks of the insurance industry. The majority of agents and brokers are honest, energetic individuals who have chosen a demanding career. The major fault of many is that they tend to push clients into buying expensive or unsuitable policies simply because they are the only policies their company happens to offer or because commission rates on them are high. Some agents are outright saints, who think selling insurance is next to godliness. Others are just hard-working men and women (albeit with the odd trick up their sleeve) hustling to put bread on the table.

"Right by Thought, Health by Habit". The daily reminder is inscribed on a small copper wall plaque opposite the desk of Garry Dukelow, a 34-year-old super-salesman for Great-West Life Assurance in Winnipeg. It is Dukelow's motto, a sort of maxim of morality that could have been handed down by the patron saint of insurance salesmen, if there were one. The words, says Dukelow, remind him "to avoid corruption, and exercise regularly." Below the phrases are rows of cryptic numbers. Only Dukelow understands what they mean. He explains that they represent goals in his work and personal life. Like a mantra, they lose their mystery and potency if they are shared with anyone else.

Sitting behind his modernistic black-walnut-and-chrome desk, Dukelow shows no sign of wear after ten years in the insurance business. In his $500 grey suit and blazing red-knit tie, he looks like a striking blond Adonis who has just stepped out of a men's fashion ad in *Esquire* magazine. There is no trace of a wrinkle in his clean-shaven, square-jawed face and no hint of world-weariness in his manner. He exudes an aura of controlled physical energy that comes from hours of advanced karate training each week.

Dukelow is an anomaly in the insurance world. "He is a super-salesman without the super ego that usually goes with it," says a colleague. In 1985, Dukelow ranked second in sales among Great-West's 658 agents in Canada. He sold enough insurance policies to customers in the Winnipeg area to bring Great-West several hundred thousand dollars in premiums. While Dukelow will not divulge his income for publication, it is well into the six-figure range—enough to turn most head office executives at Great-West green with envy.

Dukelow describes himself as a financial planner. He stumbles on the words insurance salesman; too many negative connotations go with it. "I used to have a problem with image," he says. "It took me a long time to feel comfortable introducing myself to someone at a social gathering as a—uh—financial planner from Great-West." After a decade in the business, however, he was developed a firm belief in the worthiness of his occupation. Dukelow got into insurance by chance. At his wedding reception in 1976, a family friend who worked for Great-West suggested he try it out. Dukelow took him up on the offer: the newlywed was ready for a change. At the time, he was working as a stockbroker in Winnipeg, but certain aspects of the job bothered him. "One time," he recalls, "another broker in my office had a client who lost $60,000 in five days. The broker was callous. He showed no sympathy for the client at all." Dukelow had no intention of becoming so jaded. He joined Great-West as a salesman—and made a meagre $8,900 in his first year of selling insurance.

It was only after several years on the job, he says, that he really saw the usefulness of insurance. Now, he gains satisfaction when executives retire with a good retirement income plan that they acquired as a result of his advice or when someone who dies leaves a spouse and children with much-needed proceeds from insurance. One recent case, Dukelow says, was particularly edifying for him. In 1985, a close friend in his karate club suddenly died of a brain aneurism. Before he died, the friend had bought a $75,000 life policy from Dukelow. The young widow wasn't aware of the policy, and thought that she was facing a financial crisis. When she found out about the policy she was able to pay off the mortgage on her house. At the funeral, says Dukelow quietly, "I was walking past the widow. She got up and gave me a hug and a kiss."

Life insurance has been good to Alison Jenner, a 36-year-old Vancouver businesswoman. The trappings of success include a sleek, silver 300 D Mercedes sedan, an annual income well over $100,000 and a home in Deep Cove, an upper-middle-class suburb of North Vancouver. Jenner is a brokerage manager at one of the two branches that Toronto-based Transamerica Life maintains in Vancouver. She is responsible for lining up independent brokers in the area to sell Transamerica products. Much of her time is spent on the phone arranging appointments with brokers, then meeting with them to convince them that they should add Transamerica's term or universal life policies to the product lines they peddle to the public. Currently, Jenner has about 300 brokers placing business for the branch. As well as a hefty salary from Transamerica, she collects bonuses based on the volume of business the brokers bring to the branch. She also sells policies herself. A petite brunette who speaks with a soft Scottish brogue, Jenner is happy.

But her life today is a world away from her lower-class origins in Edinburgh, Scotland. As a girl, she grew up in a family that was always trying to make ends meet. Her father, whom she describes as "an Irishman who drank too much," made a living as a travelling salesman. He journeyed about with a vanful of clothes, delivering them to a network of "agents" (usually housewives) who sold them out of their homes to their friends. Jenner's mother was a hard-working woman who held as many as five part-time jobs at one time. "She did everything from cleaning offices to working as an auxiliary at hospitals," says Jenner.

Jenner's first exposure to the insurance business came when she was just 16 years old. After graduating from secondary school in 1966, she signed on as a clerk in the pension department of Edinburgh-based Standard Life. She didn't think it was her calling. A year later, Jenner went back to school to earn a teaching diploma. Her life's path seemed set. She got married and taught physical education in Edinburgh from 1972 to 1980, but a vacation with her husband, John, to Vancouver in the summer of 1979 changed all that. "We fell in love with Canada," she says.

The Jenners arrived in Vancouver in April 1980 with little money and no jobs. "I took a series of part-time jobs," says Jenner. "I worked for Pizza Hut, Marks and Spencer and the Royal Bank." Selling pizzas paid off. One of her regular customers was the manager of a local branch of Standard Life. She convinced him to hire her as a receptionist. "The trouble was, I couldn't type," she laughs. Standard made her an administrative secretary instead. One of her jobs was to stuff agents' commission cheques into envelopes for mailing. Says Jenner: "I decided there had to be something in that job [sales] for me."

In April 1981, Standard promoted Jenner to the position of brokerage representative, a job similar to the one she now holds at Transamerica. She was reasonably successful in her new position, earning $17,000 between April and December, when she left Standard to join Transamerica. Jenner likes working for Transamerica. "The philosophy of the company has always been to sell products that are in the best interest of consumers. A lot of insurers sell policies that are good for the agents and the companies but not for the consumer." Jenner also appreciates the fact that Transamerica treats its agents well. "It treats us like entrepreneurs," she says. "Other companies tend to treat agents like the scum of the earth, and there is a wide gulf between the agents and the executives at head office."

Sometimes, Jenner feels slightly uncomfortable with her new-found affluence. "It's my Scottish Presbyterian background," she says. "I justify the fact that I drive a Mercedes by telling myself that it's a diesel and therefore uses cheaper fuel." Still, she's not complaining. "I have two philosophies," she says. "One is to have fun; the other is to make money."

John Byrne settles back in his chair, pours another glass from the bottle of Jameson whisky in his desk drawer and talks about selling life insurance. "I think it's doing good," he says. "It's a win-win situation for the agent and the customer. It's not a matter of the agent saying, 'Ha, I sold another one tonight,' and pocketing the premium." Byrne is a very successful agent for Mutual Life of Canada. His income is about $100,000 a year in an industry where the average agent's income is about $40,000. Plaques honouring his sales exploits line his office walls.

One row shows that he has done enough business in four years running to make it into the Million-Dollar Round Table (MDRT), a worldwide industry club for top-selling agents. But the success hasn't gone to his head. "The MDRT is just an ego trip," he says, grumbling that selling a few million dollars' worth of business isn't enough to join the select group; he also had to pay $100 (U.S.) to become a member and another $50 for each plaque.

It's easy to see why Byrne excels at what he does. At five feet, seven inches, with silver-grey hair and kind, Irish eyes, 46-year-old Byrne most resembles an aging leprechaun. With his puckish sense of humour and air of sincerity, Byrne can establish a relationship of trust with anyone he meets within minutes, probably the most important ingredient for being successful in life insurance sales. "I like the money I make," he says. "It gives my wife and me the freedom to do the things we like." The things they like include travelling. "I go to Ireland for four to six weeks each year, I go to Nassau for two weeks at least once a year, I go to the States and take lots of cash."

Byrne also likes the independence his job gives him. If he doesn't want to get out of bed in the morning he doesn't have to. But there are fierce pressures that go hand in hand with that independence. "It's a never-ending 100-yard dash, that's about the size of it," he sighs. One day earlier, Byrne only worked until noon hour. "The reason I went home was that I didn't feel good. I was uptight, nervous. You've got to keep selling, you've got to keep prospecting for new business. It can get to you; there are lots of pressures." When he got home, he dug dirt in the garden for four hours, then went to bed at seven o'clock and slept for 16 hours straight. "I was strung out."

Still, for Byrne, selling life insurance has been a passport to prosperity. He was born and raised in the tiny village of Clones, Ireland where his father, an army sergeant, died when John was only 16, leaving the family in relative poverty. As a youth, John bounced from job to job until he ended up in Dublin playing piano professionally with bar bands. "When I first went to Dublin in 1959, I was a country hick," he says. "I remember meeting a couple of girls from my home town who were going to university and all of a sudden they were far superior to me. They had all the right words and all the right answers. I didn't even have the right questions, let alone the right answers." Eventually, however, Byrne's musical talents made him into a star of sorts. By the 1960s he was a member of the Abbey Tavern Singers, whose "Off to Dublin in the Green" was an international hit. Then in 1968, the group went on a Canadian tour. The trip was an eye opener for Byrne. "Back in Ireland in those days," he recalls, "there were definitely separate classes." But on the tour of Canada he discovered "that you didn't have to go to university to appreciate the good things in life. I'm talking about basic things. You can go into one of the poorest homes in Toronto and they will have a shower and heating." Byrne emigrated to Canada when the tour was over.

For several years in Toronto, Byrne worked as an optician, but he didn't like the nine-to-five hours or the pay. In 1978, his last year as an optician, he made $20,000. He joined Mutual Life and made $54,000 in his first full year in the business. Now a $100,000-a-year man, Byrne says of his relative wealth: "It frightens the life out of me. I can't believe it. I left school at 16." He takes particular pleasure, though, in meeting up with some of the university students he used to envy in Dublin who have also made their homes in Canada. "I've met some of the same people by coincidence who are now doctors and lawyers, and I'm making more money than them. It doesn't do my ego a damn bit of harm."

But Byrne doesn't define success as a salesman only in dollar terms. For him, selling bigger policies with more lucrative commissions is not the point. "I regard the policy I sold this morning to a friend of mine a success because he really needed that insurance. It wasn't a big policy as policies go, but if he dies, his wife is going to get some money. And that to me is a personal success." Conversely, he says, another friend refused to buy insurance from him, even though Byrne hounded him about it for three years. He was a self-employed contractor. "Six months ago he died of cancer at 50 without any insurance. His wife is now selling her car, her garden furniture, and she had to borrow money for the funeral. For me, that is a failure."

Byrne breaks off the discussion about his job to answer the phone. It is a client calling to finalize a detail of an insurance policy he has just bought. "How the hell are ya, you're lookin' good," Byrne chortles into the phone. Then, when the conversation is almost over, he tries to get the names of other potential customers from his client: "Listen if you were to become a life insurance salesman tomorrow, who would you sell your first policies to?" Byrne doesn't like his client's reply. "What do you mean, 'Oh you guys,'" he blurts into the receiver. "I'm not one of 'you guys,' I'm John Byrne."

# PART II

## *The New Leviathans: Mutuals Turned Marauders*

"THE EXECUTIVES AT mutual life insurance companies," declares an investment dealer and vice-president of Wood Gundy Ltd., "are bureaucrats in capitalist clothing. They don't have any shareholders to report to and they do not have to make a profit." For decades, the managers of Canada's mutual insurers have conducted their affairs without fear of being taken to task for their performance by inquisitive shareholders. Theoretically, mutual companies are owned by their policyholders, and they, by and large, are a quiescent lot who don't even understand their policies let alone the bizarre jargon on an insurance company balance sheet. In business circles, mutual insurers are widely viewed as second-class citizens; as huge bureaucracies, rather than normal business enterprises.

The track record of the mutuals offers little evidence to refute the opinion of the investment dealer, who requested anonymity for fear of losing business with the companies. Life, for most of the past 100 years, has been easy for their managers: they have tended to putter about in swank offices as premiums rolled in like clockwork. It has been a family affair

107

for most of their employees, who have been promoted on the basis of length of service rather than on performance.

It was never intended to be that way. When most of Canada's insurers mutualized in the late 1950s and '60s, the purpose was to prevent foreign takeovers in the industry, not to create refuges from the rigours of business for prematurely superannuated executives. Beginning in the 1950s, Canada's life insurance companies began to feel the hot breath of American takeover artists looking for investments with sure-fire returns. Paranoia gripped the industry in the wake of one particularly high-profile episode. That involved a bid by New York financier Harold Allen to acquire control of Sun Life, Canada's largest life insurer at the time. Beginning in 1950, Allen spent the next six years trying to win control of the company by buying its shares on the open market. But he and a U.S.-based ally, Nationwide Corporation, were never able to accumulate more than 15 per cent of Sun's shares, partly because the insurance company refused to provide them with a list of shareholders. Allen's assault on Sun, which included demands for a seat on the board, finally ended in 1956, when the Bank of Montreal, coming to Sun Life's aid, bought up all the shares owned by Allen and Nationwide. Alarmed by that stormy affair and by the takeover of Dominion Life of Waterloo by U.S. interests in January 1957, the federal Parliament passed a law in December 1957 permitting life insurance companies to mutualize; that is to buy up all their shares that were in public hands and then cancel them. Most major Canadian insurers subsequently mutualized, including Manufacturers Life in 1958, Sun Life and Canada Life in 1962, Equitable Life in 1963, and Confederation Life in 1968.

Today, mutual insurance companies account for about 53 percent of the life insurance in force in Canada. But their decades-long nap is over. Consumer demands for better products and increased competition in the marketplace have placed new pressures on the mutuals to spruce up their policy offerings and take steps to replace lackadaisical attitudes toward the bottom line with a greater emphasis on efficiency and productivity. The three companies portrayed in the following pages have been among the first major companies to change their ways. They have lagged behind most smaller companies, which can update their policy lines faster without fear of disrupting a large book of business built up over decades. But to varying degrees, Sun Life, Manufacturers and The Laurentian Group have adjusted to the new realities faster than some of their large rivals by overhauling policy lines, launching progressive ad campaigns or introducing organizational changes designed to increase productivity. Sun Life is still trying to transform itself from a barge to a battleship, Manufacturers and The Laurentian Group have already made the transition.

More important, all three companies merit special attention because of their past attempts and future plans to diversify into other financial service areas. Long the sleeping giant of the life industry, Sun Life clearly intends to make use of its hefty surplus for acquisitions, once federal laws are changed to permit it to own more than 30 per cent of a financial cousin. Manufacturers, probably the most dynamic of the mutuals, has already jumped into the fray. The Quebec-based Laurentian Group, while much smaller in size, has already taken advantage of changes in Quebec legislation to build a diversified financial services conglomerate; it is the first mutual company to do so. In the financial marketplace of the future, they will be the new leviathans in the ranks of the mutual companies.

# CHAPTER 4

## *The Sun Also Rises: Sun Life Assurance*

*"Know, one false step is ne'er retriev'd,*
*And be with caution bold."*
Thomas Gray, "On the Death of a Favourite Cat"

THE 300 OR so men sat respectfully in neatly arranged semi-circles facing the podium at the front of the hall. They were all remarkably similar in appearance: a sea of grey and navy-blue suits, company men of upright bearing. Only the presence of a handful of dark-suited women interspersed among the throng provided a slight degree of variety in the dimly lit Ball Room of Toronto's Royal York Hotel. It was a sombre setting. Heavy gold-coloured curtains on the windows prevented the brightness of the spring day outside from entering. Overhead, huge crystal chandeliers added elegance but little illumination to the proceedings. The funereal cast of the affair would have made Miss Haversham, the death-haunted creation of Charles Dickens's imagination, very comfortable.

The 114th annual meeting of the Sun Life Assurance Company of Canada, held on May 7, 1985, began promptly at 11:00

A.M. and went like clockwork. Polite applause from the partisan crowd greeted the speeches of the Sun King, company chairman Thomas Galt, a six-foot-four-inch recluse making a rare and strained public appearance, and president John (Jack) Brindle, an ebullient Englishman who revels in rallying the troops as much as Galt abhors it. A slate of company directors was nominated and approved without event. There were no probing questions from querulous policyholders, who theoretically own the $15.9-billion mutual life insurance company. The only comment on behalf of policyholders came on cue from a Toronto realtor engaged by Sun Life to flog rental space in its new $100-million-apiece twin office towers in the city. He praised Sun management for sharing the fruits of its success with policyholders through generous dividend payments.

Order, Obedience and Orthodoxy, the three O's of Sun's corporate doctrine, were very much in evidence.

More than any other life insurance company in Canada, a sense of tradition dominates Sun Life. Since its founding in 1871, the company has learned by painful experience that brash experiments with change invite disaster, while reliance on old habits breeds success. The lesson was first seared into the company's collective consciousness in the 1880s when a financial scandal caused by ill-considered investments threatened the company's existence. Then came the debacle of 1930 when Sun, which had invested the majority of its assets in common stocks, was devastated by the stock market crash. The company recovered from those brushes with corporate extinction, and in each case was able afterwards to scoff at predictions in the press of its impending demise. The first newspaper headline to declare, "The Sun Is Setting" was published in the late 1800s. To this day, journalists continue to apply the easy metaphor to Sun, but the company has refused to fulfil their predictions of doom.

But then, it is difficult for a company of Sun's size to quietly fade from the scene. From its futuristic glass head-office towers in Toronto, Sun presides over an empire with 1985 revenues of $4.8 billion and worldwide assets of nearly $16 billion. That ranks it just behind Manufacturers Life Insurance Company in terms of asset size in Canada and easily places it within the ranks of the 15 largest North American companies. Through subsidiaries and branch offices, Sun operates in seven major territories: Canada, the United States, Britain, Ireland, Bermuda, the Philippines and Hong Kong. It has a total international office staff of about 3,700, and more than 3,300 field agents selling a wide range of financial services and products, including life, health and disability insurance, dental plans, pension and investment management services and mutual funds.

The real question hanging over Sun Life's future is how it will adapt to changes in the regulatory environment that are expected to permit mutual life insurance companies to become true financial conglomerates, with subsidiary operations in the banking, trust and investment brokerage businesses. By virtue of its surplus alone, Sun could emerge as a formidable competitor in the new merger-mania. Analysts point out that it could easily afford to buy control of existing financial conglomerates such as Trilon Financial Corp. or E-L Financial Corp., both of Toronto. Smaller general and life insurers or trust companies would be even easier targets to digest. The route would be clear for Sun Life to build itself into one of the nation's omnipotent corporate conglomerates. It is a dizzying proposition that brings a gleam of excitement to the eyes of Tom Galt. The canniest men and women in financial circles say it is possible.

Such a scenario would give Galt the last laugh at his counterparts at other life companies who openly criticize his management as being overly timid, and dismiss the company as a sleeping giant. But do Galt and his senior lieutenants have the wherewithall to oversee the transformation?

## A Blue-Blood by Birth

If genes can pass on a predilection for achievement through generations, Thomas Maunsell Galt is playing with a stacked hereditary deck. Galt's forbears were men who made their mark on Canada's destiny. His great-grandfather, John Galt, colonized most of the territory in what is now southern Ontario in the 1800s. His great-uncle, Sir Alexander Galt, was a father of Confederation and the first finance minister. Tom's grand-father and namesake, Sir Thomas Galt, was chief justice of the Ontario Court of Common Pleas from 1887 to 1894. Blue blood runs through Galt's veins. By virtue of both his family heritage and current social credentials, Galt is the Canadian insurance industry's only authentic patrician. His tastes run to fine art and opera. The trappings of success that surround him, from the antiques that decorate his Forest Hill home in Toronto to the beige Checker automobile he drives and the small, exquis-ite dark-brown mahogany desk that graces his executive suite, are tasteful classics. Galt's circle of friends and associates in-cludes the likes of Jean de Grandpré, the imperious chief executive officer of Bell Canada Enterprises, Senator Ian "Big Julie" Sinclair, the gruff former chairman of Canada Pacific, and Prime Minister Brian Mulroney, a long-time personal ac-quaintance of Galt's from the days when Sun Life was based in Montreal.

In appearance, Galt is blessed with strikingly handsome fea-tures. His trim physique, towering height and shock of silver-grey hair swept back from a high forehead, make him an imposing sight. With a deep, resonant voice that sounds uncan-nily like that of Gregory Peck, Galt has the rough-hewn good looks that Hollywood producers or political backroom types would kill for.

In temperament, however, Galt is suited neither for kleig lights nor the political podium. Galt is a gentle man, remarkably shy in an era when many chief executive officers are smooth practitioners of the public relations skills necessary in dealing with the mass media or in making successful appeals to legislators. In person, the lanky executive exudes an air of propriety, but he sometimes reveals a witty sense of humour that his underlings describe as slightly bizarre. A close examination of the hand-picked *objets d'art* that decorate Galt's office betrays cracks in the carapace of his otherwise austere character. On a wall not far from the desk where Galt presides over his insurance empire, a work by Russian-born painter Marc Chagall depicts two lovers in amorous repose on a hillside. On the other side of his art-strewn office, sits a small, eight-inch-high sculpture by Canadian Sorel Etrog. Exactly what the sculpture is intended to represent is not readily apparent, but Galt points out with a grin that it most resembles an interlocked couple.

For the most part, Galt is viewed as a remote, somewhat autocratic general by his senior officers. Donald Gauer, senior vice-president and chief actuary of Sun, recalls that during Galt's 1984–85 tenure as chairman of the Canadian Life and Health Insurance Organization (an industry association whose responsibilities include lobbying Ottawa on matters of financial deregulation), Galt was frustratingly secretive about important developments. Says Gauer: "He knows better than anyone else what's going on in the industry. But he is very poor when it comes to telling us about it. It's crazy. Like the cobbler's children we had to go outside to find out what was happening on the committee he was chairman of."

If Galt is reticent in private, he is only slightly more talkative than a Trappist monk in public. A senior public relations officer with the company recalls with a laugh one particularly vexing experience which occurred during Sun Life's controversial move of its headquarters from Montreal to Toronto in

1978. Hounded by the media and denounced by Quebec politicians, Galt finally conceded to holding a press conference to explain the decision. The PR man recalls preparing Galt for the event with painful care. The CEO was coached in role-playing sessions. His staff posed as journalists asking tricky questions and then helped him to formulate thorough responses. Nevertheless, the actual news conference was a disaster. "Tom," recalls the communications officer with a wince, "immediately reverted to his typical style, answering questions with curt yes or no answers."

Born in Winnipeg in 1921, Galt grew up without a natural father. George Galt was 66 when Tom entered the world, the first son after five daughters, four of whom were born to George during a previous marriage. After making his fortune in a family tea and coffee importing business, George Galt later became vice-president of the Winnipeg-based Great-West Life Assurance Company. But George died when Tom was only six.

After his father's death, Tom, his sister and mother moved to Ottawa, where his mother remarried and Tom was sent off to gain an education at private boarding schools: Ashbury College in Ottawa and later Lakefield College near Peterborough. The private school life, he once told journalist Mark Witten, was not much to his liking. "When you have to go to chapel 15 times a week," he said, "it's a bit overdone."

Marked by exceptional intelligence, Galt was a natural for the mathematical gymnastics of the actuarial profession. After a hiatus in his education during World War II (he served with a Royal Canadian Air Force radar unit in India, keeping watch over Japanese movements in the Indian Ocean), Galt studied at Queen's University in Kingston and later at the University of Manitoba. By coincidence, one of Galt's lecturers in actuarial science in Manitoba in 1947 was Sydney Jackson, who is currently chief executive of Sun's main rival, the Manufacturers Life Insurance Company. Today, Jackson is among those who regard Sun Life as a sleeping giant. "I think Sun Life has an old-fashioned style of management, sort of stodgy and auto-cratic," says Jackson. "It's the history of the company, the old Scottish Presbyterian factor." Jackson also notes: "The company almost went broke in the 1930s."

Young, well-educated and very ambitious, Galt joined Sun Life in 1948. He reasoned that it was a wise move because at the time it was the largest life insurance company in Canada. Moreover, not one to underrate himself, Galt noted that the president had always been an actuary. Eventually, Galt turned his youthful pretensions into reality. Twenty-four years of dedication later, on January 1, 1972, he became president of Sun Life.

Galt had no way of knowing then that he had achieved his cherished goal at the beginning of an era of tumult for the insurance industry in general and for Sun Life in particular. It was an era that would see a revolution in the variety and number of insurance policies made available; attacks in the media regarding the company's move to Toronto from Mon-treal; and organizational upheaval accompanied by acute ten-sion within Sun's ranks between forces arguing for and against change.

The 51-year-old actuary was certainly not chosen as presi-dent for his propensity to take the company in new directions. Galt was one of two rising stars in the company that Alistair Campbell, chairman of Sun in the 1970s, had kept his eyes on as executive material for years. The other was Anthony Hicks, who, unlike Galt, had gained experience in investments and administration during his career at the company. Galt was tradition-conscious and pensive, Hicks was impetuous and eager for change.

Too eager, it turned out. Campbell selected Hicks as presi-dent in 1970. But just two years later, Hicks was asked to re-sign. The reason: Campbell had been unnerved by the cascade of changes Hicks had immediately set in motion, including new marketing techniques and an ambitious organizational overhaul. For decades, Sun had administered its worldwide operations (apart from the British division) from head office. Hicks wanted to create separate Canadian and U.S. organizations almost immediately. A chilling rift developed at Sun as communications between Hicks and Campbell broke down. Campbell, a staid, Scottish-born mathematician, had got more than he had bargained for from his young Turk. The writing was on the wall. The company's board of directors agreed with Campbell that Hicks was trying to implement too much change, too fast. Hicks's forced resignation was effective December 31, 1971.

Chastened, Campbell turned to Tom Galt, a man he could count on to return Sun to its time-tested ways.

### Scars on the Corporate Psyche

Sun Life was founded in 1871 by Mathew Gault (no relation to Tom Galt), a hard-driven Irish immigrant who overcame hardship to assume a position of wealth and influence in Montreal. Gault's father had been a prosperous merchant and shipowner in Northern Ireland, but he was forced to emigrate to Canada in 1842 after he lost a fortune due to a series of marine disasters. At the start, the Gault family's luck was no better in the New World than in the Old. Mathew's father died within months of the move, and his mother was soon an invalid, leaving Mathew, at 22, to head a household of six younger children. A tall, handsome man with bristling mutton chops and a forceful personality, Gault eventually made his fortune in Canada's fledgling insurance industry, simultaneously serving as agency manager for two companies: the British American Assurance Company of Toronto, a general insurer, and the Mutual Life Insurance Company of New York. On the side, Gault was also manager of the Montreal branch of Toronto's Royal Canadian Bank. Those were days when an enterprising businessman could keep many irons in the fire.

Before Sun Life's creation, there was only one Canadian life insurer in existence, the Canada Life Insurance Company, which had been founded in Hamilton, Ontario, in 1847. Most of the premiums collected from the minority of Canadians who took out life insurance in those days flowed to British and American head offices. Gault decided to create another Canadian firm to wrest some business away from the foreign companies.

Gault himself became managing director of Sun Life, and the men he gathered around him for the venture attested to the standing he had reached in Montreal society. Sun's early directors included the likes of Alexander Walker Ogilvie, a former provincial parliamentarian and head of a vast flour-milling business; Alexander Buntin, a penny-pinching Scot with extensive paper mill interests in Quebec; and James Claxton, an importer of dry goods. The company's first president was Thomas Workman, who sat in the Dominion of Canada Parliament and whose interests ranged from hardware retailing to banking.

Company lore has it that Gault was an extremely capable man, but one whose varied interests kept him from paying proper attention to the insurance company's affairs. In *The Century of the Sun*, a richly detailed company-commissioned book on Sun's history, author Joseph Schull notes that Gault maintained his general insurance business when he became Sun's managing director and that later he added the presidency of the Exchange Bank of Canada to his impressive list of titles. Unfortunately, however, Gault's many duties caused more than just competing demands for his attention in a busy schedule. Conflicts of interest were also to arise that embroiled Sun in public scandal and ended Gault's career at the company in ignominy.

The problem arose over two questionable investments approved by Sun's board at Gault's behest. In the mid-1870s Sun purchased large holdings in the Montreal Loan and Trust

Company, as well as in the Exchange Bank, both institutions which Gault headed. The investments would probably never have become controversial had they not proven to be so disastrous. Within four years, their worth had been cut in half due to the serious troubles of both institutions, whose affairs were intertwined. Within a decade, the investments were worthless: the bank had collapsed and the mortgage company was barely surviving.

That financial debacle set the scene for what Schull describes as a battle of Homeric proportions within Sun that scandalized the Montreal business community and threatened to destroy the company itself. On one side of the conflict was Robertson Macaulay, a pugnacious Scot who had joined the company in 1875 as secretary, a position that put him in charge of running its operations, and who later became managing director. On the other side were Gault and the directors whose loyalty he commanded. After bringing order to the neglected affairs of the company as its secretary, the outspoken Macaulay took the board of directors to task over the two investments, declaring that they never should have been made at all because they involved the private interests of Gault and certain other directors.

Like a tenacious terrier, Macaulay fought the issue for years, attempting to convince the board to accept financial responsibility for the calamitous investments, which could have more than wiped out the company's surplus if the struggling mortgage company followed the bank into bankruptcy. Gault and his allies on the board, including his younger brother, Andrew, and Ogilvie, resisted the attack on their integrity forcefully. But Macaulay eventually won the confrontation by successfully campaigning for the support of the company's agents and policyholders. Finally, on February 25, 1887, the board agreed to Macaulay's proposal that the mistake be made good by reducing the amount of surplus distributable to shareholders, made up of largely of the directors, from 20 per cent to 10 per cent.

The battle was over but Macaulay's mission had resulted in Gault's demise at Sun. Gault resigned as managing director during the imbroglio, passing the title to Macaulay. Eventually, Gault gave up his position as a company director, too, as it became clear that Macaulay's views would prevail.

In the development of Sun's corporate culture, the impact of that historical episode was significant, but it pales in comparison with the long-lasting effects of the company's financial misadventures several decades later. The author of Sun's new bout with misfortune in the 1930s was, ironically, Thomas Bassett Macaulay, who had followed in his father's footsteps to become president of Sun in 1915.

In the wake of World War I, Macaulay had become committed to linking the company's fortunes with the rapid advances of industry. With messianic zeal, he loaded up Sun's investment portfolio with common stocks in the industries that he believed were leading North America into a new age of prosperity. By 1929, the year of the stock market crash, some 52 per cent of Sun's assets were invested in common shares, which in any era are more volatile than the usual array of more secure corporate and government bonds favoured by most of the other insurance companies. As the vicissitudes of the Great Depression worsened, Sun's existence was once again placed in jeopardy. The value of its investments plummeted, rendering meaningless the calculation of the insurance company's surplus and reserves (funds which by law must be maintained to meet future obligations). Rather than have Sun and other insurance companies in similar straits collapse, regulatory officials in Canada and the United States stepped in to give an artificially high value to their investment portfolios—a move that at least gave Sun the appearance of solvency. The catastrophe ended a period of explosive growth for Sun during the 1920s and gave Macaulay's career an inglorious end.

For two decades after that unhappy juncture, Sun Life was unable to shake off its disconcerting effects. The 1930s and

1940s brought hard times and sagging morale to the company,
according to Galt. During that period, a fortress mentality per-
vaded the company; hiring was frozen and growth was limited.
But the legacy of the crisis Macaulay helped precipitate still
endures at Sun. Since Macaulay's pratfall, there has been a
succession of chief executives at Sun for whom change is suspect and financial stability a Holy Grail. Like the ghost of
Jacob Marley, Macaulay's spectre haunts the executive suites of
Sun Life to this day, reminding their occupants of the perils of
imprudent behaviour.

### The Rule of the Sun King

When Tom Galt assumed the presidency of Sun Life on January 1, 1972, the company was financially strong. The 1950s and
'60s had been lucrative decades for life insurers. The postwar
baby boom, generally prosperous economic times and increased
demand for life insurance products from a security-conscious
population combined to enrich insurers as in no other period
in history. From a level of $1.3 billion in 1946, Sun's assets grew
to $2.1 billion in 1957 and $3.2 billion in 1967, then edged up
to $3.8 billion by 1971. Galt readily acknowledges that Alistair
Campbell passed him the reins of a buoyant company, flush
with cash and fortified by more than $19 billion worth of busi-
ness in force worldwide. Recalls Galt: "We had excellent assets,
a well-balanced portfolio; we had financial strength—in other
words a substantial surplus ($450 million in 1971) and good
earnings ($775 million in 1971)."

In assuming the presidency, Galt also effectively took over
as chief executive officer of the company. Campbell, who
was recovering from a bout with cancer of the larynx that
affected his voice, was working only part-time. Recalls Galt:
"He wasn't really running the company fully by the time I took
over. He was 65." In 1973, Campbell retired as chief executive
officer. He remained as chairman of the board until 1978,

providing his deferential protégé with avuncular advice until the end.

Galt speaks highly of Campbell's tenure at the helm of Sun Life. The two men had developed a strong rapport during the period. "We saw eye to eye on business matters," says Galt. "He was very helpful to me.... Campbell ran the company very well, but in the sixties things were not changing fast. It was a period of economic growth." By contrast, the new president faced an era of tumult that would sorely test Sun Life's time-honoured unofficial motto: "Change if necessary. But not necessarily change."

By the early 1970s, consumers had begun to wake up to the fact that the industry's most lucrative product, whole life insurance, was not designed in their best interests. Term insurance, which offered straight protection and no savings feature, was becoming increasingly popular. The surge in term sales heralded the appearance of a variety of new insurance products designed to give cost-conscious consumers a better deal (see Chapter 1). At the same time a period of legislative turmoil had begun in the United States: barriers between players in the financial services industry were beginning to fade—and the phenomenon would soon spread to Canada. Galt was by no means oblivious to these portents of upheaval. "The pace of change had been picking up—in the market and in terms of legislation," he recalls.

The manner in which Galt has dealt with changes in the marketplace and in the legislative environment over the past 15 years is a matter of considerable controversy. He has been portrayed frequently by journalists and authors as being sadly unaware of the need for Sun and other insurance companies to adjust to the new realities facing the industry. He has been cast as an almost pathetic chief executive officer, sitting sulkily in his office ready to cut any suggestion of change off at the pass and poised to banish any progressive-minded executives from the company's ranks. That depiction of Galt is overly

harsh. His scorecard does include successes. Galt acknowledges that he has been the protector of tradition at Sun
Life and the core of that tradition has been a preoccupation
with financial well-being. "Financial strength, that is our long-
term priority," he asserts. "I don't think anyone pays a pen-
alty for that." However, as if to discredit critics who portray
him as a hopeless reactionary, Galt, in an interview, brings
out some hard evidence of his early awareness of the need
for change at the company. He points to an address that he
made to Sun's board of directors late in 1971 on his appointment as the company's new president. In it, he underlined
some of the contentious issues that were to preoccupy the
company for the next 15 years, including one of Galt's major
concerns: the need for a more formalized strategic-planning
process at the company. At the time, Sun Life was using annual
sales targets and had developed long-term planning for its
investment department. But there was no planning system in
which executives could discuss and plot broader goals for
the company. Says Galt: "We didn't have a good, or any, planning system."

With rapid changes already occurring in the marketplace in
the form of demand for new products, Galt also stressed the
need for a greater decentralization of management responsibilities from head office in Montreal to national territories. But
unlike Hicks, his predecessor, Galt thought it was too rash to
split off the Canadian and U.S. operations into national offices
in one fell swoop. He proposed that Sun make the creation of
a U.S. national office a priority and delay a similar move in
Canada. Says Galt: "I decided it would be easier to do things in
two stages." By 1973, a divisional office was in place in Wellesley Hills near Boston, with a staff of about 600. The move was
overdue, in Galt's view. Says Galt: "Our U.S. business was not as
strong as it could have been. We were trying to operate it from
Montreal. There was nobody on the scene. That is not too bad
if nothing is changing but with legislation changing, with new

products being introduced, we concluded that we couldn't run the operation from a distance."

There were other problems on Galt's plate as the incoming president. Inflation was beginning a decade-long upward spiral, increasing the cost of doing business in the process. Galt warned the board of the need to reduce company expenses in order to stay competitive. "Our unit costs were above those of some of our competitors," he admits.

But the ensuing years Galt had much more to deal with than mundane matters of expense control, decentralization and long-term planning. Politically-inspired crises intervened and laid claim to his energies. The first was already brewing in South Africa when he became president. It ended with Sun Life's withdrawal from that country in 1974. "We had done business in South Africa for many years," recalls Galt, "but it was un-profitable and the political situation was worsening." Specific-ally, the South African government was preparing to introduce so-called "domestication legislation," under which Sun would have to form a subsidiary and hand over its ownership to South African policyholders. Astutely, Sun Life pulled out quickly rather than kiss its assets in the country goodbye. "In the end," says Galt, "Sun got $10 to $15 million out of the country by withdrawing."[1]

Compared with the next crisis to hit Sun, however, the South African pullout was only a minor reverberation on the Richter scale. Sun Life had watched with increasing nervousness as separatist forces in Quebec gained strength in the early 1970s, culminating with the election of the Parti Québécois govern-ment of René Lévesque in 1976. The spectre of Quebec's

[1] Sun Life was especially skittish about the "nationalization" of its foreign operations because of its experience in Cuba a decade and a half earlier. After the revolution-ary government of Fidel Castro took power in Havana in 1959, it froze Sun Life's assets in the country. By government decree, those assets are now in a bank account in Cuba earning zero interest. The Canadian Department of Insurance calculates that Sun Life's Cuban assets total $20.6 million, based on a peso being worth $1.47 Canadian.

separation created uncertainty over the Montreal-based company's future and evoked paranoia at Sun's headquarters. Galt,
who, with the help of Campbell, masterminded the move to
Toronto in 1978, still bears scars from making the controversial
step. "It was a very difficult decision," he says. "After all, the
Sun Life building was the symbol of Montreal." But Sun was
alarmed by Quebec's new language legislation, which required
that companies like Sun conduct their head office affairs in
French, a proposal Sun considered impractical. And the atmosphere had deteriorated when PQ finance minister
Jacques Parizeau publicly charged that Sun Life had invested
$400 million less in Quebec than it had received in premiums.
(The company said the figure was closer to $9 million.) Most
important, Galt argues that his hand was forced by business
considerations. "Our business was suffering, the competitors
were wooing customers away from Sun Life by casting doubt
on the future of the company." He adds: "Our sales in 1977
went down by 2 per cent. That was our problem. Our location
was being used against us."

On January 6, 1978, when Sun Life announced it would move
its headquarters, the decision sparked a strong backlash in
Quebec. Parizeau angrily denounced the move that same day
before television cameras. That reaction, Galt says, was overly
dramatic in light of the rational conversation the two had had
in a conversation hours before when Galt phoned the Quebec
finance minister to inform him of the decision. "I had been
talking to Parizeau earlier in the day and he had been calm
and reasonable," says Galt. "But that afternoon, Parizeau went
on TV and pretended to lose his temper."

Quebec Premier René Lévesque didn't mince his words,
calling Sun's executives "sons of bitches." Prime Minister Pierre
Trudeau reacted to the announcement with more *sang-froid*.
At an evening meeting arranged by federal finance minister
Jean Chrétien at 24 Sussex Drive, Trudeau discussed the move

with Campbell and Galt. Apparently accepting the move as a *fait accompli*, the prime minister asked that the company not move significant numbers of people from Montreal, a request that the two insurance men agreed to.

Parizeau's reaction, contrived or not, better reflected the depth of animosity that Quebeckers felt toward Sun Life. In 1978, 30 per cent of the company's 400-member Quebec sales force jumped ship and sales dropped by 27 per cent during the year.

The special policyholders' meeting called to vote on the issue on April 25 in Toronto was a stormy affair. Montreal lawyer Richard Holden was an outspoken critic. He headed a group of dissident policyholders opposed to the move, and had launched legal action to have the meeting declared null and void, primarily on the grounds that the company had included only information supporting the move in its mailings to policyholders. Holden was jeered at the meeting and his motions were defeated, including one to have a decision on the move postponed until after the province's planned referendum on independence. Holden did receive strong moral support from some quarters, however. The federal government, a policyholder with group life insurance worth more than $25 million covering 200,000 employees, cast its single vote against the move. But after two and a half hours and more than 20 speeches the move was approved by 84.25 per cent of votes cast, mostly by proxy.[2]

By any measure, the whole affair was a public relations disaster, poorly explained and badly misunderstood by the press and public. According to Galt, the company had decided that its priority was to get the move accomplished quickly and successfully. Communication with the press was woefully

---

[2]To vote by proxy on an issue under consideration at a policyholders' meeting, a policyholder signs a form prior to the meeting, thus handing over voting rights to company management.

inadequate; it was carried out mostly through terse press releases. Still, Galt argues that neither he nor any other executives could be very forthcoming in public because the company was being sued over the issue by Holden.

Strictly from the point of view of business, however, the move from Quebec was beneficial for Sun Life. Despite the drop in sales in Quebec in 1978, individual sales outside the province increased by 20 per cent in the same period. There were other benefits as well, according to senior vice-president John Gardner. Relocating to Toronto, the acknowledged business capital of Canada, meant that Sun could be more in tune with the thriving world of commerce and with business developments. Being the only major life insurance company based in Montreal, Gardner observes, "gave the company a certain degree of insularity." In Montreal, he says, "we were a little bit more isolated, somewhat distanced from what was going on in the Canadian industry."

But if Sun's heart is now firmly in Toronto, a large portion of its staff remains in Montreal. Gardner points out that the company still has 1,750 people on its payroll in Quebec, more than any other insurance company, and representing two-thirds of the staff of its Canadian operation. "All of our group insurance is administered from Montreal," says Gardner, "and the central part of our individual insurance administration is in Montreal also." Montreal also has a pension operation serving the Quebec market which is of a size and importance comparable to the pension function in Toronto. Gardner describes it this way: "It's almost as if we have two equally equipped, side-by-side pension operations." Overall, says Gardner, the move from Quebec "has tended to push the company into a more decentralized mode, which is by and large good. It's more typical of what you find today in the industry."

The real costs of Sun's Quebec crisis lay not in the public chastisements it received from Quebec politicians, or in the criticisms levelled against the company in the national media.

One consequence of the company's obsession with the issue, which started years before the actual decision was made, was that other necessary changes in the company's affairs were set aside. By 1978, when Galt moved up to the chairman's post at Sun and George Clarke took over as president, the company was in a twilight zone of its own making, existing in the present but living in the past. Many of its major competitors, Manufacturers Life of Toronto chief among them, had long since swept out the old, autocratic management style Sun was still practising, and introduced more modern, democratic approaches to decision making. In the fast-changing U.S. market in particular, Sun was being outsold by more aggressive Canadian competitors, including the Winnipeg-based Great-West Life and Manulife, which had armed their operations with marketing men sensitive to the changing trends in products. Sun's product line, by the company's own admission, was hopelessly outdated. Equally damaging was the fact that Sun had delayed dealing properly with a priority that Galt had identified as early as 1971: the need for better strategic planning in a rapidly changing environment.

At the end of the 1970s, Sun was trying to play catch-up to the rest of the industry, and just around the corner was another wave of changes that the whole industry would have to cope with: a trend toward increasing decentralization, a drive toward greater cost efficiency, and the computerization of field operations right down to the level of the individual agent. As Sun Life tried to respond to the need for rapid and wholesale change, serious tensions developed within the company's senior ranks over the pace at which reforms should be implemented. In keeping with Sun's conservative tradition, George Clarke, a man who tried to push things too far too fast became a casualty in the ensuing standoff. Like Tony Hicks before him, Clarke is remembered as a sort of shooting star in Sun Life's firmament; as president from 1978 to 1983, he enjoyed a brief moment of glory before he fizzled out dismally in the company's atmosphere of inertia.

On becoming president, Clarke was instrumental in introducing a plethora of innovations. His priorities were to modernize Sun's management, marketing and planning methods. Clarke's first major decision was to bring in an outside management consulting firm, P. S. Ross & Partners (now Touche Ross & Partners). As a result of its study, Sun proceeded with its long-planned separation of the Canadian division from the main corporate office; the change was completed in 1979. The company also set up a senior advisory committee (SAC), made up of the heads of three national offices, four corporate officers, the president and the chairman, which meets four times yearly to plot long-term strategy.

Clarke looked for help with his corporate overhaul both within the company and outside it. The promotion of Jack Brindle to the position of executive vice-president in 1980 brought a man with acute marketing sense into head office. (Brindle was later to succeed Clarke as president.) A Briton who rose through the company's sales ranks, Brindle became the first former salesman to ascend so high in the firm. Together, Clarke and Brindle set an executive search in motion to find a planning officer for the company. The result was the hiring in 1980 of Robert Mifflin—fresh from a job as a planner at Eaton's—as vice-president of planning. Under his direction, the old, autocratic mould of the company was finally broken. Senior executives in the corporate office were freed up from day-to-day operational decisions and left to concentrate on broader strategic issues. Says Donald Gauer: "He is just a superb planning officer…in terms of really lengthening the horizon, looking into the potential shape of the financial services industry five, ten, twenty years down the road, Bob is the guy, who at George Clarke's urging, has done that."

Clarke was a rather self-effacing actuary who had also spent some time on the agency side of the industry at Manulife before joining Sun in 1967. He was also a relentless proponent of change. In 1980, a productivity improvement committee was formed, which led to the reorganization of the company in 1982. The old function-based organization, in which the company divided its operations on the basis of types of service, was changed to a unit-based system. That meant that each unit in the field became responsible for reducing expenses and had to answer for its performance to head office. Next, in 1982, a directional planning task force was set up under Clarke's chairmanship to review the company's strengths and weaknesses by territory. Its report in mid-1983 was blunt and scathing. Among other things, it revealed a deep frustration among agents over the slow pace of change at the company, which had resulted in a four-year retention rate of only 18 per cent: of every 100 agents recruited, only 18 remained after four years. But the report did not win Clarke any kudos at Sun Life, primarily because while it was highly critical, it was badly lacking in concrete proposals for change. Complains one senior Sun executive: "It didn't provide any recommendations for action."

By the time Clarke handed the report over to Galt, moreover, the well-intentioned president had already fallen badly out of favour. For his part, Galt now refuses to talk about his relationship with Clarke, but it is clear that Clarke misgauged the pace at which innovation could be introduced at the company.

In addition, Clarke and Sun's chairman had a fundamental difference in philosophy. Clarke openly criticized the company and, by implication, Galt, for emphasizing financial stability at the expense of improved marketing and management techniques. And Galt held Clarke at least partly responsible for the financial setback the company suffered in 1982. For the year, Sun recorded a net income after dividends and taxes of $5 million; a paltry sum compared to the $100 million-plus annual income levels it had managed to harvest in the past. The company's rush to add new sales to its books had led it to make cuts in prices that were not matched by reductions in operating costs. "The major problem was over-enthusiastic pricing," says Galt. "There was also the drain of new business," he adds, which initially adds more selling expense than revenue to the company's earnings statement.

Ultimately, Clarke was tossed out of Sun Life's ranks like a worn overcoat. The end came at a meeting of Sun Life's blue-chip board of directors on October 5, 1983. When the meeting was nearly over, an unsuspecting Clarke was asked to leave the session. Minutes later, Galt emerged to inform Clarke of the decision that he had just announced to the board. After serving as president for a brief five years, Clarke was being asked to take early retirement from the company. The exchange was brief and perfunctory. As if remuneration would make up for the suddenness of the decision, Clarke's benefits and salary would continue until his normal retirement age in 1986. Even before Clarke's period on the payroll ended, however, his pleasant, usually smiling face was all but forgotten at Sun; any rare reappearances he did make only stirred up unpleasant memories.

Not surprisingly, Galt's remote manner and often brusque methods of dealing with his staff have not won him an enthusiastic personal following at the company. He is praised more for other qualities. Gardner, for one, is impressed with Galt's "very quick mind." He says the CEO "listens attentively to information and decides very quickly." Others are impressed by his scrupulous honesty. One senior executive recalls being chastized by Galt for sneaking a small item across the U.S. border into Canada without declaring it. Said the chairman: "I always declare everything." But beyond such comments, there is little evidence of loyalty. Galt rules the company by the force of his intellect and by the simple fact that the buck stops at his finely-crafted desk. By comparison, praise for president Jack Brindle is more spontaneous. While not criticizing Galt, Gardner says Brindle "brings a degree of warmth, compassion and understanding to the company."

Still, Galt has never pretended that communication skills are his strong point. His style, he says, has been to allow his subordinates to introduce innovation to Sun Life in what he considers an orderly fashion. Says Galt: "I try to encourage, to facilitate, to delegate." Chief actuary Donald Gauer, who has been at the centre of Sun's affairs throughout Galt's tenure, agrees with that assessment: "Galt takes the balanced view," he says. "He does not discourage innovation but he is not innovative personally...he leaves it to others to take the initiative."

By Galt's own favoured yardstick—financial results—he has overseen some laudible results while at Sun's helm. The company quickly recovered from its financial bruising in 1982 by taking some drastic measures. Galt decided that the main priority was "to change the mental outlook of the company, get employees to understand that the bottom line was important. People felt that the company had lots of money, a large surplus, but once earnings slow down, people realize that something has to be done." After taking some profits from investments, introducing more cost cutting, and reshuffling the product mix, the company boosted its net income back up to the $140 million range in 1983.

In the longer term, Galt's tenure has been characterized by a steady financial strengthening of the company. Expenses have been cut. Between 1982 and 1985, total office staff was reduced by 13.7 per cent, from 4,337 to 3,743. The ratio of operating expenses to revenue has fallen from 0.1203 to 0.1180 in the same time period. Return on invested assets has increased from 9.84 per cent in 1982 to 11.49 per cent in 1985. (Those returns roughly matched the average performance of the six largest Canadian life insurers.) By 1985 year-end, Sun's assets had grown to almost five times their 1971 level; its surplus had swollen to $1.8 billion from $450 million; business in force amounted to $123 billion in 1984, compared with $19.9 billion 13 years before; and annual premiums totalled $3 billion in 1985, more than six times the level in 1971.

Despite this steady financial progress, however, Sun Life did suffer the indignity of being replaced as Canada's largest life insurer (as measured by assets) in 1985. By acquiring Dominion Life in Waterloo, Manufacturers Life of Toronto vaulted itself into the lead position, which Sun had held since 1908. Galt, however, professes not to be impressed by Manulife's achievement. Mutters Galt: "There is nothing very difficult about becoming number one by acquiring another company. If you *grow* to be number one, however, you are obviously doing something better than other companies." In terms of business in force, he says, Sun Life still has the lead. As far as assets are concerned he adds, with typically dry humour, "We have no intention of staying number two."

A close scrutiny of Galt's record during the stormy years since 1980 reveals other signs of new life at Sun. In 1980, with Galt's approval, the company undertook the first major overhaul of its individual policies since 1966. Since that time, Sun Life's premium rates had remained basically unaltered, although most of the assumptions underlying the rate structure had changed. Mortality rates had declined by about 2 per cent annually, policy maintenance costs had tripled, and inflation and interest rates were far above the levels experienced in the 1960s.

Between 1975 and 1979, Sun's share of total industry premiums from new policies had dropped from 7.7 per cent to 7.6 per cent; its share of volume of new policies sold dropped from 6.1 per cent to 5.6 per cent. Since 1975 the incidence of Sun Life policies terminated within five years of sale had gone up from 30.2 per cent to 36.7 per cent. One major cause of this was the flight by consumers from whole life products to the cheaper term insurance or to new money policies. To deal with the growing problem, chief actuary Gauer introduced a host of new products (including a nonsmokers' policy in 1982), lowered premiums by reducing the cash values of policies, and threw out 11 products that were unprofitable. The revamping was no cause for rejoicing among consumers. Like other major companies in Canada, Sun Life continued to place a priority on selling Canadians traditional products, such as whole life policies and annuities. And Sun does not try to sell at the lowest prices in the market. Says Yves Laneuville, vice-president of product and underwriting for Canada: "We are not a gimmicky company. We won't lower quality too far just to lower prices." But the product overhaul did make Sun a serious competitor in the marketplace once again.

In other ways, however, Sun Life has even gone so far as to shake up the industry. As Galt puts it dryly: "We have not had a closed mind to acquisitions." Sun's competitors were caught by surprise in 1982 when the company they had dismissed as a dinosaur bought Massachusetts Financial Services Co., (MFS), the third-largest mutual fund management company in the United States. Brindle recalls: "The acquisition of MFS was totally unexpected by the financial community here and in the United States. At the time, the company managed 12 mutual funds with assets of $3.5 billion. Since that time, its assets have more than doubled to more than $10 billion."

Typically, the decision to buy MFS required a great deal of deliberation. Walter McCarthy, Sun's vice-president of investments, opposed the move. McCarthy argued that there was a bad fit between the two companies and that Sun Life "couldn't take the shock to its system." For his part, Galt played his usual part—that of the skeptic. "Galt really put us through the hoops on that one," says Gauer. Ultimately, however, the chairman approved the purchase. The main reason for his support, explains Galt, was that he wanted MFS to sell a new product Sun had developed. "We had a new annuity product," says Galt, "but it was not selling in large quantities and it made sense to get a new distribution system for it." More important, however, the purchase of MFS marked a major foray by Sun Life into wider fields in the financial services industry, a precedent that it intends to follow in the future.

### Contenders for the Throne

The two men Galt has picked as heirs-apparent at Sun Life are certainly not thumb-twiddlers who will watch opportunities pass by. In April 1985, John McNeil, who had headed the U.S. operation since 1982, was named executive vice-president of Sun Life. John Gardner was moved up from running the Canadian operation to become senior vice-president and executive officer of the corporation. McNeil, who is expected to eventually replace Galt as chief executive officer, is the man to watch. In September 1986 McNeil was named deputy chairman as of the end of the year. Gardner was named president.

McNeil is regarded with some admiration and no little wariness by his colleagues at competitor firms. Robin Leckie, chief actuary of Manufacturers, compares McNeil to Thomas Di Giacomo, the aggressive heir-apparent to Sydney Jackson at Manufacturers. The comparison has some validity. Like Di Giacomo, McNeil is an investment man, more accustomed to doing deals with bankers and brokers than talking about mortality rates with actuaries. Raised in Nairobi, Kenya, where his father was an administrator in Britain's colonial service, McNeil later studied economics at the University of Edinburgh in Scotland. In 1956, at age 22, he emigrated to Canada with his wife, Esther, an American he had met at university. They chose Canada, he says, because it seemed like a good compromise between the United States and Great Britain. After arriving in Montreal, McNeil, with the build of a full-back and the crisp bearing of a military man, wasted no time getting a job. "We got off the boat on a Thursday and on the following Monday, I had two job interviews," he laughs. In total, McNeil lined up interviews with 14 companies. "I just went up and down Dorchester Street where the major companies like Sun Life, Dupont, CPR and Alcan were located." McNeil chose a job with Sun Life's investment department.[3] By 1962 he had risen to the post of assistant treasurer in the department, but in 1966, he left the company. Then came senior jobs with a mutual funds company, an investment consulting business and, eventually, in 1975, he joined the Bank of Montreal's investment department, later becoming vice-president of investments there. Then, in 1979, McNeil got a call from Walter McCarthy, an old colleague at Sun Life. McCarthy, the senior vice-president of investments at Sun, had worked with McNeil at the company in the 1960s and was calling to offer him the job of vice-president, securities investments. McNeil took the job and now has no regrets about leaving the Bank of Montreal. McNeil admires Bill Mulholland, the fiery chairman of the bank, describing him as "an outstanding strategic thinker." But he finds the working atmosphere at Sun less antagonistic and much more to his liking. "Sure, senior executives here bitch at each other," he says, "but there is a lot less competition" in the executive ranks.

The first sign that Tom Galt had bigger plans for McNeil came in March 1982. With no forewarning Galt summoned McNeil to his office and told him he wanted him to go to Wellesley, Massachusetts, to become senior vice-president and general manager for the struggling United States operation. At the time, the division's expenses were too high and it was foundering amid the torrent of new policies that had appeared on the scene. "In the United States we got blind-sided, caught by surprise by product developments such as Universal Life, which came out of the blue," he says. "Replacements went through the roof." New products were introduced by Sun (U.S.) and corporate fat was cut. In the 18 months beginning in June 1982, McNeil slashed U.S. staff by 180 people, or about 13 per cent. Says McNeil: "We even had a whole studio producing videotapes for our sales people." The videotape technicians

---

[3]McNeil took the job vacated by a young Alf Powis, who had left to take a job at Noranda, the mining company where he eventually rose to become chief executive officer.

were among the first to go, but they, as well as other casualties, says McNeil, were laid off in a far more humanitarian fashion than was the case at some other companies. McNeil returned to Toronto in 1985, but he says there is still much work to be done at the money-losing U.S. operation. "We are just not big enough. Period," he says. "We are limping along with only 600 agents. I'd be satisfied if by the time I go out the door in 1999, we could get the U.S. sales force up to a couple of thousand agents."

Gardner, an actuary with refined tastes and an easy self-confidence, stands next in line to McNeil. Educated at the elite University of Toronto Schools, and later at the University of Toronto and Oxford University in England (where he studied as a Rhodes scholar), Gardner describes himself as a perfectionist with a cautious nature—the ideal man to maintain tradition at Sun Life.

Both Galt and McNeil are especially aware of the pace and scale of upheaval coming in the financial services sector. For years, Galt was closely involved in formulating the industry's proposals on legislative change and in presenting them to Ottawa. As the deregulatory process unfolds, he is determined that Sun will not be caught napping. To prepare for what might be cut-throat competition with banks and trust companies for consumer savings, the company has stepped up its cost-cutting measures. Staff in the Canadian operation, for instance, has been reduced by about 17 per cent since 1982. Says Galt: "We as an industry have got to get very efficient if we're going to compete successfully for saving dollars as well as insurance dollars."[4]

Despite Sun Life's decades-old tendency to be a follower in the industry, Galt maintains that a new Sun Life is emerging.

[4]Over the past ten years, the nature of Sun Life's business has changed to reflect the growing demand for annuity products in the marketplace. In 1975, 64 per cent of Sun Life's premiums came from individual and group life insurance. In 1985, less

"We intend to be, if not on the leading edge, at least right up there," he asserts. Being at the forefront could involve buying a bank "if doing so is going to be profitable for policyholders." McNeil, too, is interested in expanding Sun's operations, although he is skeptical about such ideas as one-stop shopping for financial services. "It's probably not a viable concept," he argues. "There will be some companies that stitch together one-stop shopping," he concedes. But he points out that research carried out at Stanford University has shown that the public wants a trusted financial advisor and they don't want to buy everything in one place. "The public is smart," he says. "It wants an element of competition in there. Consumers know that if they buy everything in one spot they won't get the lowest price."

Such views, however, don't rule out diversification by Sun Life. The next foray by Sun in Canada, says McNeil, could well be into the mutual funds business. Buying another life insurer, like Canada Life, is a possibility; so is buying into an investment firm. Apart from that, McNeil finds intriguing the idea of acquiring a deposit-taking institution such as a trust company. He is wary of the costs involved in building up a distribution system for a full-fledged trust business, but it is possible that the trust could stick to selling guaranteed invest-ment certificates. Expanding into merchant banking—which involves wheeling and dealing in large-scale investments for clients or for the bank itself—is also an interesting thought, he says, since Sun Life has effectively performed merchant bank-ing duties in the bond business for years. At the same time, it is not inconceivable that Sun would diversify into general insur-ance in the future, although the idea has a "low priority" at the moment.

than 33 per cent of premiums came from those two sources. Individual and group annuities accounted for 58 per cent of premium income in 1985. For the industry as a whole, about 55 per cent of total premium income is derived from annuities, compared to 45 per cent from life insurance.

Rather than following a well-defined strategic plan of diversification, McNeil believes in taking advantage of opportunities as they arise. "You have to be open-minded. I don't think you can lay out a blueprint and then start forcing things to fit into that mould. You could plough the fields looking for a property and casualty company to buy, and find nothing. Then an opportunity could come along by surprise."

For the past five years, an evolution in attitudes has taken place at Sun Life. It has been apparent most of all in the drive for greater efficiency, the acquisition of MFS, and the selection of McNeil as Galt's probable successor. There is a distinct possibility that Sun Life will soon add a fourth element to its corporate doctrine of "Order, Obedience and Orthodoxy." It could be another "O" for "Omnivorous." But if that comes to pass, it will be at a measured pace and in its proper time. Thomas Bassett Macaulay would have had it no other way.

# CHAPTER 5

## *Life Can Be Tough at the Top: Manufacturers Life*

THE YEAR WAS 1916. For several months, negotiations about a possible merger had been conducted in the boardrooms of Manufacturers Life Insurance Company of Toronto, and in those of its would-be partner, Sun Life Assurance Company of Montreal. William Gooderham, president of Manufacturers and scion of a well-established distillery family, was entranced by the idea. His counterpart at Sun Life, Thomas Bassett Macaulay, thought it just grand. Sun, already the largest life insurer in Canada by far, could chip in its $74 million in assets and Manufacturers would contribute its $20 million in assets to create a company that would control 26 per cent of the life insurance market in Canada. Everyone concerned thought it was perfectly sensible—except for the Dominion superintendent of insurance, George Finlayson. After studying the proposal at the request of the minister of finance, Finlayson vetoed the plan, arguing that it was not advisable for two such large and financially strong companies to amalgamate.

Looking back on that ill-fated romance, Manufacturers can now be glad that its adolescent brush with corporate marriage fell through. By contrast, Sun Life has every reason to curse the meddling regulator. Finlayson scuttled what proved to be Sun Life's only chance to swallow up the company that would eventually become its nemesis—an aggressive rival that, in 1985, finally ended Sun's 76-year reign as the largest insurer in Canada as measured by assets. That occurred in February 1985, when Manufacturers completed its purchase of Dominion Life Assurance Co. of Waterloo, Ontario, for more than $157 million.

In the narcoleptic world of major life insurance companies, Manufacturers has distinguished itself as an early riser. As long ago as 1970, while other large insurers were still deep in slumber, Manufacturers recognized that insurance companies had fallen almost hopelessly behind the rest of North American industry in most respects, from management methods and productivity improvement to marketing.

In the intervening years, Sydney Jackson, who became the chief executive officer of Manufacturers in 1971, revitalized the company with a series of sweeping changes. On taking power, Jackson immediately broke with the cloistered, top-down management style that had characterized head office since the days of the 90-year-old company's first president, Sir John A. Macdonald.[1] Under Jackson's leadership, innovation and risk-taking have become the dominant elements in Manufacturers' corporate culture. Perpetually restless, the Regina-born actuary has also overseen Manufacturers' rapid climb to the number one position. The company had assets of about $2 billion in 1972; at the end of 1985 that figure had risen to $16.4 billion, about $500 million more than Sun Life.

---

[1]Sir John A. Macdonald was president of Manufacturers until his death in 1891. During the same time period, Macdonald also served as Canada's prime minister. The arrangement was not unusual during the era: there were no conflict of interest guidelines to prevent politicians from combining their legislative duties with active business careers.

Macdonald's early role at Manufacturers is still a source of pride at the company. The Toronto headquarters contains a 1980 portrait of Canada's first prime minister by F. A. Verner, as well as a bronze bust of Macdonald by Silvain.

Today, however, Manufacturers has arrived at a crossroads in its development. Jackson, who turned 64 on May 17, 1986, has already withdrawn somewhat from the turbulent apex of Manufacturers' affairs. Although he is still chairman and chief executive officer, he functions as a senior statesman for the company and, more and more, has passed the reins of power to his heir-apparent, company president Thomas Di Giacomo. In 1984, when Jackson plucked Di Giacomo, then 42, from his post as head of Manufacturers' investment division, he signalled that the company was about to enter the next stage in its evolution into a modern corporation. Di Giacomo's mandate is to make the company more cost-conscious, whip unproductive divisions into shape and oversee an administrative decentralization process. Says Richard Kado, a former assistant vice-president at Manufacturers: "With the appointment of Tom Di Giacomo, Manufacturers will complete the transition from a company that was run like a small business into a professional corporation."

More important in the longer term, Di Giacomo's outstanding track record in the company's investment department earned him a reputation as a man with the deal-making instincts to help Manufacturers expand into a broader range of financial services if, as expected, federal regulations are changed to permit mutual life insurance companies to own controlling interests in their financial cousins, such as trust companies and investment dealers.

So far, however, the feisty executive has not got off to an auspicious start. Di Giacomo's demanding management style has created more uncertainty than confidence within the company's ranks. And Manufacturers' closely monitored 1985 attempt to expand beyond the life insurance industry by acquiring control of Canada Trustco ended in failure.

Di Giacomo's short tenure as Manufacturers' number two man has given renewed meaning to the saying, "Life is lonely at the top." Just how lonely was made distressingly clear to

Di Giacomo at a roast beef dinner at the end of a staff golf tour-
nament north of Toronto in June 1985. As the balding, cherubic-
faced senior executive went to the head-table microphone to
present an award to the best player of the day, someone in the
audience booed. Someone else hissed. Within seconds, a large
portion of the roughly 200 employees in the audience joined
in the off-colour reception. Di Giacomo, reputed to have a
skin as thick as a pachyderm's, appeared amused by the hostile
mood. He carried on, never losing his composure despite the
added frustration of a faulty microphone that made his remarks
almost inaudible. Some Manulifers at the event were aston-
ished, not so much by the depth of the resentment, but by the
unrestrained public display of it. Says one employee: "It was
really gauche. We used to be a classy company to work for. But
that is definitely changing."

The incident was a remarkable one for the Toronto-based
company. Its top executives are more accustomed to receiving
accolades than insults from its 4,000 employees in 138 countries. But the episode provided a glimpse of the tension that
lies just below the surface of Manufacturers' financial success.
The turmoil began in earnest in 1985 when the company
announced layoffs and relocations affecting about 500 head
office staff, necessitated by the transfer of its Canadian operations to Dominion Life's Waterloo offices, an hour's drive west
of Toronto. Acknowledges Di Giacomo: "I was the new boy on
the block. I was taking a fair bit of the resentment personally. I
could detect fear. People were frightened even though this has
always been a very people-oriented company." But now with
the move complete, the ranks of head office are still dominated by uncertainty over the direction in which Di Giacomo
will take the company as it begins its second century. Referring
to Di Giacomo's reputation as a cost-cutter, one junior super-
visor comments, "He has come across as a real hardliner. Everyone is uncertain about where it's going to go from here."
Change, it seems, is difficult even for a company whose history

has been marked by a propensity for selling harder, growing faster and innovating sooner than peers in the industry.

## Off to a Running Start

Ever since its creation as The Manufacturers' Life and Accident Insurance Company by an Act of Parliament on April 26, 1881, the company has had an insatiable hunger for expansion. Its founder and first managing director, J. B. Carlisle, was a native Yorkshireman and former auctioneer who came to Canada in 1880 as a general travelling agent for the North American Life Assurance Company. Within a short time, he had acquired many influential friends in his new country. One personal acquaintance was Sir John A. Macdonald, whom Carlisle persuaded to become the first president of the company. In fact, a company-commissioned history entitled *And All the Past Is Future*, by R. V. Ashforth, notes that the name of the company and its first advertising symbol, an arm and hammer, were intended to be tributes to Macdonald's National Policy for promoting industry in Canada. The first board of the directors meeting on July 13, 1881, included the prime minister, Sir Alexander Campbell, lieutenant-governor of Ontario and a former federal cabinet minister, George Gooderham, an influential banker and distiller, and William Bell of Guelph, Ontario, a manufacturer of musical instruments and president of the Traders' Bank.

With the company's blue-chip credentials assured, Carlisle's next step—designing the company's policies, premium rates and tables—was relatively simple. Carlisle simply copied them from the company he had previously worked for—a common practice in the era.

Carlisle himself was largely responsible for the early success of the company. An energetic salesman, he had personally peddled over $500,000 worth of policies by December 1887. He had also set up agencies to serve the provinces of Ontario,

Quebec and Nova Scotia. In the West, one agent, William Scott, served all the territories from Ontario to the Pacific Coast. His contract named him "General agent for the territory including Manitoba, the territories [the Northwest Territories and the unborn provinces of Saskatchewan and Alberta], British Columbia and that part of Ontario lying west of Rat Portage (Kenora)." By the time of the first annual meeting in January 1888, after just five months in operation, Carlisle's prodigious band of salesmen had sold 915 policies worth $2,500,000. In that same year, Manufacturers was dubbed "The Young Canadian Giant" by the press.

Over the years that followed, the company was to continue the pace at home and abroad. Expansion outside Canada began in 1892, soon reaching into all corners of the British Empire, as well as into countries such as China, Japan and parts of South America. As Ashforth records, "On the completion of its first ten years, the Company found itself well-established—and with its worldwide expansion successfully launched." In the process, Manufacturers' assets increased to $1,200,951 and its insurance in force totalled $11,326,686. By 1903, Manufacturers had also established operations in the United States and the United Kingdom.

Manufacturers' presidents over its first 75 years of existence were men of public prominence and wealth who often retained the post until death robbed them of it. One was Sir George Ross (president from 1901 until his death in 1914), who also served as premier of Ontario and was a Liberal leader in the Senate of Canada. The name most linked with the company, though, is that of the Gooderham distillery family. George Gooderham, a founding director, started the dynasty when he succeeded Sir John A. Macdonald as president at his death in June 1891. Gooderham's eldest son William, who was also the president of the Canada Permanent Mortgage Corporation and vice-president of the Bank of Toronto, held the top post at Manufacturers from April 1914 until he died in December

1935. The reins then passed to William's younger brother, Ross Gooderham, whose tenure did not end until his death at age 75 in 1951. They were prosperous decades for Manufacturers. During both world wars, the company's balance sheet blossomed with new business that more than compensated for rises in claims. Apart from the lean years during the Great Depression, the company maintained its steady expansion in business. In its first 25 years, the company's assets grew to $10 million and business in force totalled $80 million. By 1946, its assets were $330 million and business in force amounted to $970 million. Then, by the company's 75th anniversary in 1962, its assets had passed the $1 billion mark.

In many ways, Manufacturers showed that it was not afraid to be ahead of the pack. In 1925, it moved its head office from the corner of King and Yonge Streets to Bloor Street East, then largely a residential district. It was not until the early 1950s that other major insurers, including Crown Life and Confederation, moved into the area. Likewise, Manufacturers showed an early interest in technological advances for the office. In 1921, it was one of the first companies to introduce the amazing Hollerith tabulating machines, which enabled clerks to do calculations with what was considered blinding speed. In 1956, Manufacturers installed the first major IBM business computer in Canada. But in other ways, Manufacturers marched to the same drummer as its main competitors. Amid the paranoia about foreign takeovers of life insurers in the mid-fifties, for instance, the company joined the rush to mutualization. Buying up its own shares, it became a mutual company in July 1958.

Some more problematical similarities between Manufacturers and its competitors were also evident. Despite a period of strong growth during the 1950s and '60s, Manufacturers was still functioning like a small family operation with an autocratic father at the dawning of the 1970s. Company lore has it that the man who preceded Jackson, Alfred Seedhouse, believed that subordinates were best seen and not heard. He is reputed to have called in his field managers but once a year, to tell them what he expected them to do, and then send them packing back to the field.

## Smilin' Syd

Jackson changed all that after Seedhouse selected him as the next president and chief executive officer in 1972. (Until 1985 the top two jobs were president and executive vice-president). Although Jackson was a career employee—he had joined the company in 1948 after graduating from the University of Manitoba with a degree in commerce—he was no supporter of the status quo. He opened up the doors of the executive suites with his democratic style, encouraging new ideas and initiative from lower-level executives and managers. Other long-overdue changes occurred. Says Jackson: "We got into job descriptions, job evaluations, that sort of thing." At the same time, on the recommendation of a strategic task force, Jackson began decentralizing the operations of the company, splitting it into territorial divisions better suited to meeting the changing needs of different markets. Overall, he says, "it was a dramatic change in culture."

The first years were difficult ones for Jackson. He was seen as a 51-year-old upstart by his senior colleagues, most of whom were nearing retirement age. Says Jackson: "There was a lot of upset and publicity about it. That got the board of directors worried—and that, in turn, made me worried." But eventually, employee morale soared, sales (particularly in the United States) burgeoned, and company assets swelled—to $5.03 billion in 1979 from about $2 billion in 1971. The 1970s was a happy decade at Manufacturers. The company was number two to Sun Life but trying harder and growing faster.

The company's high morale was largely a result of Jackson's relaxed, unpretentious style. His performance at a 1975 conference, held at a Swiss resort for the United Kingdom division's staff, was typical. Regarded as a brilliant numbers man by his staff and standing six feet, two inches tall, Jackson has an imposing presence. At employee gatherings, he seems to tower over the proceedings like an eagle benignly surveying its domain. But at the black-tie dinner that wound up the three-day confab in Switzerland, Jackson's employees gasped when their boss from Toronto appeared wearing, beneath the mandatory dinner jacket, an extra-large pair of Swiss lederhosen. After dinner, Jackson took to the dance floor in his leather trousers. "It must have been 90 degrees in there," recalls senior vice-president John Clark, "but Syd danced all night. The band was due to pack up at 1:00 A.M. but we paid them an extra 250 francs to play until three."

When it came to working conditions, Jackson turned Manufacturers' head office employees into one of the most pampered work forces in North America. On the entire continent, there is no grander testament to the monetary rewards of selling life insurance than Manufacturers' gold glass North Tower. Opened in 1983, the $40 million, 13-storey addition married exterior architectural splendor to interior opulence. Designed by the architectural firm of Clifford Lawrie Bolton Ritchie, the new edifice is joined to the old Georgian-style limestone head office by means of a gleaming copper-domed rotunda. Designer Peter Ferguson was quoted by journalist Adele Freedman in a 1983 *Globe and Mail* article as saying that the dome has always been associated with funerary monuments and hence made sense for an insurance company. "It's a testament to the people who died at the proper time," said Ferguson. Cherrywood panelling, found even inside the Mitsubishi elevators, gives the entire new building a sort of lustrous glow of prosperity; so do the marble floors, Persian rugs, expensive oil paintings and 15,000-square-foot employee fitness centre that grace the building. Staff with more mundane matters on their mind than their swank surroundings can take advantage of subsidized dining and day-care facilities provided by the company.

During Jackson's tenure, Manufacturers achieved recognition as one of the best employers in Canada, based on such criteria as working conditions and employee benefits. The volume of business also boomed. But critics of Jackson's methods of running the company up until the early 1980s say there was very little regard for the bottom line among managers and agents in the field. "Manufacturers was a country club," says one former executive disparagingly. Jackson himself agrees that after the company reorganized into territorial divisions, proper cost controls were not put in place. In that respect, he says, the decentralization process "was an abject failure. We created divisions without having the management information that could hold them responsible. That, in fact, is still a bit of a problem. We have not got controls as well in place...as we should."

But then, Manufacturers was too busy expanding to concentrate on cost cutting. Under Jackson, the company consolidated its reputation as a major player in the worldwide insurance market. Operations and sales were expanded in the United States to the point where the company had 41 branch offices and 18 group sales offices in 48 states. "We saw the American market as a huge one that we could do very well in," says Jackson. It did. In 1985 the U.S. market accounted for more than 54 per cent of the company's total premium income. The U.K. division also set a blistering pace, and the Far East, primarily Hong Kong, proved to be fertile territory. The Pacific Asia division was bolstered to include three branch offices in Hong Kong, and one each in the Philippines and Indonesia. Explains Jackson: "We saw the Far East as the industrial giant of the twenty-first century. Selling insurance there is like selling insurance in the 1920s in North America because there is no social security."

For the U.S. market, in particular, Manufacturers dusted off its product portfolio in the early 1980s and pulled out a handful of shiny new policies, including variable life and universal life products, designed to meet consumer demand for better rates of return on their premium payments. To the company's credit, those two new product types accounted for 50 per cent of its total premium income from individual life policies in 1985; term products accounted for another 25 per cent and traditional whole life policies 25 per cent.

The emphasis on developing foreign markets soon over-shadowed the company's growth in Canada, with the result that the majority of its policyholders were non-Canadian. "We were becoming increasingly foreign-dominated and we weren't expanding in Canada because it was the least attractive area in the sense that it was the most competitive in the world," recalls Jackson. "It became apparent that we were very small in Canada and were not of a size that was economical." The best way to remedy the situation, Manufacturers concluded, was to acquire another company in Canada.

The company's first attempt to do so was a dismal failure. In 1978, Jackson set his sights on buying the Canadian operation of Edinburgh-based Standard Life Assurance Co., the first life insurer to do business in Canada. In July of that year, the two companies announced that a deal had been struck. But imme-diately, the plan began to collapse amid an imbroglio of regula-tory scrutiny, public controversy and the threat of legal action by dissident policyholders. The controversy erupted over whether Standard's Canadian policyholders were being de-prived of a fair share of the company's Canadian and world-wide surplus. Under the agreement, about $1.5 billion of Stan-dard's $1.7 billion in Canadian assets would be transferred to Manufacturers. The remaining $200 million would go to Stan-dard's Scottish parent.

Montreal lawyer Richard Holden, fresh from his unsuccess-ful fight to prevent Sun Life from moving its head office from Montreal to Toronto just six months before, seized on the $200 million discrepancy with relish. He charged that Stan-dard's 110,000 Canadian policyholders were the targets of an "old-fashioned rip-off." Toronto lawyer Robert G. Thomson, a specialist in corporate and financial law, joined in the clamour, alleging that the $200 million surplus should go to Canadian policyholders. Both men threatened to challenge the deal in court if it went through. (If the dispute had gone to court, it might have finally settled the still-unresolved issue of who owns a life insurers' surplus, the policyholders or the company.) Interestingly, the board of directors of Standard's Canadian operation opposed the deal, but were overruled by their Scottish masters anyway.

Even in Edinburgh, however, Standard's executives became increasingly disenchanted with the transaction as it became apparent that the deal might be delayed for months on end. Not only were legal actions pending, but regulators in Ottawa launched an investigation into the sale and their counterparts in Ontario threatened to do the same. By November, Standard had had enough. Standard's general manager and chief actuary, David Donald, announced in Scotland that the deal was off. Jackson's bitterness over the setback, which he blames in large part on fuzzy laws, is still sharp. "We were unsuccessful because of the goddamned laws," he curses.

The scars of the failure did not disappear until six years later, when Manufacturers stalked and captured much bigger prey. On November 16, 1984, Manufacturers acquired Dominion Life for a whopping $157.5 million from its U.S. owner, The Lincoln National Life Insurance Company. (In February, 1985, the acquisition was endorsed in a vote by Manufacturers' policyholders.) Manufacturers won the solid Waterloo-based stock company (1984 assets: $1.5 billion) simply because it wanted the company more than its rival bidders and was willing to put more money down on the table. Of the six rival companies in the final stages of the bidding, none came close to Manufacturers' offer. Imperial Life, owned by the Quebec City-based Laurentian Group, came second with a bid of $153 million, and that sum, say Laurentian officials, was arrived at as much through guesswork as through a rational calculation of Dominion's worth. Manulife paid a hefty price for Dominion. But then, the pleasure of being number one in the industry—the deal vaulted Manufacturers past Sun Life in asset size—cannot be measured in dollar terms. Neither, for that matter, can employee morale.

Under federal legislation, Manufacturers, as a mutual company, was not allowed to own a life insurance subsidiary in Canada. (The law had been designed originally to prevent over-concentration in the marketplace.) As a result, Manufacturers began merging its Canadian operation with Dominion in Waterloo—a painful process because Manufacturers' Canadian division had 500 on staff and Dominion had 550 employees at its head office, yet the target number for the merged division was a maximum of 800. There would not be room for at least 250 employees. Eventually, more than 100 were laid off; the rest found other positions in the company.

If Manufacturers' executives had had their druthers, they would have spent the months in the wake of the Dominion purchase sorting out the logistics of the move and paying attention to the insurance business. They were also aware of the need to reassure the ranks. A confidential survey of employee attitudes taken in January 1985 showed a 20 per cent decline in satisfaction with Manufacturers as a whole since July 1984. That represented "a significant downward shift," warned the report. The survey also reported that 50 per cent of employees thought that the company was becoming a less attractive place to work. The study concluded: "Since July, 1984, there has been a significant decline in confidence that MLI is doing the right things to be successful in the future." But dealing with the morale problem would have to be postponed, Manufacturers' generals were called off to do battle on another front.

### Slugging It Out with Genstar

Manufacturers had been trying for years to buy a solid foothold in a trust company, a position that would give it a jump on the competition if the laws restricting mutual insurance companies to a 30 per cent stake in trusts were changed. Says Jackson: "I think when we began to see Trilon in Canada and the same sort of thing happening throughout the world...that made us think that we should be looking a little broader than life insurance." Adds Di Giacomo: "It became apparent that we were into a potential deregulatory scenario. It looked like down the road that someone might call a new card game and we didn't have a card to attend the game."

Manufacturers' first attempt to win that card was shortlived. In 1981 it bought a 10.9 per cent stake in Canada Permanent, a Toronto-based trust company, but sold out several months later for a profit of $9 million when Canada Permanent became the prize in a takeover battle between the Belzberg family of Vancouver and Genstar Financial Corp., a financial services and real estate conglomerate based in the same West Coast city. Genstar emerged the victor in a battle that Manufacturers never really joined. "We had no axes to grind afterward," says Di Giacomo, explaining that Manufacturers hadn't had time to "grow attached" to its Canada Permanent shares.

In its next retreat from the trust industry, after a scrimmage that once again involved Genstar, Manufacturers was more badly bruised. In a protracted struggle for control of Canada Trustco Mortgage Co. of London, Ontario, Manufacturers was out-manoeuvred and eventually beated by Genstar's tough tactics.

Manufacturers had bought an initial 10 per cent holding in Canada Trustco in 1982, increasing its interest in stages to nearly 30 per cent by the summer of 1985. But the trust company's management gave Manufacturers a decidedly cold reception. Mervyn Lahn, Canada Trustco's prickly chief executive officer had repeatedly made it plain that he opposed any one shareholder owning more than 10 per cent of his company—the largest, arguably best run and last widely held trust in the country. To back up that position, a company by-law prevented anyone from voting more than 10 per cent of Canada Trustco's shares. To Manufacturers' chagrin, Lahn also contended that the insurer was a foreign-owned company under the federal laws governing loan and trust companies because most of its policyholders were non-Canadians. Because Manufacturers' residency status was in dispute, Lahn refused to let the insurance company vote at all at annual meetings of the trust company. Jackson, for his part, sat quietly on Canada Trustco's board and executive committee. He describes his relations with Lahn as "cordial but not warm," adding: "He had a style of his own." Jackson was determined to wait out the recalcitrant Lahn, hoping that as deregulation progressed, he would become more co-operative. Says Jackson: "We couldn't vote our shares, but in the short run that didn't bother me. It was a technicality—more of a newspaper item than anything."

The first hint that Jackson might not get the opportunity to wait out his stubborn counterpart at the trust company came in the spring of 1985. Angus MacNaughton, chief executive officer of Genstar, appeared in Jackson's office in March. Jackson was not overly concerned when MacNaughton mentioned an interest in buying into Canada Trustco, which would fit very well with Genstar-owned Canada Permanent. To be sure, MacNaughton and Ross Turner, his tag-team partner at Genstar (in an unusual arrangement the two men take turns as chief executive officer of Genstar) played it cool in their initial overtures to Manufacturers. At first, they talked about controlling Canada Trustco in partnership with Manufacturers. Recalls Jackson: "I said, 'Well we're allowed to own 30 per cent and if you own 30 per cent that would be 60 per cent. That's a possibility.' Then they asked, 'What if we bought more?' I replied that we weren't interested in being a junior partner."

The Genstar duo's meetings with Lahn were equally unproductive. They first raised the possibility of Genstar buying into Canada Trustco in a conference call with Lahn in late March. "They are always on the phone together," quips Lahn. A plain talker, Lahn brusquely told them he had no interest in the proposition. Undeterred, MacNaughton and Turner paid a visit to Lahn's Toronto office on May 9. At that meeting and several more that followed it, Lahn said bluntly that Canada Trustco's board was of the opinion that the trust should remain a widely held company.

At that stage, neither Lahn nor Manufacturers' executives viewed the Genstar feelers as a serious threat. Recalls Jackson, "When we thought of their owning 30 per cent, we thought, boy, they are getting into big money and where are they going to get that sort of money." But as the two Genstar executives became more pressing in their courtship, it became apparent that they were not going to be rebuffed easily. At Manufacturers, strategy sessions to assess the situation were convened. But Manufacturers' management and board had serious reservations about making a pre-emptive strike for Canada Trustco, says Jackson, because Manufacturers would have to go through a "loophole" in the law in order to get around federal laws that limited mutuals to a 30 per cent stake in trust companies. Manufacturers' management was worried about upsetting Ottawa at a time when the company was lobbying vigorously to have financial regulations changed to its liking. "We were inclined to hold off," says Jackson, "feeling that nobody would take a go at it [Canada Trustco] as long as we held 30 per cent." The company wanted more time to consider its options. "We would have been able to digest Dominion Life, which was a big management effort, we'd be able to see where the federal Green Paper [on financial services] was going." That complacency proved to be badly misguided. Just how much so became apparent on August 1, 1985, when MacNaughton and Turner arrived at Jackson's 11th-floor office in Toronto bearing disturbing news. The two men told Jackson and Di Giacomo that they intended to make a public offer for control of Canada Trustco. "They flew in and saw Tom and myself at 4:00 P.M. to say they were going to put an offer out, adding that their stockbrokers would be in to explain the details of the offer the next morning," says Jackson. "Our answer was no. We weren't interested in selling."

As promised, at 9:15 A.M. on August 2, two heavyweights of the investment community, Anthony Fell from Dominion Securities Pitfield and Jimmy Connacher, noted for his deal-making wizardry as chairman of Gordon Capital Corp., arrived at Jackson's office to explain their clients' offer. The meeting lasted only 20 minutes and no tempers flared, mainly because Fell and Jackson are good friends, having worked together closely in the Ontario Division of the Canadian Arthritis and Rheumatism Society. "We said we'd get back to them," says Di Giacomo. "I called Connacher at about 11:30 A.M. and told him there was no deal." Di Giacomo thought the offer of $41.70 a share was too low. "When that offer came out I did not think it was good enough. Us selling our shares to them was effectively handing them control of the company." Under provincial take-over rules, $41.70 was the maximum Genstar could have bid without making an offer to other shareholders. That aspect of the offer also bothered Di Giacomo. "It's not our corporate policy to take an extraordinary price for our shares and have the minority shareholders treated differently."

The next day, when Genstar made its initial $528-million bid for 40.3 per cent of Canada Trustco at $44 a share, Manufacturers was drawn for the first time into a high-stakes take-over battle. Di Giacomo, who directed Manufacturers' counter-attack, convened marathon strategy sessions with his closest advisors during the following week. They had three options, according to Di Giacomo: do nothing; sell to Genstar; or make a counterbid. By the weekend they had settled on making an offer of their own. On Saturday, August 10, they assembled their forces to hammer out the deal. Manufacturers' legal counsel, Gordon Coleman from the firm Tory, Tory, Deslauriers and Binnington, and the company auditor, Bill Archer from Clarkson Gordon, were phoned at their cottages and asked to come to Manufacturers' headquarters. A flock of company actuarial, accounting and tax experts was also assembled, and for the next two days, they discussed the legal and financial ramifications of acquiring control of Canada Trustco. The resulting proposal was put before a hastily called board meeting on Monday, August 12, and the plan was approved without event. "The meeting was pretty straightforward; we took them through the three options," says Di Giacomo. "The scenario basically was that if we got a bid in we would be more in control than the other party."

But Manufacturers resolved to make the bid (for 51 per cent of Canada Trustco at $50 a share) only if the trust firm's management welcomed the offer and agreed to hold a shareholders' vote to drop the troublesome 10 per cent ownership by-law. At a meeting that afternoon in Canada Trustco's boardroom, Lahn and his colleagues quickly agreed. Recalls Di Giacomo: "It was a very amiable meeting. There seemed to be a little relief that somebody else was coming in." That is an understatement. Lahn, who had spent the previous week frantically courting a list of about a dozen companies to counter Genstar's bid, finally had the white knight he was looking for. Lahn reasoned that ownership by a mutual life insurer, whose owners are theoretically hundreds of thousands of policyholders, would give Canada Trustco a maximum degree of independence.

Manufacturers proceeded with its offer but was stunned by the next turn of events. "When everything was a go we put out our press release to the public on the Tuesday. Then we just let everything calm down. On Wednesday we were enjoined [served with a court injunction]," says Di Giacomo. "We had to bring in the litigators." Genstar had made an application in the

Ontario Supreme Court for an injunction halting Manufacturers' offer. The Vancouver-based company asserted that Manufacturers' bid for the trust company broke federal laws limiting insurance firms to a 30 per cent interest in trust companies. Manufacturers countered in an affidavit that no federal regulations would be broken because Manufacturers did not intend to *directly* own more than 30 per cent of Canada Trustco. The rest of the shares needed to give the life insurer 51 per cent of the trust would be held by two associated companies, Dominion Life and Manuduke Ltd., a real estate investment company. As part of its defence, Manufacturers pointed to a case earlier in the year when a federally chartered life insurer, Cooperants Mutual Life Insurance Society, and two of its subsidiaries took over Guardian Trust Co. of Montreal. Manufacturers was also aware that under the federal government's financial deregulation proposals contained in the Green Paper, the legality of its acquisition of Canada Trustco would be beyond dispute.

To complicate matters further, Manufacturers faced another legal challenge to its bid. Michael Scott, a Toronto management consultant and company policyholder, filed an affidavit in the Supreme Court of Ontario asking for a restraining order against Manufacturers. In it, Scott alleged that the acquisition would be contrary to the law and furthermore that it would place policyholders' money at great risk, since if federal authorities eventually ordered Manufacturers to divest itself of the Canada Trustco shares, the insurance company might take a beating on the stock market when it sold them.

But neither court action ever came to fruition. Within days, Genstar upped the ante, putting in a new bid for 100 per cent of Canada Trustco at $45.20 a share. Manufacturers' executives first heard the news on Sunday night, August 19. Just before 9:00 P.M., Jackson got a phone call from the Genstar executives. They were calling from Windsor, where they were waiting out a thunderstorm that had interrupted their flight from

San Francisco. They wanted to meet with Jackson and Di
Giacomo at midnight at the Manufacturers office. After alerting Di Giacomo to the request, Jackson called them back in
Windsor to quash the idea. "We were all tired and didn't want
to start negotiations that night. We set up a meeting for 7:30
A.M. Monday," says Di Giacomo. From that point on, however,
Manufacturers was out of the game. It had no intention of
countering with a billion-dollar-plus offer, which would reduce
its surplus too drastically. By about 4:00 P.M. the next day, the
final documents handing over Manufacturers' interest in Canada Trustco were signed. Then Jackson got on the phone to
inform Lahn of the decision. Lahn told him: "I've got a few
phone calls to make." The Canada Trustco CEO was hoping
that another white knight would come to his rescue with a
$50-a-share bid for 100 per cent of his company. Lahn refuses
to identify the mystery suitor, but rumour had it that Bell
Canada Enterprises was interested. The trust company chief
was so certain that the new offer would materialize that he bet
$20 on it with David Jackson, Canada Trustco's legal advisor
from the Toronto firm Blake Cassels & Graydon. "If we had got
that bid," says Lahn, "it would have blown them [Genstar] right
out of the sandbox." Lahn lost his bet. His prospective white
knight dropped out just three days before Genstar's offer closed.

In the end, Genstar picked up its prize for about $1.2 bil-
lion, all of it borrowed. (Genstar's total debt load was pushed
up to about $2.2 billion by the purchase, giving it a worrisome
debt-equity ratio of 2.2:1) For its part, Manufacturers pocketed
a $150-million capital gain by selling out. But that did little to
ease the keen sense of disappointment at Manufacturers. "We
were very anxious to get 51 per cent of Canada Trustco," says
Jackson. "In retrospect, I guess we were too much the gentlemen. They were more aggressive. We saw that in their taking
things to court. If people are going to start doing that, for us to
survive we've got to be as aggressive as we can. We can't just
wait for the laws to change." Not everyone at Manufacturers

mourned the company's loss in the Canada Trustco scuffle, however. Robin Leckie, Manufacturers' chief actuary concedes, "I personally wasn't all that unhappy when we got a good result out of it....Suppose our offer had been accepted and the counteroffer by Genstar had not been in there. We would have had our work cut out for us to ensure that the investment we were making was producing a good return."[2]

For Di Giacomo, the man appointed to lead Manufacturers into the mainstream of the financial services sector, the Canada Trustco affair was not a good beginning. Manufacturers was knocked back to square one, without its long-coveted position in the trust industry. "You don't want to be a bridesmaid all your life," he says. Still, he regards it as a valuable learning experience. "We learned a lot in those four weeks. We learned a fair bit about public markets, the structure of deals."

### A Man for the Times

Manufacturers' executives have little time to fret over past tribulations, however. They have too much to preoccupy them. Despite the Canada Trustco setback, Di Giacomo has earned the respect of his senior colleagues since he was promoted in 1984. Initially, some of them regarded him as too young and inexperienced for the job. That attitude has changed. Says Leckie: "I think he has done a fantastic job in the one or two years since he was made the heir apparent. Tom has shown an emotional maturity that was perhaps very unsure at the time of his appointment. He's moved in very quickly, taken aggressive positions."

Di Giacomo has moved quickly to put his stamp on the company. He has designated like-minded men with proven

[2]Subsequently, there was another twist in the fate of Genstar and Canada Trustco. In March 1985, Imasco Ltd., a $2.9 billion Montreal-based conglomerate with tobacco, fast food and drug store interests, acquired Genstar for $ ..4 billion. Canada Trustco was part of the prize.

cost-cutting talents to head the Canadian division (John Clark) and the U.S. division (Brian Simons). One of Simons' tasks is to turn around the disappointing debut of a new variable life product in the United States. "It has not been a great howling success," concedes Jackson. Brian Buckles, formerly senior vice-president in charge of the U.S. operation, was shunted aside and given general corporate responsibilities for the division. Says a former employee in the U.S. operation: "Brian's style clashed with Tom's. Brian liked to nibble at problems. Tom takes aim and fires."

Di Giacomo plays down staff fears about who and what might come under his axe. "If my reputation as a cost-cutter had actually gone into cost-cutting," he muses, "we'd be ahead of the game." Still, Jackson describes his chosen successor as "a bottom-line, results-oriented person." If Di Giacomo has his way, he will wrench Manufacturers away from its old ways and send it further along the path to becoming a modern corporation. He is convinced that Manufacturers and the rest of the insurance industry must continue introducing modern management techniques, "promoting and hiring people on the basis of ability [instead of longevity]" in order to survive in the financial marketplace. "In the past, the life industry got out of sync with what was occurring in North America," he allows, "and I think it is playing catch-up to some extent now."

Meanwhile, Di Giacomo is scouting the financial terrain for new quarry in a broad range of financial services, from trust and brokerage institutions to real estate and mutual fund companies. The company has a bulging surplus of $1.4 billion to finance takeovers. As the financial industry evolves in the future, Manufacturers will be a contender to watch.

# CHAPTER 6

## *Setting the Pace: The Laurentian Group*

THE SIX MEN crammed into the tiny, makeshift conference room on the perimeter of Toronto's Pearson International Airport in October 1984 faced one of the most important decisions in their corporate careers. Claude Castonguay, chief executive officer of The Laurentian Group, had just flown in from his Quebec City base with his chief financial officer, Michel Durand, in tow. On disembarking from the company jet, they had hurried to the nearby offices of Innotech Aviation Limited, the company that services their plane, to hold a last-minute meeting. Now, with the roar of jet aircraft in the background, they were huddled around a small, circular table with senior officers of the group's main subsidiary, Imperial Life Assurance of Toronto. Claude Bruneau, chairman of Imperial, was in the hot seat. Time was running out for Imperial to make a final bid to buy Dominion Life Assurance Company of Waterloo from its U.S. parent, The Lincoln National Life Insurance Company. But what was the offer to be? Dominion would be a fine addition to the corporate stable of the expansion-minded Laurentian Group. Five other suitors, however, were in the running.[1] One of them, Manufacturers Life, was known to hanker after the 95-year-old company most of all.

After carrying out an evaluation of Dominion, Castonguay and his colleagues had determined that the company was worth about $140 million. But then, that was a rational, objective conclusion, and in the several months since the bidding had opened on Dominion, ardour had long since clouded out rationality in the minds of all the would-be acquisitors. Recalls Castonguay: "We knew that there were some people who wanted that company quite badly and they would have the same [evaluation] figures as ours. Even if it was a realistic evaluation, we knew we should go a little beyond it." During the deliberations, Castonguay and Bruneau stressed Dominion's attractions; Lewis Dunn, executive vice-president of Imperial, led the skeptics. Finally, a figure was settled on: $153 million. It was more than Dominion was worth but the men knew that Manufacturers' bid would be difficult to beat. Says Durand: "We knew Manulife might be the highest bidder. They are a mutual company and don't have to provide a good return on investment for their owners."[2] Durand's hunch proved true. Imperial's bid was the second highest but it fell several million short of Manufacturers' successful $157.5 million offer.

[1]At the outset of the bidding there were as many as 50 companies interested in Dominion. By October they had been reduced to five, apart from The Laurentian Group. According to industry insiders they were Manufacturers, Crown Life, Confederation Life, Aetna Canada and a group of B.C. pension funds.

[2]Durand was referring to the popular belief in financial circles that the owners of a mutual insurer, the company's policyholders, have neither the influence over, nor interest in, the financial performance of the company that shareholders of stock companies do. When taking over stock life insurers such as Dominion Life, mutual companies like Manufacturers have yet another advantage over stock companies, such as Imperial or Crown Life. Federal insurance legislation restricts how much shareholders can take out of a stock company's par fund—the fund set aside for participating policyholders (those with participating policies). Imperial or Crown would have been able to cream off only 7½ per cent of the annual earnings of Dominion's $63-million par fund. By contrast, Manufacturers, which won the bidding, could swallow up Dominion's par fund entirely after merging Dominion's operation with its own.

Claude Castonguay, 59-year-old chief of The Laurentian Group Corp., a financial services holding company with assets of more than $4.5 billion and about 4,000 employees in its various operations, looks back on the failed bid for Dominion with equanimity. "They wanted it a little more than we did," he says with resignation. Castonguay can afford to be stoic. Laurentian's acquisition scorecard over the past six years contains few failures and a series of successes unsurpassed in number by any of its competitors in Canada.

A budding international financial conglomerate with a French-Canadian soul rooted firmly in its birthplace, Quebec City, The Laurentian Group offers a glimpse at what the future will hold for mutual insurance companies intent on diversification in a more deregulated financial marketplace. The Laurentian Group Corp. is a downstream holding company created by The Laurentian Mutual Insurance Company in November 1981 to co-ordinate the activities of its member companies. The holding company was set up in order to take advantage of upcoming changes in the regulatory environment in Quebec. Jacques Parizeau, the Parti Québécois finance minister, had made it clear that financial deregulation was overdue and that many of the restrictions on the activities of mutual companies were outdated and unfair, considering stock companies did not face the same limitations. Bill 75, implemented in June 1984, freed the province's mutuals to set up downstream holding companies, through which they could raise share capital and diversify into a broad range of financial services. Using subsidiaries, mutuals could carry on activities on the turf of trust companies, take deposits, sell stocks, lease and manage real estate properties and "carry on any other activity authorized by the minister."[3]

_____

[3]Further deregulation followed when the Quebec Securities Commission altered its regulations to permit stock brokerages to own a controlling interest in insurance and trust companies, up from a previous 10 per cent ceiling. As well, banks, *caisses populaires* and insurance companies were given permission to sell Quebec stock savings plans.

Other large mutuals in the rest of Canada could only watch with envy as Laurentian Mutual used its holding company to take full advantage of its new freedom.[4] Today, The Laurentian Group has interests in everything from the life and general insurance fields to the real estate development, stock brokering and banking businesses. The acquisition binge, when added to a series of takeovers that began in 1977, has multiplied the conglomerate's assets nearly 30 times from $150 million in 1977 to their current level.

Canadians across the country have already been affected by the Group's new activities. Thousands insure their homes or cars through such general insurance operations as The Laurentian Pacific Insurance Co. of Vancouver and The Personal of Toronto, both of which are owned by the Quebec-based company. Other consumers are familiar with the life insurance activities of Imperial, Laurentian Mutual, Laurier Life, and Eaton Financial Services Ltd., and with the banking services of the Montreal City and District Savings Bank. Still more consumers do stock market investing through investment houses in which the group has a stake: Geoffrion Leclerc Inc. of Montreal or Walwyn Inc. of Toronto.

Not satisfied with only these, Castonguay is now looking for new spoils, confident that one-stop shopping in financial services, in which a consumer can arrange anything from a mortgage to life insurance at one location, is the wave of the future. The Laurentian Group Building, a new $75-million, 578,000-square-foot office tower in Montreal, offers concrete evidence of Castonguay's belief. Opened in 1986, the 27-storey, green-glass edifice, owned one-third each by The Laurentian Group, Marathon Realty Company Ltd. and Lavalin Inc., houses a diversity of financial services. Yet it is only a

---

[4]The Laurentian Group's activities in the rest of Canada were, however, circumscribed somewhat by federal regulations which prevented any one shareholder from owning more than 10 per cent of a bank.

harbinger of things to come for the Group under Castonguay's command.

Son of a Quebec City newspaper man, Castonguay is not easily deterred from his goals. He is the General Patton of Canada's insurance industry, marshalling his troops with an air of dignified, unquestioned authority honed by the rigours of his past incarnations in politics and in business. In 1966 Castonguay left an actuarial consulting firm in Quebec City to serve for four years as chairman of the Quebec Royal Commission on Health and Welfare and was the father of the province's medical insurance scheme. Beginning in 1970, he spent a controversial three years in the cabinet of Liberal Premier Robert Bourassa, serving as health minister, then social affairs minister. In the federal arena, Castonguay sat on the Anti-Inflation Review Board, set up by the Trudeau government in 1975 with powers to roll back wages and price increases. As a former politician and increasingly powerful businessman, Castonguay is a household name in Quebec and a mentor to the aggressive, canny new breed of Quebec businessman that has emerged in recent years. But his vision and plans for the group are in no way limited by political boundaries or parochial attitudes. He has already made the international financial marketplace The Laurentian Group's playing field. Expanding its presence still further in Canada and in foreign territories is his mission. By 1990, Castonguay hopes to have doubled the Group's assets—in part through internal growth, but mainly through acquisitions. "He is a mover," says Imperial chairman Bruneau. "Just look at his acquisition record."

Few doubt that the silver-haired actuary is capable of reaching his goals. Victor Koloshuk, vice-president of McLeod Young Weir, a Toronto-based investment firm, considers Castonguay "a shrewd man who never bites off more than he can chew." But, says Koloshuk, "once he decides something fits his business plans, he moves very quickly. That surprises a lot of people." The main factor working against Castonguay is time.

"Castonguay is a man in a hurry for good reason," says a senior employee. "Already nearing 60, he only has so many years to fulfil his plans." Then, too, some observers wonder whether Castonguay's lieutenants are up to the challenge. Roger McCall, vice-president of Jones Heward Investment Management Inc., a Montreal investment firm, is among the skeptics: "Laurentian has always been a homebody type of business, but the national and international scene is a whole new ball game." Adds McCall: "Castonguay has the foresight but I don't know whether his management team has the outlook necessary." The odds are, however, that men such as Bruneau, known for flair in both his personal and business affairs, and Jacques Drouin, the flamboyant chairman of the group's main general insurance subsidiary, Laurentian General, and executive vice-president of The Laurentian Group Corp., will be able not only to keep up with Castonguay, but also take up his mission when he eventually retires.

### A Company for the Québécois

The Laurentian Group's present reach and future aspirations are a far cry from its origins as The Laurentian Assurance Company, a small company founded by French Canadians for French Canadians in 1938. Laurentian was the creation of J. A. Tardif, a sombre Quebec City ophthalmologist, and his brother-in-law, G. A. Carrette, a former insurance broker. Tardif supplied the public influence necessary to create the company, Carrette brought the enthusiasm and a little know-how. The two men were irked that many of the major companies operating in Quebec at the time were draining millions of dollars' worth of premiums out of the province and not reinvesting them for the benefit of the Québécois. They resolved to create a company that would break the trend. Today, Jean-Marie Poitras, the 69-year-old chairman of the holding company's board and retired president of Laurentian Mutual, acts as the company's unofficial oral historian. He sums up its founders' motivations this way: "They founded the company with social and nationalist goals in mind. Dr Tardif got around him friends and people who believed in the need for French Canadians to be in business, to control their future."

Unlike other major insurers, the company was not born with the financial backing of the wealthy business magnates or the support of nationally known politicians on its board of directors. To raise an initial capitalization of $1 million, Tardif and his colleagues canvassed door to door among friends in Quebec City and in the decidedly unaffluent eastern region of the province.[5]

Between them, Tardif and Carrette had only a modicum of knowledge about how to run an insurance company: Carrette was the only one in the group of founders who knew anything about insurance at all. He arrived at a simple solution for designing the company's policies. In his view, Mutual Life was the best company operating in Canada at the time, and he reasoned that he could simply copy its insurance contracts to make money—and he was right. Carrette's contribution to Laurentian was short-lived, however. He died within three years of its inception. That may have been the best thing for the company, according to Poitras. "Unfortunately for him but, I believe, fortunately for the company, he died pretty young in the first years of the company. I was told that when he took a glass, he thought that he had to take more. He had problems that could have been major," says Poitras.

In the coming decades, Laurentian made steady financial progress. But the company was hampered by Tardif's

[5]The shares were cheap. They cost $100 each, but in a sort of lay-away plan, investors could buy them for $15 apiece initially and pay the balance later. Each individual was restricted to owning a maximum of 300 shares, a rule that prevented anyone from controlling the company. Several years later, the company applied to the provincial government to increase its capitalization by $1 million. Unjustly dubious about the credentials of the company, the government insisted that the shares be sold to the company's original investors, a requirement that the regulators reasoned would prove Laurentian was carrying on a sound business that had kept its investors happy. Laurentian had no trouble meeting the requirement.

haphazard management style. Although he was president of the company, Tardif functioned like an absentee landlord, continuing his medical practice full time and dropping in and spending just enough time at the insurance office to thoroughly frustrate a succession of general managers charged with running the operation. Tardif's personal style did not help matters much. Recalls Poitras: "Dr Tardif was an idealist...he had never been in business. I don't think he ever knew what discipline was. ...But he was convinced of his thinking. It was not easy to discuss things with him."

The strong-willed, idealistic doctor never did manage to get along satisfactorily with his more practical-minded managers. Finally, he gave up on being a part-time president in the early 1960s when a serious crisis erupted. The general manager at the time, Jean-Paul Guimont, and Tardif were feuding and, amazingly, had not talked to each other for two years. In 1963, Guimont walked out. "The basic problem," concludes Poitras, "was a lack of communication. It is difficult when the president is not full time." Tardif turned to Poitras, who was then running a general insurance business with his brother from an office in the Laurentian building, to help him find a new president. In 1965, Poitras himself accepted Tardif's offer to become president of the company, which by that time was called The Laurentian Assurance Company.[6] Tardif became chairman of the board and remained in that post until 1975. In 1986, Tardif still held the title of honourary chairman of the board of Laurentian Mutual.

### The Ebullient Empire-Builder

Much of the credit for The Laurentian Group's early emergence as a financial conglomerate belongs to Poitras, a tower-

---

[6]Laurentian became a mutual, rather than a stock, company in 1958 when it bought up all shares in the hands of the public.

ing, effusive man given to shaking hands with powerful sideways swings of his arm. He learned the insurance business the hard way. The oldest of nine children, his father died when Jean-Marie was 22, an event that ended the young Poitras' aspirations to become a chemical engineer. "It was a crisis. We were in debt with no money," he recalls, speaking with a heavy French accent. To help support the family, Poitras worked in the Quebec City insurance brokerage office established by his father. At night, he took social science courses and studied painting and Italian. "I am a self-made man," he declares proudly. "If I am 10 per cent less intelligent than the other people, I thought that maybe if I work 10 per cent harder, I could reach the bottom level. And if I work another 10 per cent more…"

On becoming president of Laurentian Mutual, Poitras established the business principles that still form the basis of the Group's operations today. In hiring people, he says, he always looked more for evidence of good judgement than for insurance knowledge. In acquiring companies, he always searched out good bargains and made sure that strong leaders were put in charge of each new acquisition. Early on, Poitras concluded that since Laurentian was founded about 40 or 50 years after the big companies doing business in Quebec, such as Sun Life, Canada Life, L'Alliance Mutuelle and L'Industrielle (two companies which merged in 1986), it would not be possible to catch up to them by internal growth alone. Says Poitras: "We thought that we had to grow from the inside by generating new business and from the outside by acquisitions."

Under Poitras' leadership, Laurentian grew steadily, mainly by buying up small, Quebec-based general insurance outfits. In 1967, Laurentian added a majority holding in La Paix, Compagnie d'Assurances Générales du Canada to its holdings. In 1969 it purchased the Quebec Automobile Club Insurance Company and the Universal Protection Insurance Company, two general insurers that were merged to form one, The

Laurentian General Insurance Company. Then the 1975 acquisition of The Provident Assurance Co. made Laurentian one of the largest general insurers in Quebec as well as being a major presence in the life market. The acquisitions helped boost Laurentian's assets from $36 million in 1965, when Poitras took over, to $127 million in 1977.

But Poitras' most daring move came in 1977 when his roving eye settled on Imperial Life, a slumbering Toronto-based company with assets of $700 million at the time—a company nearly six times the size of Laurentian. The idea of buying Imperial seemed preposterous to many, but Poitras thought he might be able to buy it dirt cheap. He also reasoned that the only way to expand beyond Quebec was through acquisitions. "Many companies from Quebec have tried to do business throughout Canada—opening offices, things like that," he says. "But the majority have failed. We thought we'd be better off buying a company rather than opening branches because the latter way it would be ten years before we made a profit. By buying a company we could make a profit in the first year."

Imperial was controlled by Paul Desmarais' Montreal-based Power Corp. But Desmarais also controlled Great-West Life Assurance of Winnipeg, a fact that troubled regulators in Ottawa who were concerned about concentration of ownership. Poitras knew that the federal government had turned down Desmarais' request to merge the two companies and was pressuring him to sell Imperial. Not only that, but Poitras also knew that Imperial wasn't exactly a jewel in Desmarais' crown. "Desmarais was not happy with the relationship with Imperial. He had never made money from the company," explains Poitras. Conversely, he says, "Imperial was not happy with Desmarais."

Poitras approached Castonguay, then fresh out of politics and running an actuarial consulting business in Quebec City, and asked him what he thought of his idea. Castonguay, never

loquacious at the best of times, replied: "It's a big company."
But he agreed to act as a consultant on the prospective purchase of Imperial. Poitras had offered him a carrot that he
couldn't resist. If the purchase was successful, Poitras had promised that Castonguay would take over as Imperial's new chairman. He took the job on that condition. His experience with
the challenges and responsibilities of politics had made Castonguay dissatisfied with the limited horizons of his private
actuarial business. "I was interested in being involved with a
project," he says. "I wanted to manage something fairly big.
Jean-Marie's offer couldn't have come at a better time."

To the surprise of most of the financial industry, Laurentian
and two partners, the National Bank of Canada and Groupe
Victoire, a French insurance concern, bought 99.4 per cent
of Imperial for about $24 million. For its part, Laurentian
Mutual, through a subsidiary, Laurentian Funds Inc., chipped
in $12 million for a 50.1 per cent share of Imperial. "We
bought that company for nothing," says Poitras with a grin. "It
looked like quite a *coup*," agrees Castonguay, although he
thought it was a fair price, considering the unimpressive size of
Imperial's fund for nonparticipating policyholders, from which
the earnings for shareholders (Laurentian and its partners)
are mainly derived. Nor did Castonguay consider Imperial's
financial record impressive. Guy Monfette, superintendent of
insurance for Quebec, agrees with that assessment: "They
[Imperial] had to be bought by somebody; they were just not
able to meet our financial requirements."

Laurentian's business relationship with the National Bank
and Groupe Victoire (formerly La Paix) is a secure one. The
alliance with the two institutions was already well solidified by
the time of the Imperial purchase. Both had teamed up as
partners with Laurentian in the 1975 purchase of the Provident. Presently, they are also major shareholders in The Laurentian Group Corp. The formation of the co-operative triad was
a calculated move on the part of Poitras. From the start, he

says, Laurentian wanted help in its expansion efforts. "Our preference was for two additional partners. Just having one partner would be a bit of a straitjacket; we would be exposed to fighting."

Poitras was one of the first insurance executives in Canada to recognize the growing disintegration of the divisions between the activities of insurance companies and those of their financial cousins, the banks, trusts and investment companies. Durand credits Poitras with positioning the company to take advantage of the changing marketplace. "We're trying to be prepared for the falling of the Four Pillars," he says, "and Jean-Marie Poitras started that." Says Poitras: "I like to think five to ten years ahead."

The president's appetite for expansion was not satisfied with the Imperial purchase, although with operations throughout Canada, the United States, the Bahamas and Great Britain, Imperial added an international dimension to Laurentian's holdings. Over the next five years, The Laurentian Group's major purchases included: F-I-C Fund Inc., a Montreal-based management company, for $20 million; the Loyal American Life Insurance Co., an Alabama-based life company with operations in 48 states, for $29 million; and The Canadian Provident-General Insurance Co. and its two subsidiaries, The Personal Insurance Co. of Canada and Paragon Insurance Co. of Canada, for a combined price tag of about $24 million. Poitras looks back on the growth spurt with pride. "Everything we bought, we bought for next to nothing. Basically that's the story of our acquisitions."

### Castonguay Takes Command

There have always been strong leaders in charge of Laurentian; it is a matter of tradition at the company. Claude Castonguay, who succeeded Poitras as chief executive officer of the company in November 1981, was no exception to the rule. As

CEO of The Laurentian Group Corp. and chief executive and president of its parent, The Laurentian Mutual Insurance Company, Castonguay has brought a new clarity to the group's purpose. Castonguay says that he and Poitras were the driving forces in the group from 1977 to 1981. "We felt there was a need for a group of companies offering a diversity of financial services—that it would make sense from a consumer point of view." But, adds Castonguay, "I had done my reading. I saw the need a little more clearly. Jean-Marie had spent his time just building Laurentian Mutual, trying to make it into a stronger company. His objectives were not as clear. For example, before I entered the picture the company had invested in cable TV—we got out of that." Castonguay also sold off a clutch of other holdings, including a shoe manufacturer, which didn't fit in with the Group's strategy.

Educated at Laval University in Quebec City and the University of Winnipeg, Castonguay's personality differs sharply from that of Poitras. In contrast to Poitras' ebullience, Castonguay's serious bearing strikes fear in the hearts of subordinates. "A lot of people are scared of Claude Castonguay in this building," says The Laurentian Group Corp.'s chief financial officer Durand. "I think the reason is that Claude is so well organized—he doesn't smile. You have to go fishing with him to see him smile." To get along with Castonguay, Durand had to adapt to his boss's business style. That meant foregoing small talk at the start of meetings to break the ice. Says Durand: "I won't try in the first moments of a meeting to talk about the weekend, or the last game of the Expos. He has got some business to do—we'll go through the business and then after that, he could spend five or ten minutes on topics like that."

Castonguay's impregnable aura is due, in part, to his stern visage. His craggy face appears to be chiselled out of granite to withstand the *Nordest*, the salt-laden wind that blows down the St Lawrence from the Atlantic Ocean, eroding the masonry on Quebec City's historic buildings. At the office, he has little time for procrastination. Says Durand: "In some situations where it is an important matter and people are trying to delay a decision, Claude says, 'O.K. this is what we are going to do.' "[7] Castonguay prepares well for major decisions, however. "He's a methodic guy in every aspect of this business," says Durand. "Every time he has to meet people, he prepares himself very thoroughly. With him you always have the agenda before a meeting—sometimes two or three weeks before. And before the meeting he will always phone everybody that will help him on a matter to be discussed."

The same thoroughness extends to business deals—and the results are successful. In 1984, when Castonguay was preparing to make a bid to purchase Canagex Investments Ltd., a Montreal-based funds management company, he practised his bargaining techniques with Durand—Castonguay played the suitor and Durand the reluctant seller. The session provided good practice. In the first meeting with Claude Lemire, president of Canagex, the unstoppable force met the immovable object. Laden with files bulging with information on why Canagex should sell out to Laurentian, Castonguay made his well-organized, lengthy case—from start to finish. Any interruptions were cut off with a "Please let me finish." The purchase was a good deal for Canagex, pointed out Castonguay, because with added business from Laurentian, Canagex would double its $1.4 billion in assets under management and expand into markets beyond Quebec and Ontario. Lemire seemed unimpressed by Castonguay's pitch. Like Castonguay, says Durand, "Lemire never smiles. During the negotiations it was impossible to tell what he was thinking." During the first meeting nothing was resolved. Lemire said he wouldn't sell for under $13 or $14 million; Castonguay was hoping to pay only $7 or

---

[7]There is no place for idlers in Castonguay's organization either. Castonguay calls on the services of his personal chauffeur only occasionally, and when the man isn't driving, Castonguay dispatches him to Laurentian's basement to lick envelopes and perform other clerical duties for the company.

$8 million. Eventually, in the course of future negotiations, Castonguay's determination paid off. In June, Laurentian bought Canagex for $9 million. Lemire stayed on as president.

The Laurentian chief's no-nonsense style is legendary. After the successful completion of the largest acquisition in the group's history, the $47-million purchase in 1985 of Trident Life Assurance Co. Ltd. of Great Britain and two subsidiary companies, Castonguay was ready to sleep, not celebrate. To be sure, the negotiations had been arduous. The actual deal making had been carried out in London by Roger Wain, general manager of British operations for the Group's main subsidiary, Imperial Life. Wain kept in constant touch by phone with Castonguay and Bruneau, chairman of Imperial, who were in Luxembourg for an unrelated meeting. By mid-afternoon, after numerous hectic phone calls, they had completed the deal to buy Trident from General Reinsurance Corp. of Stamford, Connecticut. Celebrations, they agreed, were called for. Castonguay and Bruneau arranged to meet Wain and an assistant in Paris for a victory dinner at an elegant restaurant just off the Champs Élysées.

Sitting at a small table in the dimly lit dining room, Castonguay and his companions were a bedraggled, subdued group. The maitre d' came to the table with a flourish, ready to suggest special dishes from the elaborate menu, recalls Castonguay. "But I asked for a plain grilled steak, with nothing else, only a glass of Perrier. I think Claude Bruneau was the brave one. He ordered a glass of wine. We looked a little silly." Castonguay says the episode illustrates his straightforward style. "I usually don't go in all sorts of directions," he says.

Castonguay is a man who combines doggedness with decisiveness, a mix that has served him well at the head of an increasingly polymorphic empire. His style was less suited to politics, where men's principles are compromised in the pursuit of the possible, to paraphrase Sir Edmund Burke, the father of Conservatism. Shortly after the election in 1970 that

swept the Union Nationale party out of power in Quebec and
elected the Liberal government of Robert Bourassa, Castonguay, as the new health minister, became embroiled in a major
controversy. In its final months in power, the Union Nationale
had unveiled a major capital works program for hospitals and
nursing homes. Even before Castonguay's arrival on the scene,
large and small communities across the province were reaping
the fruits of Quebec City's largess. With much fanfare, some
had even started the excavation for new facilities. Castonguay
put a dramatic halt to the flurry of activity. He was convinced
that "that was not the way to go." Instead, he favoured placing
more equipment in existing hospitals and establishing more
at-home services, such as meals-on-wheels, for outpatients and
the elderly. In small towns, epithets were hurled at the new
health minister.

The province's doctors were soon added to the list of the
disenchanted. Paranoia gripped the province when Quebec
doctors threatened to go on strike over the province's refusal
to permit extra-billing in its medicare plan. "Canadians had
not experienced many doctors' strikes," says Castonguay. "There
had been one in Saskatchewan in 1962 and it had been a very
traumatizing experience. So when there was the threat of a
strike people were scared." Faced by a recalcitrant government, Quebec's doctors walked off the job for a three-week
period in 1970. They were finally subdued by back-to-work
legislation. "The experience was nerve racking," says Castonguay.

By that time, Castonguay's standoffs with the electorate, which
had cost the party dearly in the opinion polls, were causing
consternation in senior party circles. There was also growing friction between Bourassa's staff and Castonguay's camp.
Bourassa lacked the experience and leadership abilities to
perform well in his first stint as premier. It was largely as a
result of this that his staff regarded the forceful Castonguay
with distrust. They thought that he was angling to take over
the premier's job—an entirely unjustified worry, according to

Castonguay. When Castonguay left politics in 1973, many provincial Liberals were not sad to see him go. "I think I had more support in the membership of the party at large than in the establishment," he says.[8]

Castonguay's experience in the political process in Quebec City, and later in Ottawa, gave him a high public profile and familiarity with important powerbrokers that were to serve him well after he joined Laurentian. In the Quebec business community, there is no lobbyist who is better connected or more influential than Castonguay. No one in the provincial or federal seats of power puts him on hold when he calls.

Although he refuses to take much credit for it, Castonguay played a key role in the formulation of Quebec's Bill 75. He did so more out of frustration than opportunism. For years, Laurentian had been frustrated by regulatory restrictions that hampered its diversification efforts. When it bought Imperial Life, for instance, Laurentian had to get around regulations that prevented it from owning a life insurance subsidiary in Canada. So it set up a subsidiary, Laurentian Funds, to make the Imperial purchase. Laurentian Funds was created in such a way that Laurentian Mutual owned only 30 per cent of its common shares, the limit permitted by provincial law. Then because the antiquated Quebec Insurance Act had no provisions regarding preferred shares, Laurentian Mutual took control of Laurentian Funds by buying its preferred shares.

There had been strong indications that the provincial finance minister, Jacques Parizeau, was aware of the need for a regulatory overhaul. In the 1960s, Parizeau had been the chairman of a task force on financial institutions that recognized the

---

[8]From the start, Castonguay had resolved to spend only one term in politics. When Bourassa first asked him to run in the 1970 election, Castonguay had only five days to make a decision. He and his wife, Mimi, repaired to a little house they owned in Mont St Anne. There, they concluded that Castonguay would try out political life, but he was not ready to make a long-term commitment to it on the basis of a few days of thinking.

trends of the future. "They saw that companies or groups of companies would diversify, that there would be a need for a broader range of financial services either through the demand of consumers or forced by competition. They saw the whole thing coming," says Castonguay.

Hopeful that he would get a sympathetic hearing, Castonguay took his concerns to the provincial inspector general of insurance, Jean-Marie Bouchard, in 1979. "I got very frustrated and fed up," says Castonguay, "so I went to see the inspector general. I told him it was so difficult to move it was becoming hopeless. He went to Parizeau and arranged a meeting." After the meeting in Parizeau's office, says Castonguay, "we had the feeling that he understood very well the kind of problems we were facing. Then we heard that some legislation was being drafted." Concludes Castonguay: "We may have been the trigger, but Parizeau had the whole thing in mind."

Castonguay's lobbying efforts with federal regulators have been more frustrating, but not unsuccessful. Since 1980, Castonguay has been squabbling with federal finance officials over The Laurentian Group's 31.5 per cent stake in the Montreal City and District Savings Bank because federal laws prohibit any one shareholder from owning more than 10 per cent of a bank. Castonguay was alarmed in 1980 when he received a letter from William Kennett, the federal inspector general of banks, directing Laurentian to reduce its holdings in the bank to the 10 per cent limit. "There was no phone call, nothing, we just received a letter," fumes Castonguay. "I felt we were treated in a cavalier way." Castonguay believed that his company's holding was entirely legal; after all, Montreal City and District was more like a trust company than a bank. Operating as a savings bank, rather than a full chartered bank, it did no commercial lending at the time and specialized in home mortgages and consumer loans.

Castonguay was not about to capitulate without a fight. In a hectic lobbying effort, he visited all the members of a

Committee of the House which was in the final stages of draft-
ing a new Bank Act. He managed to get them all to agree to
make an amendment to the Act that would give Laurentian a
five-year grace period before it had to divest its shares in the
bank. In 1986, after another round of lobbying in Ottawa,
Castonguay managed to get another two-year extension of the
grace period. His trump card, of course, was the expectation
that future regulatory changes would permit his company to
control the bank outright.

Away from the working world, Castonguay reveals a mellow,
engaging side that his colleagues at work rarely see. When he
is not travelling on the corporate Lear jet to inspect the group's
far-flung operations, Castonguay likes to go to baseball and
hockey games. But most of all, he likes to get away to his
cottage at Les Éboulements, a town 110 kilometres from Quebec
City on the north shore of the St Lawrence. The cabin is a
consoling place, with a view of the river and the Laurentian
Mountains. Its quietude gives Castonguay a chance to engage
in his favourite pastime—painting the oil and watercolour scenes
that line a room in his Quebec City condominium. There is
also another diversion at Les Éboulements. "I have a little
trout pond hidden on the property," he chuckles. Castonguay's
wife of 29 years, Mimi, also helps restore his equanimity. A
charming, unpretentious woman, Mimi is the daughter of Gas-
pard Fauteux, a former Speaker of the House of Commons
and a lieutenant-governor of Quebec.

Relaxing over a sumptuous dinner in his luxury condominium
with Mimi, Castonguay reflects on his achievements at Laurentian. He takes pride in the fact that the company has come so
far so fast. But more important, he sees The Laurentian Group's
success as an important antidote to the forces of separatism.
He points out that he joined the company just after the election of the Parti Québécois government in 1976. Says Castonguay: "It was obvious that if we could strengthen the economy—

give more confidence to the people of Quebec about going into business and creating their own companies—it would go a long way to resolving the social tensions and improving the situation." Adds Castonguay: "I saw what I was doing as a kind of counter-option to what was being proposed by the Quebec government and when I look back now, eight years later, I get a great deal of satisfaction." Still, Castonguay's horizons extend far beyond Quebec. "Inasmuch as I want to relate to Quebec," he says, "we do not want to be seen as a Quebec company."

In that regard, Castonguay has little to fear. In May 1986, The Laurentian Group further consolidated its national presence by acquiring Eaton Financial Services Ltd. from Eaton's of Canada for $85 million worth of Laurentian Group's common shares and $16 million in cash. A profitable company with $1.1 billion in assets, Eaton Financial markets mutual funds, life and general insurance and trust company products in 35 outlets across Canada. The Laurentian Group's plans for the future promise to solidify its reputation as an international player, and the United States is a favoured hunting territory. Laurentian Capital Corp., a Florida-based holding company owned entirely by Laurentian-held Imperial Life, is leading the search for U.S. acquisitions. Competition in the market has narrowed profit margins, making many regional companies easy prey. In Europe, the group is expanding steadily through Imperial Life, whose U.K. subsidiary added Trident Life's $360 million in assets to its holdings last year. According to Castonguay, the new Imperial–Trident subsidiary will serve as a stepping-stone for expansion into other European Community countries.

Castonguay has some distance to go before he rests. The Laurentian Group's assets are only about a third of those of Manufacturers Life or Sun Life. But his company, thanks in large part to Jacques Parizeau, has got a head start on its competitors—and Castonguay is not about to squander it.

# PART III

*The Corporate Sharks:*
*Stock Companies and the Search for Synergy*

IF THE GENEALOGY of insurance companies were drawn in a chart, there would be two main branches in the family tree. One would represent the mutual companies, which sprang up in the 1950s and '60s and are owned by their policyholders. The other would represent the stock companies, which didn't join in the rush to mutualization and remained owned by shaerholders. Until recent years, there was little to distinguish between the two species of insurers, apart from their owner-ship make-up. Academic studies of insurance company prac-tices into the 1970s found no discernible difference between the way the stock and mutual insurers were managed or mar-keted and priced their products. After all, when business was good there was little incentive for the owners of stock com-panies to crack down on docile management. That has changed.

The same forces that snapped some mutual insurers out of suspended animation had an impact on stock insurance com-panies first. Concerned about keeping their shareholders happy—and, for that matter, holding on to their jobs—the man-agers at stock companies generally reacted earlier than their

mutual company counterparts to the need for policy over-
hauls and better management techniques. First off the mark
among the major stock companies was Great-West Life of Winnipeg. Always a more innovative company than its eastern
rivals, Great-West's management completed the modernization process with a minimum of trauma. But the managers of
London Life and Crown Life faced the difficult task of wrench-
ing their companies from the 1930s into the 1980s in the space
of two or three years. In both cases, the feat was performed by
chief executives brought in from outside the industry. The
similarity stops there. At London Life, chief executive Earl
Orser overhauled the company without a bloodbath. The staff
of Crown Life were not so lucky.

But Great-West, London Life and Crown Life are notable
for more than the fact that their reflexes are still in working
order. All three companies are also part of larger financial
conglomerates that, for better or for worse, are shaping the
future of the financial services marketplace in Canada. Using
slightly differing approaches, Power Financial, the owner of
Great-West; Trilon Financial, the owner of London Life; and
Crown Financial, the owner of Crown Life, are trying to develop
co-operation between the different financial companies in their
corporate folds. The co-operation ranges from the sharing of
expertise and data processing facilities between subsidiary companies, to projects in which the agents of one subsidiary, say a
trust firm, are being asked to sell the products of a sister
investment or insurance company. This is called cross-selling.
Trilon has launched by far the most ambitious efforts to pro-
mote intercompany co-operation; Power Financial is a close
second in terms of enthusiasm; Crown Financial's plans are
still in their infancy by comparison. Executives from all three
conglomerates say they have studied the reasons why financial
supermarkets, where consumers can shop for a variety of financial services in one location, have been relatively unsuccessful

in the United States. The Canadian financial soothsayers say they do not intend to make the same mistakes.

The aim of increased co-operation—or "synergy"—between the member companies of conglomerates is to reduce operating costs and boost sales. But no one is sure whether consumers really want to buy several types of financial service from one company or in one location. Some players in financial services dismiss the idea, arguing that ideas about synergy and one-stop shopping are the creations of over-active executive imaginations, not a response to consumer demand. One cynic is Henry Jackman, chairman of E-L Financial, a conglomerate which controls two general insurers (Dominion of Canada and Canadian Indemnity), two trust companies (The National Victoria and Grey Trustco Ltd. and Premier Trust Co.), as well as two life insurers, Empire Life and Montreal Life. Jackman says he runs his domain without a bevy of synergistic-minded executives: his head office staff consists of himself and his secretary. He thinks synergy and one-stop shopping are nonsense. "Personally I think this talk about one-stop shopping centres is more talk than substance," he says. The folks at Trilon, Power Financial and Crown Financial are out to prove that such negative sentiments are wrong.

# CHAPTER 7

## *Manifest Destiny:*
## *London Life Insurance and*
## *Trilon Financial*

THERE WERE ENOUGH financial blue-bloods gathered in the cozy little meeting room at Toronto's Four Seasons Hotel to fill Zena Cherry's column for two months. And the wealth—hundreds of billions of dollars—represented by these denizens of the corporate stratosphere was about as difficult to comprehend in real terms as the U.S. defence budget. The 100 or so luminaries, linked by an almost overweening sense of hubris shared through knowing smiles and idle chatter, came from different ranks in the financial aristocracy of Edward and Peter Bronfman's domain. There were the dukes: Michael Cornelissen, the urbane chief executive of Royal Trust, brushed shoulders with the likes of Hartland MacDougall, a former Bank of Montrealer who became the trust company's chairman in 1984, and William Dimma, deputy-chairman of Royal LePage, the country's largest real estate company. Then, too, there was an emissary from a friendly foreign empire: Marshall "Mickey" Cohen, late of the federal Department of Finance and looking well-fed and happy in his new role as president of Olympia & York Enterprises Ltd., was there to represent the interests of real estate development billionaires Paul and Albert Reichmann. Moving up the hierarchy, there were the powers behind the throne and their senior lieutenants: Trevor Eyton, the tall, balding president and chief overseer of Bronfman-controlled Brascan Ltd., chatted a little and smiled a lot but generally kept a low profile; as did his right-hand man, Jack Cockwell, Brascan's chief operating officer, a South-African-born accountant with nimble body movements and piercing eyes. Finally, Edward Bronfman, the diminutive sovereign of all he surveyed, mingled among the throng of well-wishers; most of the time he smiled puckishly, crossed his arms, and seemed rather embarrassed by all the attention.

But this was no gathering of a feudal court. It was the April 1986 annual meeting of Trilon Financial Corporation, the financial services arm of the Bronfman holdings. Through their personal holding company, Edper Investments Ltd., the Bronfmans control Brascan Ltd., which, in turn, is Trilon's largest shareholder. Always alert for good investments, O & Y Enterprises, a subsidiary of Olympia & York Developments, became Trilon's next-largest shareholder, with 12.7 per cent of its voting shares, in 1984. The *esprit de corps* of the executives at the gathering was almost palpable. As a team, they are probably unsurpassed in business smarts anywhere in the world—and underneath their false modesty, they know it.

The news from the podium that spring day was good. Trilon president and chief executive officer Melvin Hawkrigg gave the best pep talk. Still looking ruggedly fit at 56, decades after his stint as quarterback for the Hamilton Tiger Cats football team, Hawkrigg reported that Trilon's net income (profits) had surged to $97 million from $75 million in 1984. "It was another milestone year for Trilon and its group of companies," enthused the chunky executive. The company, he declared, was "moving towards its goal of becoming Canada's leading diversified financial services corporation."

Trilon is well on its way to achieving that goal. With 1985 assets of more than $15 billion and controlling interests in five major companies with a total of $65 billion in assets under administration (client funds such as trust and estates), Trilon is the country's largest financial services holding company. Among financial companies, it is surpassed in size only by the two largest banks, the Royal, with $96.6 billion in assets at the end of 1985, and the Bank of Montreal, with $84.6 billion in assets.

Canadians can bump into some part of the Trilon group of companies on almost every streetcorner. Royal Trust, an 86-year-old company with corporate assets of $13.5 billion and another $57.3 billion under administration, remains Canada's leading trust company. (Second place goes to Canada Trust, which merged with Canada Permanent in 1985 to form an entity with balance sheet assets of $21 billion and another $25 billion under administration.) Royal Trust has 12,447 employees and 392 offices across the country. Six days a week, consumers can walk into a Royal Trust office to do their banking in savings and chequing accounts, get a mortgage, arrange to have an estate or trust fund administered, or buy anything from a registered retirement savings plan to an annuity. Royal Trust's services for corporate customers, such as pension and investment management, as well as commercial loans and mortgages, are available in North America, the United Kingdom, Europe and the Pacific Rim countries. In Canada alone, Royal Trust is the largest pension fund manager.

In fact, *largest* and *leading* are always popping up in descriptions of the Trilon group of companies. Royal LePage Limited, a Royal Trust subsidiary formed in December 1984, when the trust company's real estate operation was merged with A. E. LePage, is Canada's largest real estate company. In 1985, the company's agents participated in one of every four residential resales in Canada; that's about one sale every nine minutes throughout the year. Royal LePage's operations also extend into the United States, the United Kingdom and Europe.

The Trilon cupboard also includes CVL Inc., Canada's largest vehicle leasing and fleet management company, with more than 36,000 vehicles leased. Then there are Trilon's insurance interests. Trilon owns 100 per cent of The Wellington Insurance Company, the largest Canadian shareholder-owned general insurance company, which provides automobile and homeowner insurance to 300,000 individuals and a broad range of commercial insurance to 40,000 small and medium-sized businesses. Trilon also has a major stake in the life insurance business. Through Lonvest Corporation, a holding company which is Trilon's vehicle for insurance investments, Trilon owns 98 per cent of London Life Insurance Company. London Life's 1985 assets of $6.4 billion rank it seventh in size among Canadian insurance companies. But by two other measures, it ranks first. Its sales force of 2,664 is the largest in the country and the company has the biggest chunk of the market for individual insurance in Canada. Without foreign operations to look after, London Life has managed to sign up more than 1.3 million Canadians as policyholders and has a total $366.3 billion in individual life insurance on its books. The company has a 14 per cent share of the individual market, and has 60 per cent more of this line of business than its nearest competitor.

Considered separately, each of Trilon's five major companies is impressive in its own right. But Trilon, and ultimately Brascan and the Bronfmans, like to think that the stable of financial service companies can be forged into a cohesive unit. In the inner sanctums of Trilon and its subsidiaries, the buzzwords "networking," "cross-selling," "cross-referrals" and "co-operation" are very much in fashion. More than that, they are an integral part of the corporate mission, enunciated in almost every speech and annual report. Trilon's unique ingredient, says company chairman Allen Lambert, "is the commitment of its group of companies to co-operate with each other. By working together, group companies have pooled their capabilities to offer a wider range of high-quality products and services and are better able to meet specific and changing client requirements."

Trilon is certainly not the first company in Canada to try to develop synergy among its corporate offspring. Power Corporation of Montreal, for instance, has been trying to get its subsidiaries Great-West Life Assurance, Montreal Trust and Investors Group to sell each other's products for years, with minimal success (Chapter 8). But in terms of commitment, Trilon's efforts far surpass those of Power Corp. or The Laurentian Group (Chapter 6) or Crownx, which is also trying to develop co-operative sales efforts between its life insurance and trust companies (Chapter 9). After closely studying the generally lacklustre performance in the area by such U.S. conglomerates as American Express and Sears, Roebuck, Trilon has hammered out a strategy which it believes avoids the pitfalls encountered by the U.S. giants.

Trilon is staking a good part of its corporate reputation on its belief in the merits of co-operation in everything from cross-referrals (in which, say, a Royal Trust employee refers a client to a London Life agent), to shared expertise (a London Life executive, for example, can call on a Trilon colleague for investment advice) and, to a certain extent, cross-selling, where one company's staff sells the product of another company in the Trilon group. Trilon's efforts at intercompany co-operation are as yet in their infancy but they promise to be the litmus test for such efforts in Canada.

At 112-year-old London Life, Trilon's desire to weave the insurance company more tightly into a larger corporate tapestry is greeted with enthusiasm or at least equanimity by most employees. Considering that only a decade ago, London Life was just another stodgy, hidebound insurance company, that is a remarkable fact. But then, since Earl Orser's coming in 1978, its employees have been wrenched out of somnambulence into an environment where change is the rule, not the exception. In many areas, Orser has brought London Life's operations up to the standards of the rest of the North American financial industry. In some areas, however, London Life's methods are well ahead of any of its financial cousins, from trust companies to banks. Orser's company is probably the only Canadian life insurer that can make that claim. The methods Orser used to revive the lethargic company are generally applauded within the industry. London Life underwent a revolution without a bloodbath—unlike Crown Life, which set up a guillotine at head office and spilled buckets of employee blood to achieve the same ends. Already, Orser has fashioned London Life in his own image. His next mission, willingly undertaken, is to adapt the insurer to Trilon's grand design, to help the financial conglomerate achieve its self-proclaimed manifest destiny.

London Life is situated in downtown London, a pretty, southwestern Ontario city embraced by two arms of the Thames River. The city's streets are tree-lined, quiet and clean, lacking the polyglot pandemonium of a major metropolis like Toronto or the grime of an industrial centre like Hamilton. But London does boast a major educational institution, the University of Western Ontario and, of course, an insurance company of national stature. London Life's offices blend in well with the character of the city. They are a sort of schizophrenic mix of the old and the new. The older part of the complex, built in 1927, is a hulking grey-stone edifice overlooking Victoria Park. Behind it sits a modernistic glass-and-concrete building erected in 1965 to handle the company's expanding business. The executive offices of the company are located in the historic building, just off an octagonal rotunda with cool, green Italian marble walls. Tight security is in force. The doors to the executive office area are opened by a device which reads the palm print of the would-be entrant to see if it belongs to an approved person—something like the one the aliens use on their spaceships in the science fiction TV series *Dr Who*.

The company was founded in 1874, a time when London was little more than a military barracks town. The city had been incorporated only 19 years before; but it had been a population centre ever since 1826 when a district court was established on the site. London's first citizen, reputedly, was a man named MacGregor, who built a tavern and began selling booze off a stump in the general area of the present downtown. By the 1870s London had evolved into a respectable enough place with its own social strata. The five men who gathered in the spring of 1874 to discuss the creation of a life insurance company were merchants and lawyers from the upper echelons of those strata. They included a Doctor Woodruff, who was known for his penchant for horse racing and hunting; Edward Harris and James Magee, two law partners; a Colonel Walker, commander of the 7th regiment during the border raids by the Fenians; and Joseph Jeffery, who was manager of the London branch of the Molson's bank. Three weeks later, 105 shareholders elected London Life's first board of directors, and chose Joseph Jeffery as the first president.

Jeffery presided over the fortunes of the company for the next 20 years, thus beginning a family dynasty that lasted into the 1970s.[1] The other family name associated for decades with the company's management is Reid. Edward Reid married the daughter of the original Joseph Jeffery and served as managing director, the number two position, from 1932 to 1941. His son, Robert Reid, was a long-surviving president who served from 1958 to 1971.

[1]Joseph's son, Albert, served as president between 1920 and 1928. Albert is remembered as a remote man. He was referred to as Doctor Jeffery by his colleagues, since he held a Doctor of Civil Law degree from Trinity University in Toronto. Edgar Jeffery, another lawyer, held the top post from 1932 to 1948. He was an ultraconservative man who hated tobacco smoke and expected absolute honesty from his employees. Later, two more Jefferys took over the helm; Joseph was president in the 1950s and Alexander in the 1970s. Today, Alexander and another grandson of the original president sit on London Life's board of directors.

As a group, the Jefferys and the Reids were strait-laced individuals, in many ways reflective of the Victorian times during
which the company was founded. But London Life did have
its share of flamboyant characters. One was John Richter, who
succeeded Albert Jeffery as president in 1928. An audacious
man, Richter had originally been hired as company manager
by Joseph Jeffery in about 1880. He was a natural mathematician, who prided himself on his self-taught knowledge of actuarial science. For years, Richter would badger London Life
salesmen who came to his door, telling them he would never
buy insurance from a company run like theirs. Finally, Jeffery
invited Richter to head office for a chat and was so impressed
he offered Richter the job of manager. Thereafter, Richter
scrupulously watched over every dollar and cent that London
Life made. When the company got into farm mortgages, Richter
would travel about with a post-hole digger taking soil samples.
The man's exacting standards served the company well. As
president in the 1920s, he didn't join in the general rush by
insurance companies to buy stocks, and instead stuck to high-
quality mortgages. That helped buffer the company from the
worst effects of the Great Depression in the 1930s.

## A Corporate Lobotomy

By the 1970s, London Life, like most insurance companies,
hadn't changed much from the 1930s. It was a financially healthy company—its solid business base provided a healthy flow
of premium income—and it had a large sales force. In 1977,
several years before the Bronfmans and Trilon appeared on
the scene, London Life's major shareholders were the Toronto-
Dominion Bank, Brascan and the Jefferys, who controlled the
insurance company through Lonvest. They became concerned
about the future of the company after the president, Alexander Jeffery, suffered a heart attack. Late in the year, Jake Moore,
then chairman and CEO of Brascan, and also chairman of the

executive committee of London Life, approached Earl Orser, who had just quit his job as president of The T. Eaton Company Ltd., to evaluate the old insurer. Orser accepted the job as consultant and promised to deliver a report within six months.

The former Eaton's executive didn't have any experience in the insurance business. But his credentials for the task ahead of him were of high calibre. After graduating with a commerce degree from the University of Toronto in 1950, he had spent some time with Clarkson Gordon, earning a C.A. in 1953 and becoming a partner in 1958. After leaving Clarkson Gordon in 1961, he held increasingly senior management positions with a slew of major corporations. They included a stint as senior vice-president for Molson Industries Limited and a term as vice-president for finance of Air Canada. Then, from 1973 to 1977, Orser worked with Eaton's, becoming president and chief executive officer in 1975. A privately held company, Eaton's has always shied away from publicly divulging its finances. But observers say that it was Orser's commitment to close down the company's catalogue business that saved it from sliding down a financial precipice. Still, Orser, a strong-willed, action-oriented man, apparently stepped on too many toes at Eaton's. By 1977, acrimony between him and the Eaton family resulted in his sudden departure. Orser finds some similarity between his exit from Eaton's and the 1985 departure of Robert Bandeen from Crown Life, a company ultimately controlled by the Burns and Hennigar families. Says Orser: "The story on Bandeen is that the family probably decided to step in and manage the place. I can understand why he decided to take a walk. I have some understanding of this problem."

When he took on the job as consultant to London Life, Orser discovered enough shortcomings to fill several reports; but to him they were opportunities for improvement, rather than intractable problems. Recalls Orser: "I thought, here was this big company. The employees were loyal. The management was conservative cum paternalistic and it had this great sales force—and that, it seemed to me, was where the real potential lay. The planning and control methods were quite obsolete. They were out of the 1930s. So there was an opportunity to do something and I thought that if one simply brought good, modern management principles to bear, this company had great potential." After Orser outlined these views to London Life's board they were so impressed that they asked him to take over the job of putting the company into shape himself. Orser was hired as executive vice-president and chief operating officer in the fall of 1978. He was named president in 1980 and succeeded Alexander Jeffery as CEO in 1981.

By 1979, London Life's lines of ownership had begun to change. In that year the Bronfmans scooped up control of Brascan for $340 million; with it, they acquired a major holding in London Life. By 1985, after a major public share offering and various shuffles of London Life shares between Bronfman-controlled companies, that holding had risen to 98 per cent. But the insurance company's latest owners have no reasons to quibble with Orser's accomplishments.

At first, Orser's grand designs for change met with some resistance within the company. Says Orser: "I was told, as I have been told at other companies, that the things that work elsewhere won't work here because this business is so different; that modern management principles just won't apply. That's baloney. They have worked." One of the most important things Orser did was to bring new talent into the company's management. "I felt there was so much sameness, so much avoidance of risk taking and so much ambiguity of objectives that we'd have to inject a dollop of management who had proven records of achievement outside London Life," he says. Orser's new talent included Norm Epp, formerly with Black and Decker, who came aboard as vice-president of finance, a job that didn't exist at London Life before his arrival. Orser also hired John Andrachuk from Systems Dimensions Inc. as director of corporate planning, another previously nonexistent position, and Robert Lackey from Beneficial Standard Life Insurance Co. in Los Angeles as vice-president for corporate development. Together with several London Life veterans, such as Dale Creighton, senior vice-president for individual marketing, Orser and his team began a revitalization of London Life's operations. In the process, a dowdy old spinster was transformed into a debutante.

Orser fed the company a blend of old and new corporate tonics. For the first time, proper financial planning and control methods were put in place. Notes Orser: "Essentially, there was no financial management in the sense of the planning and control function. There was somebody called a comptroller, but he wasn't really controlling." Now the management holds a meeting every quarter to see exactly where the company stands in terms of its financial objectives and to pinpoint areas that need attention.

Product development, a largely neglected area because no one had specific responsibility for it either, became Creighton's bailiwick. Suddenly, there was a plethora of new products, such as accumulation annuities, which give purchasers the benefit of high interest rates.

New energy surged through the company after the introduction of a system to monitor and improve productivity, in other words the output per person-hour. Getting more work out of fewer workers has long been one of Orser's preoccupations. It had been one of his major concerns at Air Canada and Eaton's, and he was determined that he could achieve similar success at London Life. He called in outside consultants and set up a task force called the Operations Improvement Department. The conclusion of the exercise was that the methods used in industrial management could be adapted and applied to administrative activity. Now, every year, the company reports on its productivity achievements. In 1985 the sales force's productivity increased by 4.2 per cent. The administrative staff achieved a 9.8 per cent increase in productivity. In fact, London Life has the same number of administrative employees—2,500—as it did 10 years ago, even though the business they handle has almost tripled. Orser is particularly proud of his achievement on this front, which he thinks is unmatched in what he calls "the paper-pushing world." Says Orser: "Even in U.S. financial institutions, for example, I haven't read about or seen people who have gone at this quite as aggressively as we have." Financial incentives for employees help. Last year, London Life distributed $1.7 million in bonuses to administrative staff as a reward for productivity improvements.

### Strength in Numbers

The introduction of sales targets and new products helped rejuvenate London Life's large, loyal sales force, which Orser calls the company's "greatest strength." Even before Orser came on the scene, the sales force ranked among the biggest in Canada; but it suffered from a general listlessness, lack of motivation and sense of frustration because of the company's uncompetitive products. Under Orser, one-year, five-year, and ten-year sales targets were introduced. Rates on term insurance were wrenched downward, despite opposition from within London Life's management ranks; new money policies offering current interest rates were introduced. Whole life insurance products were also spruced up and made more price competitive. Since 1981, London Life has introduced ten new individual products and five new group products for businesses; combined, the new product lines now account for 60 per cent of sales each year.

Beneath the cavalcade of changes, however, London Life's decades-old emphasis on whole life insurance products remained the same, despite the general disregard for this relatively high-cost form of insurance by many within and without the industry (see Chapter 1). Bernie Smith, vice-president of the district sales division, notes that Current Life, the company's new money policy in which customer premiums are invested in equities offering current interest rates, hasn't sold well. By comparison, Econlife, a more traditional whole life policy, which allows customers to purchase additional protection with their annual dividends, has sold like hot cakes. Universal life products, which permit policyholders to choose how much of their premiums are going to savings and how much to insurance coverage, do not yet exist in London Life's portfolio, even though they have been a runaway success for other companies, such as Great-West Life. John Carpenter, vice-president of the general sales division, expresses skepticism about the value of universal life: "When interest rates are high, it makes sense to buy term and invest the difference, which is what universal life is; it has a lot of glamour. But we all know that interest rates go up and also go down." (Such misgivings aside, Orser says that London Life will introduce a universal life product by the spring of 1987.)

The company's sales staff is divided into two major divisions, which target specific markets. There is the general sales division, made up of well-educated agents recruited straight from university or from other careers in accounting, law or business. They are the company's elite Panzer division, specializing in sophisticated insurance planning for professionals and various plans for small and medium-sized businesses. The general division divides its market into four parts: the primary market, composed of 25- to 45-year-olds making between $25,000 to $60,000 a year; the so-called "feeder market," made up of upwardly mobile young people; the business market; and the mature market, comprised of over-45-year-olds in the middle and upper income brackets (roughly $25,000 and up). The company's foot soldiers are in the district sales division. Its 1,600 agents operate in sales territories and tailor their spiels to a young, lower-middle-class market—14- to 44-year-old individuals in households with a family income of between $15,000 and $25,000. London Life's agents sell more life insurance to individuals across the country (1.3 million Canadians) than any other company. Total premium income passed $1 billion for the first time in 1985. Individual insurance sales were up 15.8 per cent in 1984 and most of that was made up of whole life sales. Some of the sales, however, were in annuities and other retirement savings products, which are becoming increasingly popular as Baby Boomers move into their 40s. Sales of these plans rose by 35 per cent in 1985 after a 71.5 per cent increase the year before. At 1985 year-end, London Life had $36.3 billion worth of individual business in force. In the group field, the company had about $18 billion.

In several regards, London Life's sales team is among the most successful in Canada. The company's four-year agent-retention rate is high by industry standards. About 33 of every 100 agents are still with the company four years after being hired, which is roughly twice the rather appalling industry average of about 16 out of 100. The agents also keep their clients happier than most field forces do. One way to measure policyholder satisfaction is to calculate the persistency, or lapse rate, of policies—that is, the rate at which clients cancel or suspend payment on policies within 13 months of buying them. The latest survey by the U.S.-based Life Insurance Marketing and Research Association (LIMRA) shows that London Life's lapse rate for 1984 was 8.6 per cent. By contrast, the mean rate of the 13 largest companies operating in Canada was 13.7 per cent. In both agent retention and policy lapse rates, London Life is generally neck and neck with Mutual Life Assurance Company of Canada in Waterloo. There are straightforward reasons for their common success on these fronts. Both companies put their sales recruits through mind-bending training programs designed to produce high-quality, loyal graduates. (Mutual Life even goes one better: in order to avoid job-hoppers, it will not hire an agent who has worked for another company in the previous two years.) But more important, both insurers insist on single-company representation. Unlike many other companies, which permit the agents licensed with them to sell the products of other insurers as well, London Life and Mutual have so-called "captive" sales forces. Under no circumstances are their agents allowed to peddle competitors' policies.

John Carpenter doesn't like the word "captive"; it doesn't sit well with his upper-crust sales people. "That's a misnomer," he says. "They are highly intelligent, highly motivated people. It's a quid pro quo situation. We provide what we think is the finest training and the best management techniques, but it's expensive, so we expect agents to sell for London Life exclusively." The major value of the approach, he adds, is that it gives London Life "a lot of clout in terms of distribution." Bernie Smith believes the company's customers benefit as well. "The fact that our people stay with us longer than most results in better service for the client," he says.

Still, amidst all the modernization that has gone on at London Life, it is surprising that Smith's 1,600-strong district sales division uses a paternalistic approach to selling that has served life insurance companies—but not necessarily consumers—well for more than a century. Smith bridles at the suggestion that consumers need to know a great deal about insurance when they buy it. "Why do you need to know all about life insurance?" he asks rhetorically. "Isn't it enough that I sit down and try to find out what you want a life insurance policy to do and then give you a product at a rate that you can afford that will do that job for you? We could go into all the intricacies of the suicide clause and paid-up values—all of those things. But you would forget that as quickly as you hear it. What you probably won't forget is what will happen to your wife and children if tomorrow you're not here. That seems to be the key to us." Some things never change: fear has always been the best sales tool.

Nevertheless, in most respects, London Life has lapped the majority of insurance companies like a thoroughbred leading a pack of nags. And Earl Orser has been in the saddle with a tight grip on the reins. Says Smith: "What Earl expects to get done will get done. I've never seen the guy wavering in any way, shape or form."

### Forging Family Ties

These days, developing links between London Life and its sister companies is high on Orser's agenda. He is a fervent disciple of the credo of corporate co-operation. "What we really have is an objective to develop a group of financial service companies in which productivity and return will meet a high standard," he says. That includes, he adds, "a determination to exploit opportunities for the co-ordination of activities between the various companies; the so-called synergies…and we're making headway."

The term "headway," suggesting as it does the image of a runner fighting a stiff head wind, is the right word. The toughest resistance to co-operative efforts, so far, has come from the sales staff itself. According to Robert Lackey, London Life's vice-president of corporate development, the key to the whole endeavour is developing trust between the different types of sales people in the group. Traditionally, trust officers, for example, have regarded insurance or real estate salespeople as an entirely different breed, and the services they sell as foreign territory. Even getting an employee of Royal Trust to refer his client to a London Life agent for his life insurance or to a Wellington broker for his home insurance requires a great deal of coaxing. Lackey recalls a meeting Trilon arranged between top producers from Royal Trust, Royal LePage, London Life and Wellington Insurance to talk about cross-referrals. Says Lackey: "One of the women who was a top producer for Royal Trust said to a London Life salesman, 'When I send you one of my clients, I want a better client back.'" The exchange, says Lackey, "strikes right at the heart of referral selling. It shows that trust is required before people will refer their valuable clients to someone else."

Originally, when Trilon was formed by Brascan in 1982, its creators envisioned the coming of one-stop financial centres that would provide for all the financial needs of a customer in one spot. Trevor Eyton, who masterminded the creation of Trilon along with Allen Lambert, spoke in glowing terms of the possibility to author Peter Newman. In a September 1983 *Maclean's* magazine column, Newman quoted Eyton as saying: "I visualize the day when a family's entire financial services will be handled by one company. Theoretically, Canada is small enough that we should be able to have all the family units on our computers so that we know precisely how old everybody is—when each son or daughter gets out of university and is old enough to buy his or her first insurance policy, for example."

Since then, Trilon has scaled down its aspirations considerably. The group of companies is well on its way to building a shared data base containing information on a huge portion of Canada's population, but one-stop shopping, as major U.S. companies have discovered, is a questionable proposition. For instance, Sears, Roebuck's financial supermarkets, located in bright blue-and-white offices at Sears department stores, have hardly been a runaway success. The outlets, where consumers are offered the products of Dean Witter Reynolds, Sears' brokerage firm; Allstate Insurance, its property and casualty insurer, which has also begun selling life insurance; and Coldwell Banker, its real estate company, have so far been unprofitable. Certain aspects of the Sears experiment have worked. Dean Witter stockbrokers are happy about the higher volume of business they do in a store-front setting. But the endeavour has entailed huge advertising and start-up costs. "Sears has made a very heavy investment, spent millions of dollars in advertising; it'll take them a while to get that back," says Lackey. "The jury is still out on store-front cross-sales." Life insurance, in particular, he argues, is difficult to sell in such a setting, as the experience of K-Mart in the United States demonstrates. The huge retailer has given up trying to sell the life insurance products of a subsidiary in K-Mart stores. Orser shares Lackey's skepticism about the financial supermarket concept: "I don't think that one-stop shopping is on."

Even cross-selling, in which a London Life agent, say, sells a Royal Trust product has proven difficult. In a six-week pilot project in 1984, London Life agents managed to sell only four Royal Trust Registered Home Ownership Savings Plans (RHOSPs). At present, Trilon companies are achieving some success at cross-selling in a few areas. In 1985, Royal LePage sold $650 million worth of mortgages financed and administered by Royal Trust. And in the future, says Lackey, the plan is to add the insurance products of London Life and Wellington to the package. "For the homebuyer, it will be a very convenient package," he adds, noting that it is possible for the homebuyer to obtain a pre-approved mortgage under the plan. Also, sales of London Life annuities by Royal Trust have achieved reasonable success since they began in mid-1985. In another team effort, London Life is selling a mutual fund called Market Fund which was designed and is administered by Royal Trust.

At present, however, London Life and its sister companies, under the direction of a Trilon marketing committee, are concentrating most of their efforts on training staff to refer business to other sales people in the Trilon group. That is a difficult task, since offering general or life insurance agents financial incentives in return for referring business to other group companies contravenes provincial laws. Without the possibility of offering rewards to sales staff, Trilon and its member companies must rely instead on employees' loyalty and their commitment to the idea that cross-referrals will increase business for them.[2]

_____

[2] The most ambitious scheme involving intercompany referrals was launched by Royal Trust in March 1986. The project's primary purpose is to market the trust

Encouraging *employees* rather than clients to do their financial shopping with the Trilon family has been easier. In October 1985 Trilon began its "Share with the Leaders" program (every Trilon endeavour seems to have a catchy title), which company chairman Lambert calls "the first step in marketing products amongst group companies...." Under the program, which is offered to Trilon's 20,000-strong workforce, an employee who buys the products or services of another Trilon company receives Trilon shares as a reward. The number of shares is geared to the size of the transaction. If a London Life employee listed his house with Royal LePage, for example, he might receive $700- or $800-worth of Trilon stock, depending on the value of the house. The purpose of the program, says Jim Etherington, London Life's director of corporate affairs, is to "build a base of trust relationships...this all builds into the referral process eventually."

The whole point of the drive to develop synergy, of course, is to generate more business and greater profits for London Life and the other Trilon companies. Simultaneously, say group spokesmen, the client will benefit from a wider selection of products and services, sometimes with added convenience, as in the case of the home mortgage package. But consumer spokesmen are not so certain the consumer will benefit from cross-referrals and cross-selling. Robert Kerton, professor of economics at the University of Waterloo and chairman of the Consumer Association of Canada's (CAC's) Committee on Economic Reform, argues that such efforts are rife with opportunities for conflicts of interest. The quality of advice given by sales staff might be poor, he says. For example, a real estate broker

company's financial planning services. For an hourly fee of $100 or a flat fee of $1,200 financial planners dole out advice to clients on a broad range of investment matters, including income tax, investments, retirement, wills and estates, cash management, budgeting and education funding. But the financial planners do not sell financial products; they steer their customers to the products and services offered by other companies in the Trilon group. The client is under no obligation to buy those products.

might recommend that a client obtain a mortgage from a sister company, even though it doesn't offer the best terms or interest rate. In Trilon's case, the argument is undercut somewhat by the generally good quality and favourable terms of its products. (Royal Trust mortgages have very competitive terms. In March 1986 they offered interest rates lower than nearly all other financial institutions in Canada.) Nevertheless, the CAC has raised troubling issues that apply in general to the proliferation of "financial packages" being offered to consumers in Canada by numerous financial institutions.

More and more, Trilon is forging a spider's web of other, lower-profile links and relationships between its family of companies. Once again, they are designed to develop synergy and at the same time save money through economies of scale. In 1985, Trilon created three so-called synergy committees. One, the marketing committee, is working on developing the networking of product sales such as the Royal LePage/Royal Trust mortgage. Another, dealing with productivity, systems and administration, has made considerable progress in bringing the corporate clan closer together. On its recommendation, the Trilon companies have begun the joint purchasing of office equipment and furniture, an approach that allows them to buy in bulk at lower prices. The same committee is developing a system in which job opportunities within the group are tracked and passed on to prospective applicants anywhere in the group. Then, too, the committee has overseen a new, cost-saving co-ordination of computer services within the group. Wellington Insurance's business is now processed on London Life's IBM mainframe, at a cost saving expected to total $7 million over three years. And London Life is developing a computerized joint-mortgage administration system. Soon, the communications links between all group companies and their branch offices will be on one system.

The investment committee is also off to a propitious start. It co-ordinates joint investments by Trilon companies. Already, enthuses Lackey, "Royal Trust and London Life have done the largest oil and gas leasing arrangement that's ever been done in Canada." When it comes to investments, group companies can call on the expertise of Trilon and Brascan's executives; or, in the case of real estate investments, they can purchase Royal LePage's appraisal and property management services.

Through the pooling of computer systems, buying power and expertise, Trilon is putting building blocks in place that at least form the foundation of the sort of co-operation its planners envision. They are practical, money-saving measures with immediate benefits for the companies involved. Whether the resultant cost-savings can be matched by increased profits from co-ordinated sales efforts is another matter. London Life, for one, has found that training sales staff to carry out cross-sales or pass on business leads is at best a difficult task. Even action-oriented Orser doesn't expect overnight success for co-operative efforts. "I don't think that there is going to be a revolutionary rate of growth because these things don't happen that fast," he says. Indeed, Trilon's chauvinistic lieutenants have yet to prove that synergy is more than a hackneyed corporate buzzword.

### Trilon and the Regulators

Critics of corporate concentration aren't waiting around to see if Trilon's latest efforts to take a larger share of the financial services market are successful before sounding the alarm bells. Representing consumers, the CAC has already voiced its disapproval of such swelling aggregates of economic power. In a 1984 brief to Ontario's Task Force on Financial Institutions, the CAC decried the fact that financial institutions are engaging in the "perfectly legal takeover of other institutions and businesses which can assure them a continued and expanding access to, if not effective control of, a larger and larger share of the overall financial business in Canada." Added the CAC: "Perhaps the most significant recent example of this is the

development and expansion of the Trilon group of companies."
In the CAC's view, the blurring of roles between financial
institutions is not derived from consumer demand but is being
"engineered by the desire of certain corporations to gain larger
shares of the existing market in order to increase profits." The
ultimate losers from the coagulation of corporate units, says
the CAC, will be the consumers. "We, as consumers, fear that
the concentration of financial power in fewer hands is detri-
mental to the consumer interest." The CAC is opposed to the
idea of financial supermarkets and to networking. The major
fear is that the consumer will not be well served in terms of
product or price.

Not surprisingly, bankers don't like what Trilon and other
financial holding companies are up to either—they are a threat
to the banks' longstanding dominance of the financial marketplace. Robert MacIntosh, president of the Canadian Bankers'
Association (CBA) has warned that the conglomerates are growing into "huge aggregations of economic power and nothing is
being done about it." It is difficult to feel much sympathy for
the banks considering their dominance of the marketplace.

But the possible effects on consumers of increasing corporate concentration are less easily dismissed. Many, including
Orser, predict that the life insurance industry itself is in for a
shakeout. Smaller companies will simply not be able to keep
up with the larger companies, which have bigger, more cost-
effective, distribution systems, and computerized administrative networks. Orser predicts that smaller and medium-sized
companies will fall by the wayside (or more likely be taken
over) and more national companies will be formed. Says Orser:
"I don't know how they can survive with the lack of distribution...and more importantly, with administrative and technology costs the way they are, it's going to be really tough. I think
there are going to be fewer guys in the business."

Still, Orser doesn't agree that the consumer will suffer. "We're
never going to run out of competition. There is going to be

price and service competition. The consumer is going to be pretty well served."

Such issues, of course, have been seminal in the nationwide debate leading up to the overhaul of financial services legislation expected late in 1986. Orser played an important role in the consultation process between government and industry. In 1984, he served on the federal committee on financial services chaired by the former Liberal minister of state for finance, Roy Maclaren. (In March 1986 Maclaren was elected to the board of Lonvest.)

The way Orser sees it, insurance companies need to be given more freedom to move by the upcoming legislation; they do not need to be hampered by new restrictions. Says Orser: "What we really want in Canada is the opportunity to be agile and to run between the legs of the great big guys [read "banks"]…to be able to use our distribution systems and our promotion and our product strengths in the most flexible way possible. Level playing field? Sure."

Orser talks as if London Life were an independent player in the game. His imagery doesn't wash very well when Trilon's dimensions are taken into account. A common concern raised in the bevy of federal and provincial studies of financial services undertaken in the past two years has been that of the dangers inherent in so-called self-dealing between members of financial conglomerates. (As mentioned in earlier chapters, self-dealing refers to transactions, such as loans or the sale of assets, between affiliated companies or their principals (major shareholders, directors or senior officers)). The fear is that these non-arm's-length transactions could involve conflicts of interest between the companies and their shareholders, with the companies' interests being paramount (see Chapter 13). Trilon CEO Hawkrigg, for example, argues that not all self-dealing is bad, including day-to-day activities such as networking and business referrals. Hawkrigg agrees that certain dealings, such as loans between a parent company and its subsidiaries, should be closely monitored and require approval by the regulators. Already various Trilon subsidiaries, including Royal Trust and Lonvest, have set up business conduct review committees made up of outside directors who are empowered to review and stop any untoward dealings between Trilon group companies. But the probability of good conduct at Trilon is not sufficient reason to breathe a collective sigh of relief. The federal government's 1985 Green Paper recommended a general ban on self-dealing; subsequently the House of Commons committee chaired by Don Blenkarn recommended only a selected ban on self-dealing with overriding discretion given to federal regulators. Whatever laws are passed by the Commons in the fall of 1986, they should give the regulator strong powers to monitor and roll back self-dealing where conflicts of interest are involved. That would be one way of preventing what the CAC describes as the "might-is-right use of corporate power that results in the dominance of the most powerful corporate conglomerate and...deprives the consumer of market choice."

# CHAPTER 8

## *Fastest Gun in the West: The Great-West Life Assurance Company*

KEVIN KAVANAGH PACES his Winnipeg office tensely, stopping only to draw on his cigarette or to spin around and emphasize a point in his monologue. Eyes lit up, feet constantly shuffling, the president and chief executive officer of Great-West Life Assurance is extolling the virtues of a subject dear to him: the company's universal life insurance policy. "It's so flexible. It's quite a product," he declares with a genuine sense of wonderment. The customer, explains Kavanagh, has a vast array of choices, from the size of premium payments to the amount of coverage. Enthuses Kavanagh: "Universal life is the centre-piece of a wave of new ideas in insurance policies; it has introduced more dialogue between the agent and client, without all the actuarial mystique."

Whatever the merits of Kavanagh's pet policy, which has sold well for the company since it was introduced in 1982, the one-man revival meeting he stages in his executive suite offers

211

a glimpse of what really makes Kevin Kavanagh tick.[1] A tall, youthful-looking 56-year-old, Kavanagh is a senior executive with a salesman's heart. Unlike his more staid counterparts in the upper ranks of other insurance companies, Kavanagh is about as complacent as an agitated jack rabbit. Peering intently from behind clear-rimmed glasses, Kavanagh's eyes are perpetually wrinkled up in either a wry smile or a pensive frown. His mind is as restless as his feet, constantly mulling over new ideas, studying them from every angle before issuing them as marching orders to the 6,435 people in Great-West's employ. President of Great-West since November 1978, Kavanagh carries himself with the easy authority of a man used to giving orders. But as his animated little product spiel makes clear, selling is in his blood.

Although Kavanagh is an anomaly in an industry where the executive ranks are still dominated by actuaries, he is only the latest in a long line of former salesmen who have run Great-West, Canada's third-largest insurer with 1985 assets of more than $10 billion. Situated in the Prairies, far from the eastern headquarters of most of the insurance industry, Great-West sprang up 95 years ago like an aberrant growth in Canada's insurance flora. Traditionally, its managers have likened themselves more to Texans than Torontonians and have taken special pride in beating the eastern dudes at their own game. Great-West made itself so attractive, in fact, that eventually Big Money from Montreal swooped in and plucked the wild prairie flower, adding it to a bouquet that already included several other appealing blooms. In 1970, control of Great-West passed to Power Corp. of Montreal, the corporate fiefdom of Paul Desmarais, who, beginning in 1951, built his business empire

---

[1] For all his enthusiasm, Kavanagh himself does not own a universal life policy. But then he already has six policies, which include four participating whole life policies, one single-premium whole life policy and group term coverage with Great-West.

from the remains of a bankrupt Sudbury bus line into a diversified conglomerate with interests in financial services, communications and forest products. The personal wealth of Desmarais, the 59-year-old chairman of Power Corp, is estimated to be $435 million.

Today, Great-West finds itself in an identity crisis of sorts. It is a company with a maverick soul rooted in the West, but it is held in abeyance by its corporate masters to the East, who take in its profits. Great-West is a potent force in its own right: it has more than $100 billion in life insurance in force in Canada and the United States and serves more than three million people who are covered by its individual or group contracts. The company's biggest success has been in group insurance, sold to government or private-sector employers for their workforces. The Winnipeg-based operation has long ranked as the country's largest provider of group benefits, with more than $60 billion worth of group business on its books in Canada, including life and health insurance and annuities.

The chances are that, if you work for a major corporation, government department or Crown corporation in Canada, your group benefits are provided by Great-West. The company's clients include, for example, the Government of Ontario and Canadian Pacific. In the United States, too, Great-West has become a major player in the group market. Fully $27.8 billion of its $43.7 billion of life insurance in force in 48 U.S. states is in group plans. Great-West has been quick to identify new markets south of the border—it provides group coverage for a host of lottery corporations, for instance—and it has also made inroads into more traditional areas. Great-West insurance covers the teachers working in most major American cities. In 1985, its U.S. operations accounted for $1.7 billion in premium income, compared to the $1.1 billion in premiums generated in Canada.

But the company is no longer master of its own destiny. Power Corp.,[2] which owns Great-West through its holding company Power Financial Corp., sees the life insurer as one element in a broader scheme to expand and integrate the services of the various financial services in its domain. That means more co-operative marketing efforts between Great-West and its cousins in the Power Financial orbit: The Investors Group of Winnipeg, Canada's largest provider of investment funds, and Montreal Trustco, which became the fourth-largest trust company in the country with its May 1986 purchase of Crédit Foncier from the Montreal City and District Savings Bank. Internationally, Power Financial also has a minority holding in Pargesa Holding S.A., a Swiss-based international banking and investment group, which, in turn, has interests in a host of other European financial institutions and the New-York-based investment underwriting powerhouse, Drexel Burnham Lambert Inc.

Power Financial president Paul Desmarais, Jr., one of two Desmarais sons being groomed to eventually take over the reins of the empire (the other is André, who is vice-president of the parent company), sees the vast network of sales outlets maintained by the company's subsidiaries as the key to success. A crucial player in Power Financial's integration strategy, Paul, Jr., boasts that the financial services group under its wing already has one of the largest distribution networks in North America, with a total of 220 regional offices in Canada and the United States. "The key to growth is the distribution network which we now have," says Desmarais.

[2]Power Corp., a $1.6 billion (assets) conglomerate 60 per cent owned by Paul Desmarais controls:
• Just more than 70 per cent of Power Financial, which in turn holds 96.2 per cent of the Investors Group, 55.4 per cent of Montreal Trustco Inc., and just less than 10 per cent of Pargesa Holding S.A.
• Gesca Ltd., a communications holding company, which publishes *La Presse*, Quebec's second-largest daily newspaper.
• Approximately 40 per cent of the pulp, paper and packaging giant, Consolidated-Bathurst Inc.

To exploit that network, Power Financial is constantly devising ways in which its operating companies can co-operate by selling each other's products—so far, with limited success. For its part, Great-West, if left to its own devices, would probably be happier sticking to its time-tested, simpler ways. Mutters Kavanagh: "I tend to think that the gluing together of different financial services is not what most consumers are looking for."

### Family Feuds

At Power's urging, Great-West, Investors Group and Montreal Trustco have been experimenting with cross-selling, and so far, it has proven to be a difficult undertaking. Grand designs for product networking and customer referrals have fallen victim to intercompany competition and mutual suspicion. The only notable success has been in term insurance. "Investors' Personal Financial Planners," enthuses Kavanagh, "are writing about 50 per cent of Great-West's term business." In 1985, Investors Group sold nearly 6,000 Great-West term insurance policies with total annual premiums worth more than $2 million, up from about 4,000 policies with $1.6 million in total premiums in 1984. Investors also sold 852 Great-West individual disability income insurance policies with premiums worth $416,000 in 1985[3] and 946 single premium, immediate annuities[4] for its insurance cousin. But the traffic has been mainly one way. John Butcher, a Toronto-based division manager for Investors, points out that all but a handful of his company's 1,300 sales force are dual-licensed to sell both mutual funds for Investors

---

[3]Great-West has also had an agreement with Toronto-based Manufacturers Life since December 1983, under which Manulife sells Great-West disability income policies. During 1985, ManuLife sold 1,277 Great-West disability income policies, with total premium income of $865,985. Few companies in Canada offer this type of policy, the only significant competitors in the Canadian market being Great-West and The Paul Revere Life Insurance Company of Worcester, Massachusetts.

[4]Single premium, immediate annuities are the kind consumers buy when they cash in their RRSPs at age 71.

and insurance for Great-West. By contrast, Butcher estimates that only about 14 of Great-West's 658 Canadian agents are dual-licensed. That means that they sell plenty of insurance for their own company and precious few mutual fund units for Investors. "There is very little contact between the two companies," says Butcher. The major problem, he says, is a difference in attitudes about what is good for consumers. At Investors, planners like to advise clients to buy term insurance and invest the difference, whereas Great-West's agents still espouse the merits of whole life insurance. "It's a philosophical difference," agrees a Great-West agent. "The two companies have a conflict of attitude about what is best for the consumer." Kissin' cousins, they are not.

There have been even fewer efforts to encourage co-operation between Investors and Montreal Trustco. Investors encourages its staff to sell Montreal Trustco's investment certificates, but with only marginal success. In general, the field forces at the two companies see themselves more as competitors than as allies. They compete head-on in trust services—Investors has its own trust subsidiary—in investment funds and in RRSPs. Robert Gratton, chairman of Montreal Trustco, revealed a rather dog-in-the-manger attitude about the whole idea of co-operation in a 1984 article in *Canadian Business* by journalist David Olive. "We offer a complete range of products in-house," explained Gratton, "because there's a valid fear of losing a client's business should he or she have to get a particular product elsewhere."

Power Financial sits above its feuding family like a patient patriarch who won't give up on the idea that, working together, the corporate clan would be an unstoppable combination, equal to far more than the sum of its parts. If anyone can get the family together in joint undertakings, it is Jim Burns, the hyperactive chairman of Power Financial who regards homeostasis as a state of sin. Burns takes a grassroots approach to the whole endeavour. "We don't believe integration will ever come at the board level," he points out. "It has to happen at the field level. The field people will make it happen." Making it happen will not entail handing the sales staff a briefcase full of different products and ordering them to go forth and sell. John MacBain, director of marketing at Power Financial, has studied cross-selling efforts by major U.S. financial conglomerates such as Sears, Roebuck and Prudential Bache. So far, they have had poor results, he says, because they simply plunked new products on their sales staff's desks and told them to sell them.

Power Financial, MacBain points out, is taking a more careful approach to developing cross-selling. To encourage Investors sales staff to sell Great-West term insurance, MacBain says, the policy applications were greatly simplified and stamped with the Investors name-brand so they appealed to Investors sales staff. More important, Power Financial's strategy is first to develop an economical *system* for cross-selling. "What is important is the system; the distribution is what counts," says Burns. "The key is to get the cost down and offer various products at a low price." To explain, Burns recalls that Henry Ford once scoffed at his own reputation as a marketing guru. Ford attributed his success not to marketing genius but to the simple fact that he saw the potential of selling a lot of cars for a low price. He determined that if he could sell an automobile for $800, he could sell millions of them. He did, says Burns, using an assembly line. "The assembly line alone made it possible," notes Burns.

### Project Power

Power Financial is trying to apply the lessons of Ford's assembly line at a rather secretive pilot project involving Montreal Trust and Great-West in Toronto. For several months, Montreal Trust has had a crack team of personal finance experts testing whether there is a market for the comprehensive financial advice they offer. According to Tom Thompson, the trust company's manager of personal financial planning, select groups of customers have been invited to participate in the project, in which they attend a financial seminar at Montreal Trust and later sit down with a "financial planner"[5] to analyse their complete financial situation and goals. To a certain extent, the project simply sounds as if Montreal Trust is trying to get in on the latest industry craze by calling its sales force financial planners. There is much more to it than that, however. Once the system is in place, any number of products designed by Power's stable of companies can be added to the store shelf. "The idea," says Thompson, "is to get an umbrella effect. Looking down the road, the combinations are unlimited." But, echoing Burns, Thompson emphasizes that the key to success is getting an efficient and low-cost adminstrative apparatus in place. It is a worthwhile objective. If consumers can get cheap, well-designed products—from life insurance to RRSPs and investment funds and GICs (guaranteed investment certificates)—at one source, they won't feel the need to shop around for bargains at a number of financial institutions.

Kavanagh does not show as much enthusiasm as Power Financial executives about the idea of offering a variety of financial products in one place. Great-West's president says he "has a great deal of reservation" about whether any company will experience great success in offering every kind of financial service in one location. "One-stop shopping won't stop people from shopping," he quips. In the future, says Kavanagh, customers such as self-employed professionals or business owners will continue to require specialized treatment. That sort of

---

[5]Everyone, it seems, wants to be called a financial planner. The term certainly has more cachet than, say, "insurance salesman" or "mutual fund marketer." At present, virtually anyone in Canada can hang out a shingle and sell advice on family budgeting, investments, and retirement planning. "Financial planner" is a catch-all title that, in legal terms, requires no special training or a licence. An infant agency called The Canadian Association of Financial Planners has tried to bring some discipline to the burgeoning field by offering educational courses and granting the designation "chartered financial planner" to graduates. But there is as yet no regulation in the industry and anyone with a calculator and sharpened pencil can call themselves a financial planner. For a good discussion of the need for regulation in the industry, see Cathryn Motherwell's article "Financial Planning's Present Failings" in the December 1985 issue of *Report on Business Magazine*.

business, points out Kavanagh, has been characterized by the individual's accountant, his lawyer and life insurance agent sitting down together to work out a strategy. But he concedes that one-stop shopping might appeal to consumers with less specialized needs. "Looking down the pipe I see a continuance of the theme of specialization. It's neither black or white in my head; it's kind of grey. I think the Sears type of thing for particular kinds of customers will probably be a growth factor in the business."

Still, on the individual side of the business, Kavanagh believes agents must become able to advise customers on the full spectrum of their financial needs. "There will be a meaningful trend toward the agent taking a broader view of the customer," says Kavanagh. To explain, Kavanagh goes to the blackboard and scribbles down the four categories of financial service offered to consumers. They are: (1) risk management (insurance); (2) asset management (investments and retirement planning); (3) credit services; and (4) transactional services (bank or trust accounts). Traditionally, he says, life insurance agents have been most active in the first category, and, to a lesser extent, in the asset management area, where they have sold annuities and RRSPs. But increasingly, he says, life agents must play a more important role in their older clients' asset management beyond simply advising them on tax-favoured retirement funding. They must function more as "financial planners," scrutinizing their clients' entire financial picture and giving advice on investments in everything from mutual funds to CSBs, as well as on insurance and annuity purchases. The new buzzword in the insurance industry is "wealth accumulation," says Kavanagh. "There's a big market out there where people, particularly in their late 40s or 50s, are asset rich and don't know what to do with their money."

The scenario Kavanagh portrays, however, is far less ambitious than the sort of one-stop shopping system envisioned by Burns and MacBain. Kavanagh's approach involves improving the existing skills of life insurance agents and reorienting them toward giving counselling on wealth accumulation rather than simply on protection against financial disaster. Summing up his attitude to Power's plans for the gradual integration of the services offered by its subsidiaries, Kavanagh asserts: "The success of conglomerates like Power Financial and Trilon will not depend on product cross-selling but on the individual operating success of the companies in their respective folds." Perhaps Kavanagh's horizons are simply more limited than those of Burns and others at Power Financial. Kavanagh certainly reveals none of the excitement about the potential of further integration that Burns demonstrates. Burns talks about the future with his characteristic "get on with change" approach to business. Kavanagh is proud of Great-West's record as an innovator in the insurance field, and is less eager to mess with a gameplan that has proven successful for decades.

## The Lure of the West

Great-West was founded in 1891 in Winnipeg at a time when the idea of basing an insurance company west of Toronto brought snickers of disbelief in established insurance circles. That the company survived at all and later thrived was due to the efforts of Jeffry Brock, a transplanted Easterner who founded the company with a determination based on the belief that the West had been exploited long enough by the major companies from Montreal, Toronto and New York. Brock's 21-year tenure as Great-West's managing director (as insurance company heads were then called) set the company on a salesoriented tack that, to varying degrees, has dominated its activities throughout most of its existence ever since.

A small man with a quick mind and an outgoing personality, Brock was born on January 6, 1850, in Guelph, Ontario, and attended private and public schools in the southern Ontario city before going to the High School of McGill College in Montreal. Brock's family was prominent in the Guelph area;

his father, Thomas Rees Brock, was a well-known registrar for Wellington county. Still, Brock's origins in the business world were hardly auspicious. Fresh out of school, Brock entered the retail trade as a clerk in Shewman's book and stationery store in Guelph. Then, after a few years, he left Shewman's to apprentice at Barclay & McLeod, a dry goods store in nearby Georgetown. For a time, dry goods appeared to be Brock's calling. His skill at peddling everything from hammers to haberdashery later took him to St Louis, Missouri, where he worked as a salesman for S. Duncan and Company, and then to Troy, New York, where he moved merchandise with characteristic flair for another major dry goods retailer.

By 1872, the diligent clerk turned master salesman was back in Canada, working for a Toronto wholesaler. Later, in 1877, Brock and a brother set up their own dry goods business in Toronto, but within two years, Brock had sold out his interest. Like many ambitious entrepreneurs at the time, Brock had the foresight to realize that there was a lot more money to be made selling insurance policies than curtain material. Besides, Brock and his new bride, Louisa, had heard the call of the West. As the decade of the 1880s began, Brock joined the flood of humankind surging toward Winnipeg, where he started his first venture in insurance with a partner, Captain Carruthers. Like thousands of others, Brock was lured to the "Gateway to the West" by a great real estate and investment boom sparked by the building of the transcontinental railway. To the west of Winnipeg, the CPR's prairie construction was well underway, and to the east, the government was building a line between Red River and Fort William (now Thunder Bay). Winnipeg itself was a polyglot collection of fortune hunters and drifters. Its broad, muddy avenues were filled with workmen, stray horses and a growing abundance of garbage. New buildings were being erected almost as quickly as the tent colonies that were springing up as homes for job-seekers. Real estate speculation became rampant as the population of the city doubled each year. In 1882, Winnipeg's population of 16,000 supported no fewer than 300 real estate dealers.

Brock and Carruthers prospered amid the boom. A decade later, the popular duo had turned their operation into a thriving business and both had achieved a measure of wealth and respectability in Winnipeg. But the ever-ambitious Brock decided to strike out on his own to form the Great-West Life Assurance Company. Canada's first western-based insurance company was officially incorporated by a special Act of Parliament in 1891. (The hyphen in the name Great-West resulted from a typographical error.)

It was not a propitious time to start any new venture in Winnipeg. The boom of a few years before had turned into a bust, now that the railway furor had subsided, the region was facing a recession. But the emigrant from eastern Canada had put down his roots in the West and was convinced that Manitoba needed a home-grown life insurance company. It would be a company that, unlike the major firms from the East, would reinvest the money of Manitobans in the region, fuelling its economic development.

Selling insurance was a peculiar business in those days. The companies presented themselves to the public as models of Victorian respectability. Their executive officers fostered an image of staid propriety; Brock himself stares from early photographs with a look of decorum and chilling severity. In reality, those same executives were on the front lines of a rough and tumble business. As managing director of Great-West, Brock personally ensured the early success of the fledgling company by selling policies at a formidable pace. In an article published in 1911, the Winnipeg *Tribune* described his ambitious undertaking: "So this little man, he is no giant physically, set to work and with courage as indomitable as Horatio Nelson, plunged in and started his big Company. He took off his own coat and went to work. He induced practically every friend and acquaintance and hundreds who were neither, to take either a policy or some stock in the Company." The secret of success in the insurance business, it seems, has never changed.

Brock was prodigious in other ways as well. The same article added parenthetically: "Oh! Yes! Mr Brock has a wife and a large family. These men of small stature always have both." In fact, Jeffry and Louisa raised a brood of eight children, an impressive number even in the late 1800s.

Including Brock, the company had a sales force of three in its first year of operation. The energetic team sold an amazing 834 policies, providing more than $2 million in insurance protection in the first 12 months. That means that, on average, each man had to sell more than five policies every week for 52 weeks straight. Today, an insurance salesman is doing well if he sells an average of one policy a week, excluding holidays.

Brock served as managing director of Great-West until shortly before his death in 1915, and oversaw a period of steady, rapid growth. Just two years after its founding, the company entered the competitive eastern market when it established a branch in Toronto. By the turn of the century, it was represented in every province. In 1906, Great-West entered the U.S. market with the creation of a branch office in Fargo, North Dakota. Company literature describes Great-West as "Canada's fastest-growing insurer" during the period. But that is a contested title, since several other insurers make the same claim.

Nevertheless, Great-West had proved its detractors in the East wrong. As a company director, the Honourable H. J. Macdonald commented in 1904: "When this company came into existence the people in the East, and many in our own province, were in the habit of looking on it as almost a still-born child. They thought there was little chance of a life insurance company with its head office in Winnipeg meeting with success." The company had easily rid itself of the "What good can come out of Winnipeg?" stigma. When Great-West celebrated its 22nd anniversary on August 18, 1913, it had business in force exceeding $92 million, assets exceeding $12.5 million,

income for 1912 of more than $3.5 million and more than
44,000 policy holders.

The Winnipeg press celebrated Brock's achievements with
parochial enthusiasm. In 1914, one year before Brock's death,
the Winnipeg *Saturday Post* said that Brock and his staff had
"gone upon the principle that to be successful, an insurance
company must be like Caesar's wife, above suspicion." But the
success of the company also caught international attention. A
profile of Great-West in the *Illustrated London News*, on March
28, 1914, rhapsodized over the company's achievements,
describing them as a metaphor for business development in
western Canada. The story of Great-West, said the British paper,
"was, in effect, that of the early days of Western Canada; of
great opportunities then foreseen by few now enjoyed by
many—a story of enterprise, of hard-won achievement…" The
writer credited Great-West's success in part to the fact that
Canada was "a new country, peopled largely by the young and
vigorous," the sort of people who provided "a most desirable
field of risk-selection."[6]

### Cut from a Different Cloth

In the history of life insurance, the nature of Brock's exploits
was not unique. Most of the major companies were formed by
energetic types with visions of premiums dancing in their eyes
and who could sell a policy to anyone who gave them two
minutes of their time. In the late 1800s, the captains of the
insurance industry sat squarely in the mainstream of capital-
ism. Actuaries were used insofar as they were needed, sometimes as consultants who sold their services and sometimes as

---

[6]The article went on to note, however, that the company had done very well
financially by grossly overestimating annual mortality rates each year and setting
more than enough money aside in reserves. Typically, projected death claims were
often exaggerated by 80 per cent or more. Apparently, despite his aggressive
nature, Brock liked to have the odds stacked in his favour.

staff employees of the richer companies. Most insurers, however, designed their policies by copying the mortality tables
and policies already in use by other successful companies.
Gradually, however, actuaries did move out of the backrooms
and into the boardrooms. But Great-West bucked that trend,
even though Great-West sits next door to one of the oldest and
most prominent actuarial schools in North America, the University of Manitoba. The result, arguably, has been a succession of chief executives who never let entrepreneurial flair
take a back seat to the ultraconservative tendencies and mysterious rites of actuarial science.

In the year's following Brock's death, Great-West was buffeted by a series of near-disasters. Almost immediately, the
company had to cope with the effects of the First World
War. Unlike some of its competitors, which actually thrived
on a torrent of new business during the war, Great-West's financial stability was challenged during those years. By the time
the war ended, the company had paid out $1.5 million in
claims. Then came the deadly flu epidemic that swept North
America after the war, costing Great-West another $1 million
in claims.

By the 1920s, however, the company's fortunes were on the
upswing again. Then, amid the widespread excitement over
the future of industry in North America, Great-West's managing director, C. C. Ferguson, initiated the company's first tenta-
tive moves into a line of business that only years later would
prove to be a seam of pure gold. Recognizing the potential of
the continent's great industrial enterprises, Great-West, in 1920,
became one of the first companies on the continent to enter
the infant field of group insurance. At the time, providing
group benefits for employees was a novel idea; and as it turned
out, its time had not quite yet come. Group insurance plans
sold poorly for Great-West during the 1920s and sales pretty
well dried up when the Great Depression struck—a period
when neither employers nor employees had money for fringe

benefits. As of 1940, group plans accounted for only 9 per cent of Great-West's insurance in force.

The man who pulled Great-West out of the doldrums brought on by the Depression was Henry Manning, who left his sales job with Home Life in New York to become the Manitoba company's chief executive in 1938 and stayed in the post until 1955. In management style, Manning had certain things in common with other insurance executives of the era. James Burns, the Power Corp. president and Power Financial chairman who was president of Great-West from 1971 to 1979 began his career at the insurance company while Manning was still at the top. He remembers Manning as an "autocratic kind of a guy." Says Burns: "You never took Henry Manning lightly. You took him very seriously and he took himself very seriously."

But he was not stodgy. In key areas, Manning did things differently. Most major insurance companies in Canada began peppering their jargon with talk of the need for a "market-driven" approach in the late 1970s and 1980s. Manning was on to it in the 1930s and '40s. From the start, says Burns, Manning was very field-oriented; he put an unprecedented emphasis on hiring top agents and paying them well. Manning's strategy sometimes sparked angry clashes with Great-West's board of directors. In Burn's estimation, "the single most important thing Manning did was hire a young salesman named Earl Schwemm to run the company's Chicago branch." Manning proposed to pay Schwemm, a young man in his thirties, a salary that was more than one-and-a-half times greater than the chief executive's salary. At the time, 1936, that was simply unheard of. Says Burns: "Manning really had to bully it past the board." In no time after being hired, Schwemm was bringing in unprecedented amounts of business to Great-West. Before Schwemm's arrival, Great-West's branches were considered to be doing well if they did $1 million worth of business annually. Schwemm regularly drummed up $20 to $25 million worth of business a year.

Kavanagh credits Manning with giving impetus to Great-West's U.S. operations in particular. Says Kavanagh: "Manning modernized the company's approach to the market in terms of the way in which our field force was compensated. He thought it was most appropriate that a branch manager make more than the president if he got the sales job done in outstanding ways."

Manning's other major hobby horse was group insurance. Says Burns: "He had the wits to hire top group people. His emphasis was always on the group side." In that regard, Manning's most important acquisition was Stefan Hansen, a University of Manitoba-trained actuary who headed Great-West's group operations in the 1950s. "Hansen had a missionary approach to selling group insurance," recalls Kavanagh, who was hired by Hansen in 1953. At the time, Great-West was hardly known to major Canadian corporations. "I'm sure major companies like Air Canada and Dofasco wondered who the hell Great-West was," says Burns, "but Hansen would always come up with some new wrinkle in group coverage to win their business." By the 1960s, Great-West was no longer a nobody in the group field: it could already lay claim to being one of the largest group insurers in Canada.

Manning had a great style, recalls Burns: "He was always talking ten years ahead, always talking as if the company were ten times larger than it was." The positive thinking paid off. When Manning retired in 1955, he had transformed Great-West from the small, parochial company he took over in the 1930s into one of Canada's largest companies, with $556 million in assets and $2.47 billion worth of insurance in force. Says Burns: "Manning was the guy who put the foundation in place for the subsequent success of Great-West."

Since Manning's time, his successors haven't strayed from the priorities he established. Relative to the rest of the insurance industry, Great-West's managers have traditionally shown more willingness to innovate. David Kilgour, who replaced Manning in 1955, was another sales-oriented leader who had previously made his mark at the company as director of marketing for individual insurance. Kilgour, whose offspring include Edmonton Tory MP David Kilgour and Geills Turner, wife of federal Liberal leader John Turner, was a dynamic, outgoing chief executive who cut a wide swath at the company and on the national scene, regularly taking the federal Liberal party to task on pension issues in public forums. Like Manning, Kilgour ruled Great-West with an iron hand. Says Burns: "Nothing was terribly democratic at Great-West when he was there. He was number one and he didn't have a hell of a lot of time to talk with other people."

From the viewpoint of business, Kilgour presided over the company's fortunes at a time when making money in the insurance business was almost as easy as waking up in the morning. The 1960s was a boom decade for the economy and, by extension, for insurers. Great-West was no exception. Its assets had surged to about $1.5 billion by 1969. The only worrisome threat to insurance company profits in the period came from the introduction of nationwide medicare in 1968. As a result, Great-West and other insurers lost a large portion of their health and accident business in one fell swoop.

Still, as a widely held company, with insurance in force of more than $11.6 billion in 1969, a fat surplus of $84 million and a thriving U.S. business that contributed $800,000 annually to profits, Great-West was a prime target for takeover, a fate eventually suffered by all the Canadian life insurance companies that had not mutualized in the 1950s. The first threat to Great-West arose in January 1969, when an uppity little outfit called the Great Western Saddlery Co., publicly announced that it intended to make a bid for control of Great-West. Kilgour was affronted by the Toronto-based company's bid, which he and the rest of Great-West's management considered inadequate. Saddlery's holdings in computer services, space research and urban development companies were worth a mere $25 million, compared to Great-West's $1.5 billion in assets. Still, Saddlery had the financial backing of its controlling shareholder, Edper Investments Ltd., a holding company owned by Peter and Edward Bronfman. Saddlery never did make a public bid for Great-West, although it quietly accumulated 194,000 Great-West shares on the North American markets. Just as Kilgour was devising his strategy to fight off Saddlery, Investors Group of Winnipeg bought out Saddlery's shares and followed up with a public offer, which netted it 50.1 per cent control of Great-West, for about $70 million. At the time of the takeover in April 1969, Investors was 77 per cent held by a clutch of five Canadian companies: the Royal Bank of Canada; the Canadian Imperial Bank of Commerce; Canadian Pacific Investments Ltd; James Richardson & Sons, Ltd; and Imperial Life Assurance, a Toronto-based insurer then owned by Power Corp. Within a year, however, Power Corp. had bought a controlling interest in Investors and hence won control of Great-West Life Assurance, an even bigger prize.

### The Gunslinger Takes Charge

The Burns era at Great-West, which lasted from 1971 to 1979, was like no other before it and the odds are, like no other after it. As Burns tells it, he sauntered into the chief executive suite of Great-West with his six-guns drawn, ready to clear the place of anyone who thought like an actuary or had grown too complacent with the company's success. Although Burns was only a boyish-looking 41 when he became president, he was bristling with ideas for change developed over nearly two decades with the company. Born in Winnipeg on December 29, 1929, Burns graduated with a degree in Commerce from the University of Manitoba in 1951, and then went to Harvard, where he earned an MBA in 1953. Upon graduation, Burns signed on with Great-West's marketing division and spent the better part of his career in the company's U.S. operation. Burns credits his U.S. experience with forming his attitudes toward business. "I spent all my working life in the United States and my orientation was to the American way of doing things."

For one thing, the culture of insurance companies, including Great-West, infuriated Burns. "I always thought that the culture in insurance companies was strange," he says. "There was this mystique about reserves and all this other actuarial mumbo jumbo. It wasn't run like any other business. As long as you didn't lose any money, it was inevitable that you'd be profitable." Burns had different ideas. "I was determined that I was going to run it like any other business," he says.

In the early 1970s, a full decade ahead of most of Great-West's competitors, Burns introduced the idea of profit centres to the company's sprawling operations. That involved scrutinizing all its component parts to see which areas were making money after expenses and which ones weren't. Burns also beat his competitors to the draw in terms of hiring and promotion standards. John Green, Great-West's current vice-president and number two in command to Kavanagh, was a group agency manager in Winnipeg during Burns' tenure. Says Green: "Burns started the company's practice of recognizing people according to their performance and contribution rather than their seniority." The new president also broke down career stereotypes at Great-West. Traditionally, different specialists at Great-West, as at other companies, had advanced through their careers on a single track. Actuaries did actuarial things, marketing experts stayed in sales-oriented jobs. Burns shook that up by starting an exchange program in which actuaries, for instance, were rotated through different types of jobs, from personnel management to group sales.

Burns was not pressured to instigate the upheaval because Great-West's profits were in any jeopardy. Early in his tenure, Burns made an intriguing discovery about the company's earnings outlook by having his actuarial staff develop a computer model of Great-West's operations. To Burn's amazement, the model showed that if Great-West simply managed to keep its existing group business on its books, the company would double in size in five years. Any other insurance executive might have giggled at his good fortune, taken the rest of the afternoon off to play golf and spent the next five years merrily counting premium payments. Not Burns. He launched an unprecedented campaign at the company to increase the quality of service to keep its customers happy and make sure they maintained their business with Great-West. Names of whole divisions were changed in the ensuing campaign. The administrative services division, for instance, was rechristened the policyholder's service division. In addition, the company became the first to set up local payment offices in major centres across the country to speed up the claims-payment process.

The strategy also involved boosting the morale of the agents, the front-line troops who dealt directly with customers. Says Burns: "I tried to get rid of the idea that agents were second-class citizens and elevated them to the first rank in terms of importance at the company." The salaries of agency managers in the group insurance field, which had fallen behind those of managers on the individual business side, were immediately increased. Says Green: "Burns put our very best people in charge of group offices and paid them better than managers at any other company."

Burns introduced a decentralized management style to a company that had always been run on an autocratic, paternalistic basis. His speciality was ideas, not operational expertise. "Burns was a very conceptual boss," says Kavanagh. "He didn't involve himself with the intricacies of underwriting and policy design." Burns liked to prod newly promoted employees into action. Recalls Kavanagh: "I remember he could needle you. His favourite question was, 'When are you going to do something?' It used to goad the hell out of us."

During Burns' tenure, Great-West's business in the United States increased by about five times, and the company cemented its predominance in the Canadian group market. In 1978, the last full year of Burns' presidency, premium income from all lines of business at Great-West topped $1 billion for the first time. Says Burns with satisfaction: "The greatest pleasure in life for me was to beat the hell out of the Toronto companies. And we did." A self-described "gunslinger" in terms of management style, Burns attributes Great-West's success in part to its Western character. "The advantage of being in Winnipeg, was that the orientation was to the South. We're more like Texans than the old-school English types in the East," he says disparagingly.

Still, in February 1979, shortly after Power Corp., through Investors Group, increased its stake in Great-West to 95.7 per cent, Burns packed his gear and headed East himself to take over as president of Power Corp. (In 1984, Burns also took on the presidency of the newly created Power Financial Corp. In 1986, he was promoted to chairman of the latter company.)

### The Turbulent Eighties

The building rises like a Greek temple, strangely transported in time and place to the Canadian Prairies. The entire six-storey corporate headquarters of Great-West Life Assurance is clad in grey-white Manitoba Tyndall Stone, adding to the classical theme. At the front of the edifice, eight majestic, ten-foot-wide Doric columns rise to the underside of the fifth floor. At their feet a huge, rectangular metal slab sits on two concrete walls. Anyone using the main entranceway to the building must pass underneath the modernistic portal. From a distance, the slab looks eerily like a sacrificial altar. Walking into the building, one almost expects to hear the chanting of priests. The symbolism of the building is fitting for an insurance company, suggesting as it does that the corporate entity housed therein is worthy of reverence, trust and obeisance.

The new, 188,000-square-foot, $10 million corporate headquarters building was completed in 1983 by Great-West to handle the overflow of staff and equipment from its existing headquarters, which remained linked to the new structure by an underground office complex containing another 51,000 square feet of space. The construction of the new edifice was a testament to Great-West's burgeoning size and wealth. But that prosperity also necessitated the far-reaching operational changes which Kevin Kavanagh introduced at Great-West shortly after he succeeded Burns as president of the company in 1979.

No sooner had Kavanagh taken over the job than he began the process of splitting Great-West's North American operations into distinct parts. Previously, all management decisions and administration had emanated from Winnipeg, but by 1983 the American operations were split off from those in Canada and housed in a spanking new U.S. head office tower in Denver, Colorado. In both countries, separately administered group and individual insurance divisions were created in an attempt to make each branch more attuned to changes in its own marketplace and better able to respond quickly to them. The new headquarters in Winnipeg became the domicile of Great-West's corporate office, where the senior officers of the company oversee the performance of all divisions. The old headquarters complex became home for the Canadian operation.

It was a painful period for Great-West. First, the splitting up process proved to be much more difficult than anyone in the company's management had anticipated. Kavanagh and his senior colleagues were soon bogged down in the logistics of the project—including setting up separate computer systems in each country. More important, there were serious customer service problems in the United States as Winnipeg-based staff were moved to Denver and hundreds of new recruits were hired for the expanded U.S. operation. "In that period, there were times when we had seven or eight green people for every one or two experienced staff across the whole country," recalls Kavanagh. "It compromised our service standards. We were struggling all during that period." To add to their problems, the expenses associated with the reorganization soared beyond expectations, seriously depressing the return on the equity held by Great-West's shareholders.

More trouble was to come. Beginning in 1979, Paul Volcker, chairman of the U.S. Federal Reserve Board (the American central bank) began cranking interest rates upward to unprecedented levels. For the North American economies, the process precipitated the worst recession since World War II. For insurance companies, says Kavanagh, it also added another kind of misery. As interest rates soared into the low 20 per cent level, consumers became increasingly disgruntled with the low, 3 to 4 per cent rates of return offered by traditional life insurance policies. Like other insurance companies, Great-West was blindsided by the consumer rush to higher-yielding investments, such as plain savings accounts and term deposits. Says Kavanagh: "It became clear to us that in order to participate in financial services we had to have products that were much more sensitive to interest rates." Great-West's strategic thinkers were drawn away from dealing with problems generated by the reorganization of the company to the task of designing new policies.

By 1981, Great-West was putting the final touches on a new money policy that reflected current interest rates. But in the fall of that year then Liberal finance minister Allan MacEachen introduced a budget which contained new taxation provisions for life insurance policies with a high cash value. The new measures scuttled Great-West's shiny new policy. So it was back to the drawing boards. Then, early in 1982, Great-West introduced its universal life policy, which permitted buyers to share in the benefits and risks of interest-rate fluctuations, but which also offered them an unprecedented degree

of choice in various aspects of the policy (see Chapter 1). Kavanagh states proudly that Great-West's Living Life policy was
the first Canadian-designed universal life product. He adds
that Dominion Life of Waterloo was first off the mark with a
universal life policy in Canada, but it was designed by the U.S.
company which owned Dominion at the time.

Other costly miscalculations were also made by Great-West
during the period. For example, the company owned a 10 per
cent state in the Edmonton-based Canadian Commercial Bank.[7]
By the time the CCB failed in 1985, amidst a hurricane of
headlines and speculation about the stability of the banking
system, Great-West had totally written off its $10-million invest-
ment in the bank.

Great-West stumbled again, this time in a major foray into
the property and casualty business. In 1979 Great-West transformed Harriot and Associates, a subsidiary in the property
and casualty business, into a new company called Gold Circle
Insurance Co. Gold Circle, based in Toronto, had an exciting
mission. It was intent on forging a new market by selling group
property and casualty insurance plans to major employers. For
decades, employees have been able to get low-cost term life
insurance coverage through their employers, but Gold Circle
offered plans that would give employees low-cost general insurance on their cars and homes as well. Group property and
casualty insurance plans like this have never been popular
with Canadian insurance companies. Under insurance law, if a
consumer determines that he fits into the same lifestyle category as the members of a firm or professional association covered by such a group plan, he can walk in off the street and
demand the same low-cost coverage. That means, for example,
that if a teacher discovered that the teachers in another board

---

[7]Twenty-one institutions, mainly pension funds, held 94 per cent of CCB's stock.
Aside from Great-West, the major shareholders were the Caisse de Dépôt et
Placement du Québec and the Canada Deposit Insurance Corporation, each with
about 10 per cent.

of education were covered by a Gold Circle group plan for insuring their cars or homes, he or she could go to Gold Circle and legally request the same terms of coverage.

Gold Circle's sales were not complicated by this legal technicality, since almost no consumers are aware of it. But the company's business was hampered by employer resistance to the idea of providing group property and casualty coverage to employees. The resistance was based in part on managers' worries that the new kind of benefits might become the subject of contract bargaining with unions. Founded with high hopes, Gold Circle has since lost money in every year of its operation. In 1984 alone, the company had an underwriting loss (premiums less claims) of $4.9 million, investment income of a meagre $412,000, and a return on equity of minus 220 per cent.

In an attempt to dig Gold Circle out of its financial abyss, Great-West struck a deal in September 1985, with The Laurentian General Insurance Co. of Montreal, in which The Personal, a money-losing general insurance company owned by Laurentian, was merged with Gold Circle. The resultant company, which retained the Personal name, is majority-owned by Laurentian. The plan is, however, that Great-West will eventually inject enough capital into the Personal to give it a 50 per cent share. John Green, Great-West's vice-president, explains that both companies were having difficulty because they were too small to be cost effective. "Too much of the premiums was being eaten up by overhead," he says. "They really didn't have the necessary critical mass." By merging Gold Circle's block of business (about $12 million in annual premiums) with the business of The Personal (about $24 million in annual premiums), Green thinks the two companies have attained that critical mass and will be able to make a profit. Kavanagh concurs: "Growth is the solution to the problem," he says.

Summing up the tumultuous early 1980s, Kavanagh says stoically: "We endured short-run pain for long-term gain that we can see starting now." Kavanagh speaks of the stormy period as if it were an ordeal by fire designed to knock the feet out from under a fledgling insurance company president. Kavanagh withstood the test, but it is clear that the rash of problems he had to deal with served to reinforce his pragmatic nature. Unlike the high-flying Burns, who had little time for the nuts and bolts of day-to-day operations at the company, Kavanagh had little choice but to involve himself with the various crises that erupted. Around the company, he is known as a much more "hands-on" boss than Burns was. After creating the separate Canadian division, for instance, Kavanagh personally took charge of it for several years before he appointed Green to head it up in 1982. Says Green: "Kevin tends to know at all times what's going on in the company." Burns, too, recognizes that Kavanagh brought a different management style to the company. Says Burns: "Kevin is less of a gunslinger than I am. He is more thoughtful. He goes around and around a problem, studying it from every angle before he has it right."

Kavanagh's 32-year career at Great-West prepared him well for his role as an involved boss, with a penchant for keeping a finger in every dyke. Born in Brandon, Manitoba, on September 27, 1932, he began his career at Great-West immediately after graduating from the University of Manitoba in 1953 with a Bachelor of Commerce degree. Kavanagh was one of a stable of bright young men hired and then converted to the virtues of selling life insurance by Stefan Hansen, the legendary one-time head of Great-West's group operations who is remembered reverentially at the company.

For the next 14 years, the young recruit excelled at selling group insurance for Great-West in Winnipeg and Toronto. Then he began a rapid ascent to the upper echelons of the company. In 1973, Kavanagh was sent to Denver as vice-president, marketing, for the United States, and succeeded in expanding its operations from 28 states to 44 states in his two-year posting. In 1976, he returned to Winnipeg as vice-president, group operations, and within three years, he had taken over as president and chief operating officer.

Kavanagh's rise to the top brought him a comfortable lifestyle and a large house in Winnipeg's fashionable Tuxedo area, but it also brought a desk-full of responsibilities that leaves him little time for the wise-cracks and practical jokes that marked his earlier years with the company. In the past, he delighted in pulling the legs of his more taciturn colleagues. One such victim was Arthur Brown, an investment officer who worked with Kavanagh in the United States. "Brown was a very conservative kind of a guy," recalls Kavanagh. To shake Brown up a bit, Kavanagh had a plastic urinal installed in a room adjoining Brown's office, and then arranged for a staff meeting which Brown would preside over. In the middle of the meeting, Kavanagh had a caretaker interrupt the proceedings by walking in with a large wrench and proceeding to fix the urinal. Brown was startled, and then amused when he discovered what was going on.

Later, while Kavanagh was based in Winnipeg, he conspired to victimize Ron Galloway, a consultant working at the company who was known as a great practical joker himself. On the day the local phone company delivered new phone books to Great-West, Kavanagh arranged to have hundreds of employees put their old phone books in Galloway's office. Chuckles Kavanagh: "Galloway arrived to find about 300 phone books stacked up on his desk." The next year, Galloway got even. On the day of the annual delivery of new phone books, Galloway filled Kavanagh's car to the roof with discarded directories. Says Kavanagh, "I had to get a truck from a local garage to unload the books and cart them away."

Today, Kavanagh hasn't the time for such frivolity. The only hint of his lively sense of humour is the impish school-boy look that sometimes comes over his face. But he remains a popular figure at the company. According to surveys by outside consultants, morale is good among the company's staff. In a 1985 study, 92 per cent of employees rated Great-West as a very successful company; 62 per cent of employees said they felt a high degree of loyalty to their employer; and 76 per cent said they thought it was a good place to work. Seventy-two per cent said they were satisfied with their job. The high level of staff loyalty can be explained in part by the fact that Great-West didn't go through a traumatic period of extensive layoffs in the early 1980s, as did other companies like Crown Life, Manufacturers Life and Sun Life. Answers to a host of other questions in the survey revealed that employees generally regard Great-West as a well-managed place. As a chief executive officer with a strong grip on all aspects of the company's operations, Kavanagh must be given credit for that achievement. Managing people, putting out brush fires in the company's operations and marketing are Kavanagh's areas of strength; devising grand designs for the company is not one of them.

Kevin Kavanagh begins the slide show in the darkened board room of Great-West with the enthusiasm of a man showing slides of a just-completed vacation trip. Only days before, Kavanagh's audience was the company's blue-chip board of directors, which in addition to Paul Desmarais and Jim Burns, includes the likes of Robert Campeau, chief executive of Campeau Corporation of Toronto; Jerry Nickerson, chairman of Nova Scotia's H. B. Nickerson & Sons Limited; and J. Blair MacAulay, a partner with the prestigious Toronto law firm, Fraser & Beatty. The board of directors was generally pleased with what they saw in Kavanagh's slide show, and on this February day, Kavanagh is giving a repeat performance for the interviewer.

As the president of Great-West stands before the screen, clicking up different slides with a hand-held control, his feet, as usual, are in perpetual motion. They shuffle, pivot and pace as he explains the significance of each set of financial figures that appears on the screen. The numbers look good. They show that in the previous year, 1985, Great-West had a total profit of more than $85.6 million, up from about $77.6 million in 1984. The series of graphs are a financial roadmap of Great-West's operations, showing strengths and weaknesses as they impact on the company's bottom line. Profits in the United States are lacklustre, dragged down in part by a fall-off in health insurance sales. "Health insurance is the number one strategic issue facing U.S. operations," says Kavanagh. The good news in Canada, where profits are higher than in the United States, is that individual life insurance sales have continued to soar. New sales of life insurance, measured by face amount, totalled $5.4 billion in 1985 and $3 billion of that was sold to individuals, as opposed to groups of employees covered by company plans. In Kavanagh's view, the surging life sales point up the success of Great-West's policy overhaul since 1982. He boasts: "Ninety per cent of the products we sell now we didn't have four years ago."

Kavanagh revels in the nuts and bolts of the business; he is in his element talking about sales results, new products and profit figures. He foresees Great-West expanding in the future through internal growth—by building on its existing business base—rather than making acquisitions. Kavanagh leaves the crystal-ball gazing to his corporate bosses at Power Financial. They can talk all they want about intercompany integration and achieving synergy through co-operative marketing efforts. Kavanagh has difficulty working up any enthusiasm at all for such lofty intentions. Great-West may be part of a Montreal-based corporate leviathan, but as long as Kavanagh, the boy from Brandon, Manitoba, runs the company, it will not easily give up its maverick Western ways.

# CHAPTER 9

## Never Look Back:
## The Resurrection of
## Crown Life Insurance

MICHAEL BURNS STEERS the four-wheel-drive truck around the country roads with the deftness of a champion rally racer. Gravel flying, the vehicle bounces onward as the chairman and chief executive officer of Crown Life Insurance waves a hand toward points of interest on the left and right. This is Burns country: 600 acres of crops and cattle-range near King City, 45 minutes north of Toronto. He wheels into a driveway and pulls to a stop at a barn where there are some new-born calves. Hopping out of the truck he strides inside and, oblivious to the mud and manure, enters a stall to pat a two-week-old calf. "It's a beauty," he says adoringly. Dressed in blue jeans, a flannel shirt and Wallaby shoes, Burns is in his element. A boardroom brahmin during the work week, Burns is a country boy at heart, who spends his weekends engaged in his favourite pastime: raising Simmental cattle for show and sale.

Despite a long career in the family investment business, Burns Fry Ltd., and his latest incarnation as an insurance executive, Burns is most at home on the farm. After all, he grew up milking cows and pitching hay just a stone's throw away from the antebellum-style mansion he built for himself on the family acreage in 1974. A tall, heavy-set man with a ready smile, 49-year-old Burns combines the wiliness of a Bay Street broker with the amiability of a Hoss Cartwright, star of the 1960s TV series, *Bonanza*.

There isn't much money in raising livestock. Even though Burns' exotic herd of cattle, imported from France, has won him a wall-full of ribbons from shows at various North American fairs, sales of the brown-and-white animals have kept profits only slightly ahead of expenses over the last 15 years. The stable of winning thoroughbred racehorses he keeps on one of his several farms hasn't added much to the bottom line either. But it's the nature of the farm work Burns likes. "The thing about farming," he says, "is that you can look back at the end of the day and see what you've done. In business you've got to wait for the quarterly financial results."

Burns' predilection for fast results explains his obvious pleasure with the turnaround at Crown Life Insurance over the last few years. The fortunes of the Burns clan rise and fall with those of the life insurance company, which is the lodestar in the corporate universe of Crownx Inc., a Toronto-based conglomerate with a bevy of other subsidiaries in the nursing home, information technology and financial services businesses. Burns is also the president of Crownx, an ideal vantage point from which to keep an eye on the Burns family's wealth—about $100 million—which is tied up entirely in Crownx shares. When Crown Life prospers, its parent company's shares take on an added lustre in the view of stock market investors. That, in turn, gives Burns a more secure feeling about his own well-being. Between six kids, four dogs, 120 cattle, 70 sheep, a dozen or so horses, a donkey and the hired hands who take care of them, there are a lot of mouths to feed at Kingswood Farm.

Depending on who you listen to, the events at Crown Life between 1982 and 1985 were either a godsend or a cataclysm. At the instigation of Burns and 47-year-old David Hennigar, who represents the holdings of Crownx's other major shareholder, Nova Scotia's wealthy Jodrey family, the 86-year-old life insurance company was gutted like a tumbledown building and then rebuilt from the inside out. Lifelong employees and executives filed out of Crown Life's doors in numbed disbelief as the man hired to revamp Crown, Robert Bandeen, fired 25 per cent of the payroll in a two-year period, brought in new executive talent and generally modernized the way the company's affairs were managed. When Bandeen suddenly quit as Crown Life's chairman in the fall of 1985 he left a company poised to make record profits but saddled with a shell-shocked workforce with abysmal morale. Says an appalled chief executive from a competing company. "It wasn't what Bandeen did. It was the way he did it. I don't know if Crown Life will ever recover from the ordeal."

Whatever the merits of Bandeen's methods, their impact on Crown Life's bottom line has been substantial. In 1982, Crown Life's common shareholders made a meagre 6.16 per cent return on their investment. In 1985, the rate of return was 19.39 per cent. The net income of the company rose from $14.6 million in 1982 to $71.6 million in 1985. More than $56 million of that 1985 profit flowed through to Crown Life's 94 per cent owner, Crownx, helping to boost the parent company's profit to $66.1 million for the year. But Canada's eighth-largest life insurer is more than just a cash cow for Crownx and its major shareholders, the Burns and Jodrey families, which together hold 49 per cent of Crownx's voting shares. Crown Life has also been spruced up and recharged to provide a solid revenue base for Crownx's further expansion in the financial services sector.

Crown Life is one of several companies in the Crown Financial Group, a Crownx subsidiary formed to oversee the conglomerate's financial subsidiaries. As well as Crown Life, which had assets of $5.9 billion at the end of 1985 and $76.5 billion worth of life insurance in force in Canada, the United States, the United Kingdom, the Caribbean and the Pacific Rim, the group includes a long list of other enterprises. Among these are Coronet Trust Company, a Toronto-based operation with $165 million in assets; Caruscan Corporation, a real estate development and management company with interests across North America; Private Ledger Financial Services, Inc., a California-based broker-dealer that sells everything from stocks to mutual funds through 650 brokers across the United States; and a 40 per cent stake in Beutel, Goodman & Company Ltd., a Toronto-based investment counselling operation that handles Crown Life's equity investments. Burns makes no secret of the fact that he is looking for additions to the corporate stable. Buying another life insurance company is near the top of the list; trust companies and property and casualty companies are also potential targets.

There is a new confidence in Crownx's executive suites (even if morale is still low in the trenches) that comes from counting an influx of cash. On the balance sheet, things are looking up in two of the three major arms in the Crownx domain. Not only are earnings from Crown Life at record levels, but the profits of Extendicare, a Crownx subsidiary with 180 nursing home centres in North America, reached $55 million in 1985. Such gains have made the small $6.7 million loss suffered by Crowntek, Crownx's struggling information technology subsidiary, easy to swallow. They will also enable Crownx to live up to its billing as a player to watch in the financial services market. Crown Financial is smaller than conglomerates like Trilon Financial, which has assets of more than $15 billion, but its goals for building an integrated financial services empire sound remarkably similar. Crownx literature declares that the objective is to build the Crown Financial Group into "a series of autonomous companies linked by shared management expertise, distribution systems, technology and investment activities." Still, Crown Financial is pursuing that strategy at a more measured pace than either Trilon or Power Financial. They are the hares. Crown Financial is the tortoise.

The purpose of all these plans is not to build some grand tower of Babel where masses of consumers will pay homage with their chequebooks—although the image isn't unappealing to Crownx's owners. Instead, the corporate entity is driven by a more mundane, capitalistic motive: to maximize the return on investment for shareholders in the companies. As far as Burns and Hennigar are concerned, that leaves no room for dallying with outdated, inefficient attitudes and habits. The family welfare comes first.

### The Desperate Decades

Crown Life was not always a family-owned enterprise. It spent the first few stormy decades of its life as a rather risky investment for various groups of wealthy Torontonians. When Crown Life began its existence in June 1900, life insurance appeared to be a lucrative business for anyone with the capital and know-how to start a company. At the time, Canada was still fertile territory for a new life insurance enterprise. There were already 39 companies—18 of them Canadian—serving the needs of the country's population of 5 million, but insurance was an infant industry. At the turn of the century, the average family owned only $450 worth of life insurance—about enough to take care of unexpected burial expenses.

The nation's nineteenth Canadian-owned insurer opened for business in a small room in the downtown Toronto headquarters of *The Mail*, a morning newspaper that later became *The Mail and Empire* and, eventually, *The Globe and Mail*. Crown Life's founders were two prominent Toronto residents, William McMurrich, a lawyer who had served as mayor of the city from 1881 to 1882, and Harley Roberts, an insurance man who had sold policies in Canada for New York Life and the Equitable Life Assurance Society, both U.S. companies. These two men used the same recipe for starting an insurance business that had served other companies so well. They raised a dollop of capital and added a liberal helping of prestige by convincing Sir Charles Tupper, a father of Confederation and a former prime minister, to serve as the first president of the company. Tupper was the first of a long succession of prime ministers and politicans to serve as the company's president or on its board of directors. Former presidents include Sir Robert Laird Borden (1928–37) and George Howard Ferguson (1937-46), a premier of Ontario. The roster of the board of directors has included C. D. Howe, Lester Pearson and John Turner.

Despite its pedigree, however, Crown Life got off to a shaky start. Although the company was incorporated in 1900, it didn't start business until the next year. The founders had hoped to be able to raise $1 million in capital with their first share issue in 1900, but it met with a decidedly underwhelming response. The $45,000 worth of shares they sold wasn't enough to pay the $50,000 required for a federal licence to do business. By July 1901, however, the company had sold another $10,000 worth of shares, bringing its capital to $55,000. That was enough to buy the federal licence, but after expenses the company started business with only $4,000 in cash on hand.

The company's experience during the next nine years was no more auspicious. Sales were strong, but the high administrative costs of the new business depleted the insurance company's coffers. Although Crown Life had agents selling across the country, by the end of the decade cash flow at head office diminished to the point that the company's board was wrestling with the idea—eventually rejected—to merge Crown Life with another insurer. Tumult within Crown's management continued throughout the period. In 1904, Crown brought in a consulting actuary, William Standen of New York, to examine the company's business. Standen produced a scathing report that suggested cutbacks in such expenditures as advertising and directors' fees. Standen's austerity measures were approved when the president, Sir Charles Tupper, was absent, and when he discovered that his salary had been cut in half he resigned. Between 1901 and 1910, Crown Life went through three presidents and four chief executive officers and moved its headquarters five times. By then, it was time to settle down.

The man who brought a semblance of order to Crown's affairs for the next four decades was Herbert Roy Stephenson. He was hired in 1912 as company actuary at an annual salary of $1,800, and by 1916 he was also managing director of Crown. (Managing directors in those days were comparable to chief executive officers today; the president's role was largely that of figurehead.)

Under Stephenson, the company struggled along for years, buffeted by the rising claims experienced during World War I and the great flu epidemic that swept North America in 1918, taking twice as many North American lives as the war did. By 1921, however, Crown Life had absorbed the heavy claims from the war and the flu epidemic, and Stephenson was plotting expansion. To win new business in the face of competition from his much larger rivals, he designed a new, cheaper life insurance policy. By lowering the first-year commission levels paid to agents and reducing the cash surrender value of the policies, Stephenson was able to decrease premium rates considerably. Sales increased exponentially. In 1924 alone, Crown Life sold more than $14 million worth of new insurance. By 1930, Stephenson had also expanded the company's operations into Michigan, the West Indies, Bermuda, Great Britain, Africa and Hawaii.

Known to this day as the architect of Crown Life, Stephenson continued to head Crown Life right up to the time of his retirement as chairman of the board in 1959. (He continued on as a director until his death at age 85 in 1973.) Stephenson saw Crown through the arduous 1930s; during those years it was one of the few life insurance companies that increased its business every year. (Insurance in force climbed to $220 million by 1939.) And Stephenson continued to govern that pattern of growth right through the war-torn 1940s.

## Forging Family Ties

Although Stephenson held the managerial reins at Crown Life for decades, control of the purse strings landed early on in the hands of the Burns and Jodrey families, two prominent business clans, whose origins were in the Maritimes. The Burns family's association with Crown Life began first. Herbert Deschamps Burns, grandfather of Michael, the current chairman, was elected to the board of Crown Life in 1927. He was associated with Crown for the next 33 years, becoming president in 1946 and chairman of the board in 1956. Herbert Burns hailed from Moncton, New Brunswick. His father, Charles, had moved there to work in a textile mill after spending several years in Digby, Nova Scotia, where he tried fruitlessly to earn a living trading goods back and forth between Digby and the Caribbean Islands.

Herbert's climb from Moncton schoolboy to a monied member of the Canadian business establishment owes as much to his ability to withstand the peripatetic life of a bank manager as to his financial savvy. At age 15, Herbert Burns joined the Bank of Nova Scotia at $1.50 a week because another offer he had received—as a labourer in a lumberyard—paid only $1.25 a week. He stayed with the bank for another 65 years, moving from branch to branch across the country and eventually rising to the post of president, and then chairman of the board. When he first signed on as a director with Crown Life, Burns was manager of the Bank of Nova Scotia's main branch in Toronto. His increasingly senior duties at the bank were apparently not too onerous to prevent him from playing an active role at Crown as well.

Herbert's son, Charles F. W. Burns, picked up the family mantle at Crown Life in the 1940s. As with Herbert, the life insurance business was a sideline for Charles, whose primary occupation was running the stock brokerage he had founded. Charles had borrowed money from his father in the early 1930s to form Toronto-based Burns Brothers, which eventually became Burns Fry Ltd. As well as running the investment company, Charles Burns became a director of Crown Life in 1946, president in 1959 and chairman of the board in 1964.

The increasingly important role the Burns family played in Crown Life after 1946 was no coincidence. In that year, the Burns clan bought a major stake in the company, along with George McCullagh, publisher of *The Globe and Mail*. When McCullagh died in 1952, Charles Burns convinced a prominent Nova Scotia businessman, Roy Jodrey, to buy up the McCullagh holdings. Charles Burns and Jodrey had been friends ever since the early 1940s when they were introduced over dinner one evening at the Hotel Nova Scotia in Halifax. Roy Jodrey had turned his back on the family's farming roots in the Annapolis Valley and built a business empire centred on the Minas Basin Pulp and Power Co. Ltd. The much younger Burns became an investment advisor to Jodrey, patriarch of one of Nova Scotia's most wealthy families. The Burns–Jodrey tie at Crown Life has continued right up until the present. Today it is carried on by the close working relationship between Michael Burns and David Hennigar, whose mother, Jean Hennigar, is a daughter of the late Roy Jodrey. Hennigar devotes most of his energies to controlling the Jodrey family's $3.5 billion empire and running Burns Fry's Atlantic region operations from Halifax. But as vice-chairman of Crown Life and chairman of the board of Crownx he also spends one or two days a week at Crownx's Toronto head office.[1]

---

[1] The Burns interest in Crownx is held through family-owned Kingfield Investments Ltd.; the Jodrey interests are held through Scotia Investments Ltd. But the families'

Throughout the 1950s and '60s, the Burns and Jodrey families didn't have to worry much about the welfare of their
holdings in Crown Life (Crownx, the parent holding company,
wasn't created until 1983). Insurance company managers had
to bend over backwards not to make money in those heady
economic times. Says Alan Morson, current president and a
28-year veteran of Crown Life: "Back in the fifties and sixties
incompetence couldn't ruin a life insurance company; only
malevolence could. Things were going right, we had improving mortality rates (resulting in lower than expected death
claims) and some good margins in the business." That all
changed, however, in the 1970s and '80s. "The business became
much tougher," says Morson. "There was more competition
with other financial institutions and more competition among
ourselves, the life insurers."

Under Arthur Williams, president from 1964 to 1971, the
company was a contented, paternalistic place. Williams, a
former agent, was "a peach of a man, very well-loved and
respected," says Morson. But then, there was very little adversity to test his mettle during his tenure. In 1971, chairman
Charles F. W. Burns reported with pride to the annual meeting that life insurance sales had reached a record $1.6 million
in 1970, up 26 per cent from the previous year—not much to
worry about there. But Robert Dowsett, who succeeded Williams in 1971, did not have such an easy ride. A pleasant,
quiet-spoken actuary who had joined Crown in 1950, Dowsett
made some attempts to modernize the company. He introduced productivity improvement programs and monthly financial reports—efforts designed to try to focus more attention on
the bottom line. Such palliative measures, however, were not

ties to Crownx and Crown Life don't stop there. John Jodrey, son of Roy Jodrey
and chief executive officer of Minas Basin Pulp and Power, sits on the board of
Crownx. Joan Addison, eldest daughter of Charles Burns, was elected to the board
of Crown Life in 1986, making her the first woman on the company's board in its
86-year history.

enough to shake Crown Life out of its torpor. By the early 1980s, a crisis had developed. "Our profits were eroding," says Morson, "especially in the U.S. health insurance market, which was a large bucket of business." Premiums from American sales had always formed the lion's share of Crown's revenues. But between 1979 and 1980, the contribution of U.S. sales to total premium income had fallen from 58.7 per cent to 54 per cent. At the same time, Datacrown, a data processing subsidiary formed by Crown Life in 1970, was in difficulty as a result of the spread of microcomputers in the business world, which was resulting in lower demand for Datacrown's central data processing services. Crown Life was suffering badly because management, for the most part, was continuing in its time-worn, outdated ways. Says Morson: "Crown tolerated some inefficiency. It was a place where people kept their job just by showing up for work, not by achievement."

### *Plotting the Palace* Coup

The man who took the initiative to change all that was Michael Burns. He came late to the insurance business, having spent most of his career working for the family stock brokerage. After completing two years of a four-year program in agriculture at Cornell University, he had joined Burns Brothers as a messenger in 1958 and had worked his way up to its executive ranks in 1977, when he abruptly resigned. "I was not enjoying going to work in the morning and wanted to take a break," he recalls. Burns was also weathering the break-up of his marriage to his first wife, Judy, and repaired to his farm for two years to reconsider his future. "I did nothing during the period," he says. "I only went into town [Toronto] one day a week."

By 1979, Burns was ready to go back to work. "I started to get more involved with Crown Life," he says. That year, he succeeded his father, Charles, as chairman of the company. A veteran of the fast-moving investment business, Michael Burns didn't like what he found at the insurance company. "Tragically, the life insurance business in Canada had become an industry where nobody ever lost their job. If an employee stayed long enough, he would eventually rise to the top," observes Burns. He and David Hennigar, who had become friends at Burns Fry, put their heads together on what should be done at Crown. Says Burns: "We realized that we had a huge asset there that wasn't being realized to the best advantage of either the Burns family or the Jodrey family." Their conclusion was that they "should either find a way to use the company or else dispose of it."

The ambitious young scions knew they couldn't give their joint heirloom a facelift without the blessing of their families' ruling patriarchs. "I went back to my father [Charles]," says Burns. "David went back to his uncle, John Jodrey. We were dealing with assets that we had not created; they were assets created by our respective families." With the necessary approvals obtained, Burns and Hennigar set about looking for a major investor willing to inject cash into Crown Life in return for shares in the insurer. The objective was "to end up with a company with large assets and some cash in it. Then we would go on and try to expand the company," says Burns. In 1980, Crown Life began courting potential suitors to invest in its shares, but the company suddenly switched strategy and launched plans to acquire Extendicare, the fourth-largest nursing home operator in North America. Recalls Burns: "We had found a group to invest in Crown Life and we were in the planning stages of how we might proceed when we started having discussions with Extendicare." Burns and Hennigar—neither of them slouches in the arcane science of corporate finance—thought the nursing home company attractive for several reasons. For one thing, it had plenty of potential for growth. For another thing, they reasoned that it could be used as an upstream holding company for Crown Life through which they could launch takeover raids. As a life insurer, Crown Life was limited to a 30 per cent stake in other companies by federal law.

Early in 1980, Burns proposed to Harold Livergant, founder and chairman of Extendicare, that Crown Life acquire the nursing home empire. Six months later, the deal was consummated in an exchange of shares. The Burns and Jodrey families handed their Crown Life holdings to Extendicare in return for 6 million shares of the nursing home giant. That gave the two families control of Extendicare and left them as the ultimate owners of Crown Life as well, since the insurer became a subsidiary of Extendicare. After the deal, Extendicare owned 35 per cent of Crown Life but an immediate follow-up offer to Crown Life's minority shareholders and other transactions since then have boosted that holding to 94 per cent. (In 1983, the name of the holding company was changed from Extendicare Ltd. to Crownx Inc., which became the parent of the Crown Financial Group, the Extendicare Group nursing home business, and the Crowntek Group, a new subsidiary created that same year to oversee the conglomerate's information technology interests.)

The reverse takeover of Extendicare in 1980 was only the first sign that Michael Burns was back in fighting form. There was much more to do. He and Hennigar had created a parent holding company for Crown Life and its sister companies that would enable them to build the multifaceted conglomerate they envisioned. But now it was time to attend to the ailing insurer itself, which was still by far the most important company in their shared corporate realm. There was little point in having a flashy new parent company at the top of the pyramid if its main underpinning was in decaying condition.

While Burns thought that no part of Crown's operations should be immune to change, including the management, the rest of Crown's officers, from president Dowsett down, felt that there were only a few problems that required attention. Some subterfuge on Burns' part was necessary. Unbeknown to Crown's management, Burns held private conversations with McKinsey & Co. Inc., a New York-based management consulting firm.

Burns asked it to send in a team to do a complete review of Crown's operations and make proposals for wholesale change. Meanwhile, Dowsett and his fellow executives thought *they* had hired McKinsey. They had no idea that their own jobs were on the line or that, all the while, McKinsey was acting on direct marching orders from Burns. Says a Crown executive close to the events: "McKinsey had a direct pipeline to Burns. Management thought they had hired the consultants, but Burns had hired them first. After they got inside the company, they sorted out the problems and went back to Burns with suggestions." Apart from proposing drastic measures to improve Crown's management methods and operating efficiency, McKinsey recommended that Crown's executive suites be cleaned out.

Burns liked the idea of changing management, but he was at a loss about exactly who would carry out the task. This was Crown Life after all, where corporate family ties had always come first. The potential victims were more like relatives than employees. At the top of the list was Dowsett, an amiable, intelligent actuary who had joined the company in 1950 and had played a major role in many of its achievements, including a growth spurt in the early 1970s. Dowsett and the vice-presidents below him were career employees, well-liked by staff and colleagues. Says Burns: "Crown Life was a very homey place, with executives that had worked there all their lives and never had a job anywhere else and whose wives were friends."

Burns knew he didn't have the stomach to carry out a purge himself, nor did Hennigar. "It's not my style," says Burns, "and David [Hennigar] couldn't have done it either." But they knew that an outsider like Robert Bandeen, president of Canadian National and a director of Crown Life, would be a good man for the job. After becoming head of CN in 1974, Bandeen had slashed the payroll by 11,000 to 75,000, reorganized the Crown corporation into profit centres and pushed it into the black by 1976. Burns and Hennigar talked about hiring Bandeen, but decided that they couldn't steal him away from CN. "We put the idea in the back of our heads," says Burns, "and went about our business, keeping our eyes out for the right person."

Fortuitous circumstances made Bandeen ripe for the picking by early 1982. Late in January of that year, Bandeen began placing calls to Burns' Toronto office to let him know that he was about to step down as CN president. It was an excruciating time for Burns. "We kept missing," recalls Burns. "The worst fears were running through my head. I wondered if he was phoning to tell me he was resigning from Crown Life's board of directors." Finally, on a Saturday afternoon, Burns reached Bandeen by phone at his farm in the Eastern Townships of Quebec. Bandeen told Burns of his decision to resign from CN and asked if he should step down as a Crown director as a result. Relieved, Burns said no, wished Bandeen luck and hung up the phone. Immediately he realized that he had just missed a golden opportunity to make a job offer to the tough guy from CN. "I thought to myself, 'You damn fool,'" says Burns. Then, he spent the rest of the afternoon trying unsuccessfully to get back in touch with Bandeen, who was out with his family. That evening Burns was preparing to go for dinner at his parents' home when he decided to make just one more phone call to see if Bandeen was at home. Success. The offer was made, Bandeen reacted with delight, chortling, "You've made my weekend," and asked for some time to think. Four days later the two men struck a deal over lunch in Toronto, and on June 1, Bandeen took over as Crown Life chairman, president and chief executive officer. The old insurer would never be the same again.

## The Bandeen Legacy

Robert Angus Bandeen was born in Rodney, Ontario, the son of a Presbyterian minister. During his three years at Crown Life he functioned like St Peter at the Gates of Heaven, selecting the chosen few who had a place in Crown's future and casting the rest into the outer darkness. Bandeen was educated at the University of Western Ontario in London and at Duke University in Durham, North Carolina, where he completed a doctorate in economics. But his performance at Crown Life showed he was more interested in practical results than ivory tower musings. Even before he took over at Crown, Bandeen had become familiar with some of the company's deficiencies while sitting on its board of directors. Says Bandeen: "The whole company wasn't run in an entrepreneurial spirit. I tried to give people a sense of accountability and responsibility." The people he kept on staff, that is. An endless stream of executives and lesser employees came before the hulking, six-foot-two-inch Bandeen, who, seated behind his desk, perfunctorily told each one his or her fate. A total of 750 employees were lopped from the payroll between June 1982 and November 1985. Employees were treated "like turnips falling off the back of a truck," says Alastair Rickard, editor of the *Canadian Journal of Life Insurance*. Rob Dowsett was treated more tenderly. He was shunted aside to a small office and given the title of vice-chairman. But Dowsett didn't last long as an executive with no power. He left a few months later to join William M. Mercer, a major international consulting firm specializing in pension and employee-benefit plans.

Applying some of his experience from 27 years at CN, Bandeen reorganized Crown Life into seven profit centres based on geography and product line. Operations in Canada and the United States were split, with each country having a separate profit centre for group and individual insurance. More profit centres were established for operations in Britain and other foreign countries (the Caribbean Islands, Jamaica, Barbados and Cuba) as well as for Crown's life reinsurance business.[2]

[2]Like some other large insurers, Crown Life also runs a life reinsurance operation, in which it shares the risk on life insurance policies sold by other companies. In 1985, sales of reinsurance totalled $11 billion, making it the fifth-largest life reinsurer in North America.

The reorganization was aimed in part at improving results of the U.S. health business, which, Bandeen says, had become "a large money loser." The U.S. market still accounted for the majority of Crown Life's premium revenue but, according to Bandeen, from 1981 to 1982, the company was profitable only because of an accounting manoeuvre that boosted Crown's U.S. assets to reflect the rising value of the U.S. dollar in relation to its Canadian counterpart. As another remedial measure, the company raised its health insurance premiums in the United States and became more selective in the quality of business it wrote.

As the purge at head office continued, the general agency system in the United States was left largely untouched. Since general agents finance and run their own operations, they do not pass on overhead costs to the company. But agents in the Canadian operation's branch system were not spared. (In a branch system like the one in Canada, agents work out of offices provided by Crown, which pays all operating expenses.) Bandeen closed down about 50 branches across Canada, determined that business should be sold through insurance brokers who pay their own way.

As well as slashing staff numbers and reorganizing operations, Bandeen began to transform Crown Life into a performance-oriented workplace. He introduced an annual training course for middle management at Bishop's University in Lennoxville, Quebec, where lecturers imbue 30 to 40 staff for four weeks each June with the knowledge of a newly minted business school graduate and the enthusiasm of a Dale Carnegie disciple. And to reinforce the idea that productivity pays, Bandeen introduced bonuses for managers who reach yearly profit targets. In a more fundamental shift, Bandeen made Crown's employees focus on the marketplace to a greater degree than before. "The company had not done market research (to find out what consumers want) prior to Bandeen's coming," notes Al Morson. There has always been a tension in

life insurance companies, explains Morson, over whether the
real client is the agent who must sell the products or whether it
is the consumer. Bandeen left no doubt that Crown was placing a priority on selling what the consumer wanted rather than
just the products the field force asked for. Crown Life's annual
advertising budget was boosted from zero to about $2.5 million.
"We adopted a go-go, alive image," says Morson.

Bob Bandeen was not a man with limited perspectives who
could regard himself simply as a hired gun to do the dirty
work for his bosses. He also believed his mandate was to build
a dynamic financial services empire based on Crown Life. To
that end, Bandeen acquired the titular power to perform his
role as empire builder. As well as running Crown Life, he
assumed the presidency of Crown Financial Services when it
was created in 1982. Bandeen also took on the more important
post of president of Crownx after it was formed in 1983. His
horizons appeared to be unlimited.

Between 1982 and 1984, Crown Life and its associated companies had mixed results in their acquisition attempts. Some,
including a 1983 bid for control of Crown Trust of Toronto by
Extendicare Ltd., failed. Other bids met with success. In 1985,
Crown Financial bought a 40 per cent share of investment
counsellor Beutel, Goodman & Company Ltd. of Toronto for
$16 million to handle Crown Life's equity portfolio. Crown
Financial also bought 75 per cent control of North Canadian
Trust Co. of Edmonton, which was renamed Coronet Trust
and moved to Toronto in 1985.

As an upstream financial holding company, Crown Financial had greater freedom than Crown Life to make acquisitions. But the insurance company also made its share of
purchases in the period, particularly in the United States where
it bought up several medium-sized insurers and turned them
into subsidiaries. An early addition was the 1982 purchase of
Annapolis Life Insurance Co., a small Baltimore-based insurer.
(Three years later, Crown sold the company for $4.6 million,

about $800,000 more than it paid for it.) Subsequently, in 1984, Crown Life bought Independence Life and Accident Insurance Company of Kentucky and changed its name to Crown America Life Insurance Company. In the same year, Crown also acquired California-based Private Ledger Financial Services, which sells investment-related products throughout the United States.[3]

Bandeen played a key role in the expansion of Crownx's financial services holdings. It was he, for instance, who hired Donald Payne, a former Bank of Montreal vice-president, as Crown Financial's vice-president for investment operations in 1983. It was also Bandeen who fired him 20 months later. "Payne wasn't a team player," explains Al Morson. "He was a tough-nosed guy with good financial knowledge but he kept everything close to his vest." But more and more, Bandeen wanted greater power to run the full gamut of Crownx's affairs. That, as he discovered, didn't sit well with Michael Burns and David Hennigar. "When I was hired, Burns and Hennigar said to me, 'You do the running, we're passive investors,' " says Bandeen. "They watched me turn around Crown Life but when it got to Crownx it was a different matter. Basically, they wanted to run it. That was valid, since they own the company." Bandeen says it was this clash of wills that led to his unexpected departure in November 1985.

But there were other disagreements between Bandeen and the Burns-Hennigar team. For one thing, Burns and Bandeen disagreed about whether to fire Duncan MacLachlan, who had been hired by Bandeen to turn around Crowntek, Crownx's

---

[3]The acquisition of Private Ledger in 1984 was, in fact, a damage-limiting move by Crown Life. Originally, Crown Financial had paid $9 million for an interest in Private Ledger's California-based parent company, American Principals Holding Inc. (APHI), a developer of tax-sheltered housing investments. But the Securities and Exchange Commission pushed APHI into receivership after squabbles developed between its partners. Since Crown's investment in APHI was secured by debentures in Private Ledger, Crown picked up 100 per cent control of Private Ledger when the parent company went into receivership.

ailing computer services subsidiary, in 1983. MacLachlan had led Crowntek on a two-year acquisition binge, buying businesses involved in everything from fibre optics to software marketing and microcomputer retailing. In 1985 Crowntek suffered an operating loss of $6.7 million on revenue of $168 million. Burns was determined that MacLachlan was not the man to lead Crowntek back into profitability. "MacLachan was a great acquirer, a great visionary," says Burns, "but he was not a good operator." Bandeen didn't want to let MacLachlan go. Says an observer: "I think the job Bandeen did at Crown Life drained him more than anybody dreamed of. He couldn't act on a person [MacLachlan] that he had brought in." Bandeen counters that the suggestion that he ran out of steam is nonsense. It was simply a matter, he says, of a disagreement over who was going to run the company.

If Bandeen's current business endeavour is any indication, the balding, interloper from CN hasn't lost his taste for carrying out turnarounds. In 1985 he joined with two other partners to form Cluny Corp., which specializes in modernizing and streamlining stagnating companies for their owners.

The Bandeen name is rarely uttered in Crown Life's headquarters these days. If it is mentioned by lower-level employees chatting over coffee, it is invariably with an awe that borders on terror. The remaining staff, after all, are the survivors. The Bandeen era is like a painful memory for many, a memory best tucked away in the recesses of the mind. Better to focus on the record profits the company is making. Crown Life is a company concentrating with all its might on the future and trying to forget the past. Only in-house staff surveys, which reveal that morale is still at subterranean levels, expose the scars that still exist a year after Bandeen's departure. "The morale problem was inevitable, but there has been some pick-up," argues Morson, who was elevated to president by Bandeen in 1984. "I guess that's because people are getting used to living with uncertainty. It's also because our managers are getting training in how to fully appreciate the importance of people." An ironic observation.

Bandeen's detractors dot the insurance landscape. They range from the victims of his axe to executives at other life insurance companies who think his methods were too abrupt. Mike Hutchison, one-time vice-president and director of marketing at Crown Life was fired by Bandeen in October 1982. Now a vice-president with National Life, Hutchison is unwilling to give Bandeen credit for anything. "The money Bandeen saved by cutting staff," says Hutchison, "is being eaten up by the huge costs of the advertising campaign he started." Continues Hutchison: "The changes that helped turn around the U.S. group health business were put in place by the guy who was fired on the same day as me [Jack Roberts]." Admitting that his comments may be "sour grapes," Hutchison adds: "The really frustrating thing was that Bandeen never made any attempt to learn anything about insurance. He had designs on taking over the whole company—Crownx, too—but this brought him into a direct clash with Michael Burns, who is a very strong-willed guy."

Bandeen has no regrets about his actions, although he allows, "there are always things that you'd do differently with hindsight." Responding to the sniping of his critics, Bandeen points out that Crown Life achieved record profits in 1984 and 1985 because of his actions. The once-troubled U.S. operations accounted for a healthy 65 per cent of the company's premium revenues in 1985 and 80 per cent of its $71.6 million profit. The only trouble spot on the 1985 earnings statement was a drop-off in new Canadian business, to $933 million from $976 million in 1984. That was a result of Bandeen's dismantling of the branch system of agencies in Canada, which cut the company's distribution network dramatically. Over all, however, Morson is delighted with the financial results. He laughs: "The question now is, 'What do you do for an encore?' " Michael Burns and David Hennigar have a few ideas.

## More Jewels for the Crown

Burns and Hennigar are now firmly esconced at the helm of the conglomerate Bandeen resuscitated. In appearance, they are an unlikely twosome. Burns, a swaggering giant of a man given to wise-cracks and self-effacing jokes, towers over Hennigar, his portly, bespectacled partner, who most of all resembles a friendly clerk at a corner grocery store.

Together, Burns and Hennigar have great plans for the conglomerate they jointly rule. One minor game-plan—to split each Crownx voting share into one voting and one nonvoting share—had to be shelved in May 1986, when the company's minority shareholders voted down the idea. Burns was disappointed by the turn of events. A major reason: increasing the number of nonvoting shares in Crownx would have permitted him to sell shares without diminishing his controlling position in the company. "It was for estate-planning purposes," he says. "Sometime in my lifetime or in the Jodrey family's lifetime there is going to have to be some estate planning done."

That minor setback behind them, Burns and Hennigar are plotting a steady expansion in financial services. Hennigar points out that Crownx has used share issues to reduce its ratio of debt to equity (shareholders' investment) from an unhealthy 1.2:1 at year-end 1984 to 0.5:1 in 1986. "We have the capital to do some fairly major things," he says. Burns elaborates on what they might have in mind. "We would like to acquire another life insurer in the $200 million range," he says. "In Canada if we can, but more probably in the United States." Already, the company has acquired an interest in a merchant banking company whose operations will eventually extend from Canada into the United States and the United Kingdom. Picking up a mutual fund dealer is another possibility. But Burns finds the idea of buying a property and casualty insurer less interesting; it ranks lower on his shopping list, he says. Noting federal regulations may be changed to allow insurance companies to control trust companies or banks, Burns adds: "If we decide we should get into the deposit-taking business we will do so."

Crown Financial will not move too far too fast, however, if Burns' right-hand man, Robert Luba, has his way. As president of Crown Financial and executive vice-present of corporate investments and finance for Crown Life, Luba plays a pivotal role in formulating the conglomerate's acquisition strategies. His credentials for the job are impressive. A stout man with a droll sense of humour, Luba joined Crown Life in 1984 after a successful 17-year career with Labatt's, the London, Ontario, beer and food company. At Labatt's, Luba was a boy wonder, becoming vice-president of finance at the tender age of 29. Bandeen hired Luba as Crown's chief financial officer in order to bolster the company's ranks with talent from outside the insurance industry. When Donald Payne was fired, Luba took charge of Crown's investments as well.

Luba is not about to repeat what he sees as Payne's mistakes. "There was a loss of confidence in Payne," says Luba, "because he tried to move too fast. His approach was 'Damn the torpedoes. Full speed ahead.'" Luba is more cautious. He warns that there is "an atmosphere of hysteria" in the financial services industry about the need to diversify through acquisitions. "That hype is dangerous," he says. "You've got to keep your head. One bad acquisition and you can wipe out all your gains."

Where is this cautious acquisition strategy supposed to lead? Burns reflects on the question as he turns the four-wheel-drive truck into the laneway to his house, the tour of the Burns farms completed. He sees great possibilities for cross-selling products among Crownx's subsidiaries—an activity that has already begun at Crown Life. The insurer's agents already sell registered retirement savings plans (RRSPs) and guaranteed investment certificates (GICs) for Coronet Trust. And in a newer venture, Crown Life is training a team of 13 recent university graduates as financial planners who, working out of an office in Toronto, will sell insurance, GICs and mutual funds. But Burns has even grander visions. One possibility, he says, is for Crown Life to sell life insurance policies that include a condition that the policyholder is entitled to a bed in one of Extendicare's nursing homes in old age. "I see a real opportunity to create products that allow people to live in a nursing home without depleting their wealth," he says. (The nursing home care could be paid for in advance by adding the cost on to an individual's life insurance policy premiums.) Burns also suggests that blue-collar workers might want to pay $1 a month extra for group insurance offered through their employer in return for a guarantee that they would receive counselling services if they are laid off or retire. "I see all sorts of add-ons to policies," he says, slapping his hands down on the steering wheel of the truck, which is idling in front of his country home. He also sees great potential for various financial services being sold in a store-front operation. "They will be like shopping centres," he says, "where one company leases space to a number of different companies, from banks and trust companies to life insurers and real estate firms." Crown Life is already trying out such a concept on the ground floor of its Toronto headquarters.

Michael Burns regards the past with resignation. Recalling the shake-up at Crown Life, he says, "I don't think there is anything I'd do differently today than I did then." But he talks about the future of Crownx and Crown Life with an enthusiasm that he usually reserves for a ribbon-winning Simmental bull. For Burns, after all, more than just a company's profits are involved; the prosperity of the family heirloom is at stake.

# PART IV

*Interlopers from Abroad*

# CHAPTER 10

## *The Foreign Insurance Companies in Canada*

THE FIRST INSURANCE company to be established in Canada was an invited guest. That was in 1804, when a group of prominent residents of Montreal, concerned about the absence of insurance protection against fire in Lower Canada, made a plea to the Phoenix Insurance Company of London, England, to offer its services in the colony. Phoenix, which operated out of an office on Lombard Street, complied on March 7, 1804, when the board of directors appointed Alexander Auldjo, Esq., as the "Agent for the Company in the Provinces of Upper & Lower Canada." The directors of the Phoenix approved the venture because the young colony met the conditions they thought were necessary for a profitable business operation. "Insurance against fire," stated a company document, "has only prevailed in those States where Civil Liberty is enjoyed and where Public Credit and Commercial Honour mutually supporting each other, inspire Confidence of Mankind."

While the Phoenix's early confidence in Canada's progress as a civilization proved to be well founded, the company could not forsee the adversity—whether the product of catastrophic fires, nature's wrath or government legislation—that was to assail it and the hundreds of foreign general and life insurance companies that have sent agents, created branches or bought out Canadian operations in the country since the turn of the nineteenth century. Making profits in Canada has been no cakewalk for the foreign interlopers.

## Trial by Fire

Throughout the nineteenth and early twentieth centuries the major challenges to the well-being of foreign property and casualty companies—and indeed to their Canadian counterparts—came from catastrophic fires. St John's, Newfoundland, was practically destroyed by fire in 1816; in 1845, Quebec City suffered two great fires in one year, which destroyed the suburbs of St Roch and St John. Seven years later, 10,000 people in Montreal were left homeless by fire. The list goes on: another blaze in Quebec City in 1866 consumed 2,100 houses; a fire in 1877 turned a good portion of Saint John, New Brunswick, into tinder; and similar conflagrations struck Ottawa in 1900 and Toronto in 1904. To besieged insurance companies, it was as if the gods had turned into pyromaniacs.

The series of disasters, which was made worse by the prevalence of wooden buildings, had an important effect on the make-up of the general insurance industry in Canada. During those harrowing times, numerous Canadian companies suffered serious financial reverses. Foreign-owned companies, backed by capital from abroad, withstood the ordeal better and moved to increase their share of the marketplace. In 1869, Canadian-controlled fire and casualty companies had written 28 per cent of the business in Canada. By 1925 that had declined to only 7 per cent.

Today, foreign insurers[1] still dominate the general insurance market in Canada. Roughly two-thirds of the property and casualty insurers operating in the country are foreign-controlled, and they account for more than 70 per cent of the business written each year. The spectre of horrific fires no longer haunts the foreign insurers. Instead, they see their worst enemies as Mother Nature, which tries them with everything from tornadoes to hailstorms, and, most of all, the Canadian court system, which they allege is following the lead of the American system by awarding too much money to too many people in settling accident and liability claims.

That view is shared by the more than 40 foreign-controlled reinsurance companies that dominate the Canadian market for property and casualty reinsurance. The five largest reinsurance companies in Canada, measured by annual premiums written, are West German-owned Munich Reinsurance; Swiss-owned Canadian Reinsurance Group; West European-owned Universal Reinsurance Group; Italian-owned Adriatic Insurance of Canada; and U.S.-owned General Reinsurance. Together, they account for more than 40 per cent of the business written by reinsurance companies operating in Canada each year. The foreign reinsurers have never thought much of Canada's climatic and geographic conditions. A description of Canada in a brochure prepared in 1985 by Munich Re's German parent, the largest reinsurer in the world, is revealing. States the booklet: "The exposure to the hazards of blizzards, droughts, floods, devastating hailstorms and tornadoes, forest fires, and, in the provinces of Quebec and British Columbia, earthquakes, makes the country prone to loss of life and damage to property."

Overall, Canadians have benefitted more from the assets that foreign-controlled general insurance and reinsurance companies have invested in the economy—more than $7 billion in 1985—than they have suffered as a result of the tumult in

---

[1] The terms "foreign-controlled" and "foreign-owned" include Canadian companies that are majority-owned by foreign interests, subsidiaries of foreign-based companies, and Canadian branches of foreign companies.

the marketplace that followed the companies' competitive excesses in the early 1980s. Between 1981 and 1985, doing business in Canada reached a low point for the foreign property and casualty insurers, as well as for the reinsurers to whom they ceded business. While the general insurers engaged in a competitive binge of rate slashing to attract new business, the reinsurers followed suit by slashing the rates they charged the primary insurers for taking on part of the risk of the policies they had written. That subsequently proved to be shortsighted, as rising claims outstripped premium income for most companies. Rates to consumers were then jacked up sharply and some lines of coverage became difficult to obtain. (See Chapter 11.) For Canada's largest general insurer, Royal Insurance Company of Canada, a subsidiary of U.K-based Royal Insurance, the last few years have been a time of testing.

### Riding Out the Storm

For the terror-stricken residents of Barrie, Ontario, it was as if the Four Horsemen of the Apocalypse had arrived in fury. Late on the afternoon of Friday, May 31, 1985, the skies over the southern suburbs of the small city of 45,000, 100 kilometres north of Toronto, turned an eerie black-green colour. Children playing after school in neighbourhood backyards looked up in wonder as the skies above them darkened and the winds gathered force. Some began to make a dash for home. Mothers busily preparing dinner dropped what they were doing and worried about the whereabouts of their families. But there was no way anyone could protect themselves against what was to strike within seconds. Nine-year-old Jonathan Peochman was at a favourite fishing hole with his buddies. As the tornado approached he jumped on his bike and began pedalling for home. He never arrived. Bill Vandebergt was standing next to his 25-year-old son David at the door of a tire retreading factory when the tornado struck. Seconds later, Vandebergt regained consciousness to find his factory demolished and his son dead; David had been picked up and carried 300 metres in a hail of rubble by the winds. The scenes of tragedy were replayed across the area as the tornado's winds ripped up trees, tossed cars and trucks in mangled heaps and obliterated homes and factories. Barrie was one of about a dozen small Ontario communities that lay in the path of three separate storms, each containing a pack of twisters with winds up to 500 kilometres per hour, that cut a 50-kilometre-wide swath of destruction that spring day. When it was all over there were 12 dead, between 400 and 500 injured, 300 houses destroyed, thousands homeless and 20,000 people without electricity. The total cost of the material damage was about $150 million. It was the worst natural disaster in the province since Hurricane Hazel struck in 1954.

In Toronto, Edward Chick, vice-president of claims for Royal Insurance, first heard of the devastation on news reports on Friday evening. He knew immediately that the company had to put its Emergency Response Plan, prepared in advance for such disasters, into action. By 8:00 A.M. on Saturday morning, Chick was in his office in downtown Toronto. First, he notified other Royal executives that he had declared a state of emergency. Then, following the sequence of steps laid out in a Royal manual, he called regional managers in Hamilton and Toronto and two head office claims executives to enlist their help in getting emergency staff on the scene. After about 60 fruitless phone calls, he was able to contact Ontario centre manager Phillip Bellinger, who lived in Barrie. Bellinger, in turn, was able to reach Barrie agent Bob Sarjeant, who offered his office as headquarters for the Emergency Claims Centre. By Sunday afternoon, 11 Royal staffers were at the headquarters. Chick himself took a helicopter tour of the Barrie area to get an overview of the destruction. "I was horrified. It was staggering that there wasn't more loss of life," says Chick. Early on Monday morning Royal's claims staff were out in the rubble

assessing damaged homes, vehicles and businesses. The staff
was authorized to sign cheques for up to $15,000 on the spot
so residents could buy clothes and begin repairs on their
dwellings immediately. On the same day, full-page ads appeared in the Barrie *Examiner* and were played on local radio
stations, alerting insured people how to get in touch with
Royal. Similar emergency plans were put into action by the
roughly 20 other insurance companies with clients in the affected area. But Royal, beams Chick, "was the first company on
the spot."

In terms of damage, the tornado's rampage ranked ahead
of other famous recent disasters in insurance annals, including
a 1984 fire at the Syncrude plant in Fort McMurray, Alberta,
that will eventually cost insurers $100 million; and a 1979
hailstorm in Calgary that dented $1.6 million worth of mer-
chandise. After the Ontario tornadoes, insurance companies
were left with the tab for most of the $150 million in damage;
about 25 per cent of it was not covered by insurance, according to the Insurance Bureau of Canada. Royal alone received more than 1,000 claims for a total of about $10 million—
a distressing but unavoidable setback that came at a time
when the company itself was trying to get its balance sheet into
the black after losing $3.5 million (before tax) on its operations
in 1984.

Royal Insurance Canada, the largest general insurer in the
country, is one of the more than 200 foreign-owned companies that represent about two-thirds of the 314 property and
casualty insurers operating in Canada. Owned by London-
based Royal Insurance—a company with 95 subsidiaries and
22 associated companies in 80 countries around the world—
Royal has been operating in Canada since 1850.[2] It employs

---

[2] Royal likes to date its origins in Canada to 1833, since that is the year in which a
company that it took over in 1961, the Western/British America Group, began its
operations in Canada.

more than 2,000 people and has another 2,000 independent agents and brokers selling its wares, including auto, home, marine and commercial policies, across the country. For Royal and the rest of Canada's foreign-owned general insurers, 10 of which hold places in the list of the 15 largest general insurers, the country has been a pretty inhospitable place in recent years. During the past several years the entire industry—Canadian-owned and foreign-owned companies combined—has suffered underwriting losses. Only earnings from investments have kept most companies in the black. Royal is among a minority of companies that have suffered losses even after investment income was taken into account. Another is Zurich Canada—owned by the Swiss-based giant, Zurich Insurance Company—which suffered the ignominy of recording an overall loss of $1.5 million in 1984 and $5.6 million in 1985.

In terms of 1985 premium income, Royal regained the number one rank it had temporarily lost in 1983 and 1984 to The Co-operators Group Ltd. of Guelph, Ontario, a Canadian company owned by 35 co-operatives, credit union centrals, farm groups and other co-operative associations across Canada. At the end of 1985, Royal had $494 million in premium income (not counting reinsurance) compared to the $484 million in premiums taken in by The Co-operators.

In the past decade, the executives at Royal's downtown Toronto office building have been on a roller-coaster ride as their business expanded rapidly, and then shrank, savaged by the severity of the industry's business cycle and the vicious tactics of less conservative companies. Somewhat shell-shocked by recent developments and chastened by past mistakes, Royal's managers have adopted a more cautious attitude to both the volume and type of business they will write. More than anything, however, Royal's experience in Canada over the last ten years highlights the glaring flaws in the way the property and casualty industry operates and how little power any one company has to correct the situation.

The late-1970s were expansive years for Royal, partly because of Royal's position within the industry. Many of the other companies that had been chasing business aggressively by offering low premium rates to clients were now cutting back on business and recovering their equilibrium. This inevitable contraction after the binge gave large, stable companies like Royal the opportunity to move into the market, offering policies to a wide variety of clients who suddenly found it difficult to find coverage elsewhere. That is exactly what Royal did, beginning in 1976.

From a standing start in 1975, when premium income totalled $280 million, Royal increased its premium intake to $400 million in 1976 and $484 million in 1977. "It was a hell of a rate of growth," reflects Royal's executive vice-president Roy Elms. Directed by then-president Alan Horsford, who now runs Royal's London parent, the company operated under a philosophy of public service. While it did not take on bad or overly risky business, it did develop a wide-ranging book of business, from product liability to medical malpractice coverage, rather than concentrating on the cream—very low risk types of business such as coverage for office buildings. Royal's policy reflected its belief that insurance should be easily available to all sectors of the public. The public-spiritedness of Horsford, who arrived from Britain to take over as head of Canadian operations in 1974, was also reflected in a series of new programs designed to keep customers happy. The wording in policies was simplified to make them more understandable to clients. In 1976, an ombudsman program called Royal-Aide was introduced for personal lines customers; that is, customers with home or auto policies. Under Royal-Aide, the customer could appoint an expert "aide" at Royal's expense who would meet with a Royal representative to adjudicate a dispute over a claim. The decision of the two would be binding on both the client and the company.

The aim of all these activities was to boost Royal's market share, and it worked. Between 1975 and 1982, Royal's portion of the Canadian market jumped from 5 per cent to 9 per cent. "It was a euphoric period," says Elms. The company hired hundreds of new employees and busily opened up new branches across the country. By 1979, Horsford had passed the reins of Royal Canada on to Jean Robitaille, a Montreal-born dynamo who had joined Royal in 1951 as a trainee and quickly rose to become the branch manager in Quebec City, where he stayed for 19 years, expanding the operation dramatically. In 1974, Robitaille went to Toronto to become vice-president for marketing and development. The French Canadian from the rough streets of Mile End in Montreal obviously impressed Horsford with his tireless energy and outgoing personality. In 1976, Robitaille was made a senior vice-president and in 1978, he was made executive vice-president. When Horsford left for London in 1979 to take over as general manager of the world-wide operation (he later became the parent company's chief executive officer), Robitaille replaced him as president of the Canadian subsidiary.

But by the time Robitaille moved into the president's suite, Royal had already reached the top of its roller-coaster ride, and unbeknown to Robitaille or anyone else, it was about to start a downward plunge. The slide was not caused by the company itself so much as by the next severe cyclical slump that hit the industry as a whole. To their credit, Robitaille and other Royal executives realized by 1982 that the latest competitive binge of price cutting in the industry could not continue. Elms (who was acting as chief executive officer for the company in early 1986 because Robitaille was recuperating from an operation for throat cancer), shakes his head as he thinks back to the industry's state in the early 1980s. Royal knew that premium rates would have to be raised industry-wide if companies were to stay on a stable financial footing; that is, have enough money set aside in reserves to meet future claims from policyholders. "We perceived a need to increase prices based on our own observations and actuarial calculations," he says. "We thought we could lead the market up by increasing our premium rates." Royal did try to do that. The trouble was no other companies followed suit. "It's all very well to think of yourself as a leader," says Elms, "but to be a leader you've got to have followers. There were no followers."

For a time, the rest of the industry scoffed at Royal's predictions of trouble to come. Unforeseen circumstances intervened to postpone the day of reckoning that Royal was predicting. Elms notes that warm winters in the period kept claims in the all-important automobile insurance side of the business very low, which deluded many insurers into thinking their rate slashing to win new business could continue without consequence. But the delay only made the industry's premium rate increases, which began in 1985, more dramatic—and painful for everyone from day-care centres and car owners to municipalities and truckers, who suddenly found insurance very expensive or difficult to obtain.

Royal paid dearly for its foresight. Because it alone raised its rates in 1982, it forfeited market share to more aggressive competitors offering cheaper insurance. Royal's premium writings (revenues) plunged from $500 million in 1981 to $400 million in 1982. In the process, its share of the market shrank back to 5 per cent. According to Bryan Glendinning, Royal's vice-president of commercial lines, the trick to riding out the cycles in the insurance business is to be the first company into an upturn and the last company to slide into a downturn. Using that yardstick, Royal failed miserably in the latest down cycle. It led the pack down in terms of losing business because it made the "mistake" of trying to act responsibly and raise its rates. Royal was also very vulnerable to the latest downturn, notes Glendinning, because it is a multiline insurer that has tried to keep its brokers happy by taking most of the business they line up. "We've tried to be all things to all people," he says, noting that small companies that try to cream the market, taking only low-risk business, suffer less when a slump occurs because they don't have high claims to worry about.

Elms attributes much of the excessive price cutting in the industry to small companies that passed on most of their risk to international reinsurers. "Some companies have been nothing more than reinsurance brokers," he complains, noting that several small companies that failed in recent years fall into this category. "Because of their reliance on reinsurance they were not subject to the discipline of being a true risk taker, and as a result they went to the wall." Elms also criticizes the reinsurers for taking on so much business from that type of small operator. "There is no doubt that a lot of the blame rests at the feet of international reinsurers."

Since it stumbled in 1982, Royal has been trying to regain its balance with a program of drastic cost-cutting and reorganization. The overhaul was designed to restore profitability in the face of the sudden slump in business and, more generally, to transform Royal from a paternalistic operation into a more efficient one. Total staff numbers, which stood at a high of 3,720 employees in 1979, had been slashed back to about 2,000 by 1986. It was a trying period for both Robitaille and Elms, who had to wield the axe together. "It was as painful for Jean and me as it was for the people we let go," says Elms. He means it. Both Elms and Robitaille had spent most of their careers with Royal and they were products of its culture, which emphasized a cradle-to-grave approach in dealing with employees. Understandably, morale at the company plunged and has not recovered much since. Says Elms: "The transition from a paternalistic operation to a hard-nosed commercial operation was hard for the long-time employees to take." Even small measures, such as increasing the work week from 33¾ hours to 35 hours, caused grumbling in the staff.

The company reorganization also reduced the number of bureacratic levels in the operation. Fourteen of 19 district offices across the country were closed in 1984. Elms was particularly bothered when it fell on him to close down the Winnipeg branch, where he had worked as manager for many years. Company divisions were also reorganized, based on product line rather than on a branch/head office split. The position of vice-president for branches was abolished. Vice-president positions were created for each type of business, from personal lines to commercial risks. That means that the vice-president in charge of, say, personal lines, is responsible for the marketing, underwriting and ultimately the profits of that type of business across the country, and the branch managers report directly to him. The reorganization, says Glendinning, "has changed the corporate culture dramatically. There is more accountability. If anything goes wrong with the commercial lines division, for instance, it's quite easy to identify where the responsibility for it is. The buck stops with the vice-president."

Like most general insurers, Royal is pulling back from certain types of high-risk business. Since early 1985 it has refused to write medical malpractice policies. "Our results historically in the area have been horrendous," explains Glendinning. Royal is also reluctant to provide product liability coverage— for companies that transport hazardous chemicals, for example. Liability coverage in general is regarded with suspicion. "We're very restrictive in that area," says Glendinning. Chastened by its experience at bucking an industry trend—its attempt to lead the market in raising prices only led to trouble—Royal now seems content to batten down the hatches and ride out the storm.

### Life's Adversities

Foreign-controlled life insurance companies operating in Canada over the last 150 or so years have had a smoother road to travel. Ever since the first life insurer in Canada, Edinburgh-based Standard Life, began doing business in Quebec City in 1833, the foreign life insurers have cashed in on the same improving mortality rates and high profit margins that have bolstered the coffers of Canada's entire life insurance industry. On the debit side, they also suffered through economic down-turns such as the Great Depression and the rising claims brought on by two world wars, but those setbacks were hardly specific to Canada.

The most puzzling question is why foreign life insurance companies have not come to dominate the Canadian scene as their counterparts in the general insurance and reinsurance businesses have done. The reason for that, according to insur-ance historians, can be traced back to events in the late 1800s.

During the first two-thirds of the nineteenth century, the life insurance business in Canada was conducted almost exclu-sively by American and British companies, which had been founded decades before insurance became available in Can-ada. The first Canadian company, Canada Life, was established in 1847, but by 1869, it was still greatly outnumbered by the 23 foreign companies licensed to sell life insurance in Canada, and it had only 15 per cent of the total business in force. Then, during the 1870s, a clutch of Canadian companies sprang into being. They were Mutual Life (1870), Sun Life (1871) and London Life (1874).

The fact that these Canadian companies flourished despite the headstart of the foreign insurers is attributable to federal legislation such as the first Federal Insurance Act, which was passed in 1868. In large measure, this Act was designed to correct what legislators saw as an untenable situation: the for-eign companies could spirit policyholders' money out of Can-ada without keeping any assets in the country as security for future claims. The new Act changed all that. It required that all federally registered life insurance companies deposit $50,000 with the federal government. For foreign companies, the amount was increased to $100,000. All companies were also required, for the first time, to file annual financial statements with the minister of finance. Then, a few years later, the government decided that a $100,000 deposit was not enough. The major life companies had books of business worth many times that amount. Two new Acts, passed in 1875 and 1877, established the principle that foreign life insurers must maintain assets in Canada sufficient to meet their obligations to Canadian policyholders. Those companies, which had long regarded Canada as a gold mine, reacted with horror. About half of the two dozen foreign insurers stopped writing business in Canada. U.S. companies pulled out in droves. Nine of the 17 American-based insurers doing business in Canada closed up shop in 1868 alone. By 1873, four more had withdrawn. No similar flight of foreign general insurers occurred because the deposits required of them by the new law were much smaller. But the effect for Canadian life companies was dramatic. In "The Story of Foreign Activity in the Canadian Life Insurance Business," which appeared in a 1984 issue of the *Canadian Journal of Life Insurance*, the magazine's editor, Alastair Rickard, notes: "The reaction of the foreign insurance companies to the regulatory legislation of 1868, 1875 and 1877 constituted the most important factor in the subsequent burgeoning of Canadian life insurance companies, and the increase in their share of the life business."

From that point on, Canadian life insurers never looked back. By 1900, foreign companies accounted for only 29 per cent of the life insurance owned by Canadians. After rising marginally to 34 per cent in 1920, the foreign companies' share of the business slipped to 32 per cent in 1940, to 29 per cent in 1960 and to less than 15 per cent in 1984.

Today, 82 of the 169 life insurance companies in Canada are Canadian incorporated, 67 are American, 9 are British and 11 are from Continental Europe. Only 5 foreign-owned life insurance companies hold positions in the list of the industry's 15 largest companies ranked by assets (see Appendix). And even the largest foreign-owned insurer, Standard Life Assurance Co. of Montreal, with 1985 assets of $4.1 billion, is dwarfed by the largest Canadian company, Manufacturers Life, which had assets of $16.4 billion. The next two largest foreign-owned insurers are Metropolitan Life (with 1985 assets of $3.7 billion) and Prudential Insurance Co. of America (with 1985 assets of $2.9 billion).

The ten largest foreign-owned life insurers, mainly from the United States and the United Kingdom, have roughly $20 billion worth of assets in Canada, assets which are invested mostly in government bonds, mortgages, real estate and common shares. That is a substantial contribution to Canada's economic system. Equally important, some of the smaller foreign companies in particular have been responsible for adding much-needed competition to the Canadian insurance market. Almost every company in Canada now offers term insurance, universal life products and nonsmoker rates on policies that are as much as 50 per cent lower than the rates charged to smokers. Just seven years ago, most of these innovations were even rarer than good bargains in the Canadian life insurance industry. The companies that first introduced these overdue changes in spite of the protestations of the old-line insurers were foreign-owned mavericks. These same companies have also been among the first to modernize management methods in the industry. Among their ranks can be found companies like Maritime Life, National Life and Transamerica Life. All three are U.S. owned; all three have been able to seek out new business aggressively while relying on the financial backing of their large foreign parent.

### The Charge of the Life Brigade

Mahogany row is mainly empty these days. Just a year ago, the back-to back office suites that lead off the corridor, named for its rich brown mahogany walls, were occupied by various vice-presidents and other senior officers of the National Life Insurance Company. Today, most of the spacious aeries overlooking Toronto's University Avenue are vacant. In 1985, Ross Johnson, president of National, kicked all the executives downstairs or upstairs—wherever the staff of their various departments were located. "It's the only way they can really keep in touch with what is going on," remarks Johnson, a towering, grey-haired man with the build of a linebacker and the enthusiasm of a revivalist preacher.

Johnson, who became president of National in 1979 after New York Life fired him as manager of its Canadian operations, has a contagious good nature that has infected National Life from top to bottom. Giving a whirlwind tour of his headquarters, he hardly has time to explain the various operations to his guest as he exchanges robust greetings with employees at every turn in the hallways. From accounting and data processing staff to a busboy in the cafeteria, Johnson knows them all by name and he takes time to banter or joke with each one. This is not only a show put on for the interviewer. Rather than being surprised by the attention, the staff respond in kind, cracking jokes and generally carrying on with their boss in a casual manner, no matter what their rank. In one vacant meeting room, where a management improvement course for staff has broken off for lunch, cards bearing the first names of participants sit on the tables. Johnson takes one look at them and is able to identify which group of employees is attending the session. "Oh, it's junior-level managers," he says, identifying them from the approximately 500 employees who work at National's headquarters. This is management by walking around—the technique popularized by the best-seller, *In Search of Excellence*—to the $n$th degree. But Johnson clearly didn't get it from any book. It's in his blood.

Innovation has been the rule, not the exception, since Johnson took over the reins of National, which is owned by

New York-based Continental Corporation, a property and casualty insurer. His democratic management style has paid dividends in terms of company morale, earning National a place in *The 100 Best Companies to Work for in Canada*, published by *The Financial Post* in 1986. A carefully cultivated spirit of egalitarianism permeates the company. The little things help. Every month, departments that have made significant improvements in productivity are paid surprise visits by Johnson, who joins them for a coffee break. All senior executives, including Johnson, are expected to spend one day a year with an agent in the field. Every head office employee, including Johnson, is required to sell at least two life insurance policies a year (or at least give a licensed National agent two customer leads that result in sales). Pointing out that he sold six policies himself in 1985, Johnson declares: "We do this so no one forgets what business we are in."

New attitudes have been applied to the marketplace as well. National lays claim to being one of the first companies in Canada to introduce attractive, universal life policies, which pay near-current rates of interest, and offer maximum flexibility to policyholders. Johnson thinks very little of traditional whole life products. "We sell only a smidgen of them," he says, holding up his thumb and forefinger to illustrate the point.

Johnson is National's high-octane fuel. He won't rest until he has built National from one of the smallest operators on the Canadian scene into one of the largest. His strategy to achieve that involves trying to sell more new business every year than any of his competitors. In 1980, National sold $259 million worth of individual policies. By 1985, that figure had soared to $1.9 billion. In the same period National's group business in force increased from $5.4 billion to $9.9 billion. Total assets swelled from $690 million to more than $979 million, making National the eighteenth largest life insurance company in Canada. "We are the fastest-growing company in North America," claims Johnson.

The rapid expansion began in earnest in 1982. At that time, says Johnson, "a decision was made to either reduce head office staff and overhead or find additional sources of business." The company chose the latter course. The number of agents operating in branches across the country increased from 84 in 1980 to 222 in 1985. (During the same time period, the average annual income of branch agents went from $31,000 to $56,000.) The main reason for National's growth spurt, however, has been the business brought to the company by the PPI Financial, an insurance agency with 1,000 independent general agents operating from Montreal to Vancouver. Originally, in mid-1982, National signed an agency agreement with PPI's precursors, the Dickstein Insurance Agencies operating in Ontario and Quebec and James A. Burton Insurance Agencies of Winnipeg. In 1983 the two agencies merged and PPI, the resultant company, maintained the selling agreement with National. Johnson can be thankful for that. In 1985, PPI produced about 60 per cent of National's business.

Such rapid expansion involves enormous costs because of the up-front administrative expenses of selling new business and of hiring and training new agents. In 1980, the company had a profit of $6.4 million; in 1981, $5 million; and in 1982, $3 million. Then the company suffered a $1 million loss in 1984 which grew to a $7 million loss in 1985. (The large 1985 loss was caused in part by a writedown in the value of National's real estate assets in the western provinces.)

To Johnson, losses are an unavoidable consequence of trying to win a larger piece of the market. His goal, he says, is to be the largest insurer in Canada in terms of individual business in force. He thinks National has the products and the agents to do it. "We *are* the competition," he says, glowering. Still, Johnson admits that he had better start producing a profit pretty soon in order to keep his bosses at Continental Corporation happy. They will subsidize the company's operating losses for only so long. "We should be in the black next year," Johnson says. "Otherwise there may be some other grey-haired guy sitting in National's chief executive office."

### Maritime Life's Race to Beat the Wind

National Life is by no means the first insurer to launch an assault on the mainstream companies. No life company has sounder credentials as an iconoclast than Maritime Life of Halifax, which is the largest life insurance company based in the Atlantic provinces, and has been owned since 1969 by the Boston-based giant, John Hancock Mutual Life Insurance Co. Maritime's corporate symbol, proudly displayed in company literature, is the schooner *Bluenose*. An oil painting by Jack Gray of the famous Nova Scotian vessel in full sail hangs in the company boardroom. The painting depicts the *Bluenose* surging ahead over the sea, and for a time in the late 1970s, Maritime Life was very much like that. It set a blistering pace both in terms of sales and asset growth. Today, the company is still forging ahead at a good clip, but not at racing speed. There is a new, more cautious captain at the helm who knew enough to slow the vessel down before it foundered.

For decades after it was founded in 1924 by a group of Nova Scotia families, Maritime Life showed little sign that it would ever be much more than an also-ran in the industry, a reasonably profitable regional operation. True, it did make a concerted foray into the armed services market beginning after World War II, which quickly established it as the largest supplier of life insurance to Canada's armed forces at home and in Europe—a position it still holds today. This was accomplished mainly by hiring as agents Halifax soldiers and sailors, who then sold insurance to other military personnel. Otherwise, Maritime developed slowly and steadily as a regional company. Says company president and chief executive officer J. D. "Dick" Crawford: "It was a very traditional company in terms of products and the way it distributed them."

In 1948, after 25 years of existence, Maritime was still a small company with only $37 million worth of business in force. In the 1950s, the company ventured forth into other territories, setting up branches throughout the Maritimes and in Quebec and Ontario. By that time it also had well-established branches in Bermuda, Nassau and the West Indies. In the 1960s, Maritime Life grew rapidly, as did most companies in the industry during the economic boom of the time. But it was only when John Hancock bought Maritime in 1969 that the company set off on a course that was to rankle the entire life insurance industry.

John Hancock paid out $7 million for the small Halifax-based insurer that had about $30 million in assets. The deal seemed to satisfy all parties concerned. The U.S. company was looking for a toehold in the Canadian market and Maritime's major shareholders, who included Reuben Cohen and Leonard Ellen (better known as the owners of Halifax-based Central Trust) knew that Maritime needed more capital to expand. They were also insistent that any new owner should continue Maritime's business focus on the Atlantic region and retain its headquarters in Halifax. John Hancock fit the bill.

Between 1969 and 1985, John Hancock became Maritime's sugar daddy, pumping a total of $60 million in capital into the Halifax subsidiary. Maritime used the cash to finance an explosive period of growth. Between 1970 and 1979 alone, premium income from individual policies ballooned by 1,198 per cent and group insurance premium income increased by 2,450 per cent. By 1983, Maritime's assets had reached $1 billion, almost 2,000 per cent above the level reached ten years before.

The sea change at Maritime Life can be understood only when the company's character is taken into account. Executives and employees at Maritime have never really felt as if they were part of the industry fraternity. Says Ted Moffatt, director of marketing for individual life policies: "We don't have too much contact with the rest of the insurance people.

We are isolated geographically and to some extent by the way we operate."

That outsider mentality lay behind Maritime's decision in the early 1970s to design and launch a new kind of life insurance product called new money policies. They bore that name because, for the first time, they offered consumers current interest rates on the cash values in the policies. Launched in 1974 under then-president Orville Erickson, the new money policies were able to offer better rates of return for a simple reason. In traditional whole life policies the premium payments, face value and cash surrender value are determined by the mortality-rate and interest-rate assumptions prevailing at time of issue. The terms of a policy issued, say, in 1960 would be based on mortality rates at the time and on an actuary's conservative assessment of what the level of interest rates in the economy will be over the life of the policy. (A company wouldn't want to build in a 5 per cent annual rate of return on the policy's cash value if there was a possibility that the interest rate the company could earn on its investments in long-term bonds might fall below that level.) As was explained in Chapter 1, Maritime's new money policies were very different. They provided that every five years, the face value, premium level and rate of return on cash value could be updated based on the level of interest rates in the economy. Maritime was able to provide this flexibility because it invested the premiums in five-year mortgages, rather than long-term bonds. If, at the end of five years, interest rates had risen, the policyholder would receive added coverage at no extra cost. If they had fallen, the policyholder would have to increase his premium payments or else the face value of his policy would decrease.

The rest of the industry was variously appalled and frightened by the new type of policy, since it was so much more attractive than the tired old gruel they had been serving up for a century. The mainstream companies were particularly upset with Maritime's first new money policy, called a single premium whole life policy. It enabled a consumer to cash in an existing $100,000 whole life policy, for example, and then use the cash surrender value of, say, $8,000 to buy the Maritime new money policy, which had a much larger face value. Moreover, under the single premium plan, no further premium payments were required, while with the original policy, the consumer would have had to pay tens of thousands of dollars in premiums over the life of the policy. As interest rates rose in the late 1970s, consumers turned in droves to Maritime's new money policy, cashing in their less attractive policies and buying Maritime's products in order to take advantage of rising interest rates. The old-line companies were flummoxed at the thought of losing so much business, especially when other upstarts, including Vancouver-based North West Life Assurance Co. of Canada, a small Canadian company, brought out similar new money products. The larger companies didn't respond in kind at first (most have their own versions of new money policies today) because their large asset bases gave them less flexibility. They had billions of dollars invested in low-yielding, long-term bonds, which were falling in value as interest rates rose. (Bond prices always drop as interest rates rise.) The big companies wanted to stem, not encourage the rush by consumers to cash in their old policies because it threatened to erode their asset bases further. They were also quite happy with the tidy profits they were making on traditional policies that offered policyholders measly rates of return of 2 to 3 per cent.

Maritime had another factor working in its favour. Under president Michael Hepher, who succeeded Erickson in 1975, the company phased out its branch system and replaced it with the general agency system already common in the United States. Under the branch system the company is responsible for paying the costs of training the agent (who works exclusively for the company) and pays for his office and overhead. General agents, on the other hand, are independent business people who pay their own office overhead. Although they must be licensed with one company, they are free to sell the products of any company they choose. Maritime chose the general agency route because it was the only way it could expand quickly across the country without facing horrendous costs. Says Crawford: "Maritime could see the potential for rapid growth coming out of this new product line but the cost of building a traditional [branch] distribution system to carry that right across the country looked awesome." By January 1977, Maritime had moved exclusively to the general agency system. That change also brought recriminations from the mainstream companies. Insurers using the branch system regularly brand companies relying on general agencies as "prostitutes" because they do not have to incur the costs of training agents. The agents are always hired away from other companies that have already paid their training expenses.

Industry outrage mounted as Maritime's sales climbed. The headiest sales period was between 1979 and 1981, when interest rates peaked in the 22 per cent range. But the cat-calling didn't bother Maritime executives much. The president from 1979 to 1982 was the kind of man who liked to break taboos and do things differently. Ray MacEneaney was a man in a hurry, who had risen rapidly through Hancock's ranks in Boston. In 1979, at age 38, he was airlifted in to run the bustling Halifax subsidiary with a mandate to continue its expansion. An odd-ball actuary who sported a beard and wore cowboy boots, MacEneaney's efforts paid off in spades. Under his leadership, Maritime's assets surged from $350 million to $950 million when he left in 1982—and he didn't care if the rest of the industry didn't like the way the growth was accomplished.

By the time MacEneaney left to become a private consultant, however, Maritime's headlong rush had run into trouble. The first shoal to appear was the November 1981 federal budget which effectively killed Maritime's single premium whole life policy. Previously, the lump sum premium payment had been tax deductible; the budget made it taxable. Sales of the product, as well as those of certain annuities affected by the tax provisions, began an immediate nosedive. Maritime reacted by bringing out other new money policies without the single premium feature, but the damage was already done.

At the same time Maritime's spectacular growth rate had become impossible to sustain. Even with a general agency system, selling and administering a slew of new policies entails a lot of up-front costs. In 1981 alone, Hancock pumped $41 million into Maritime in order to keep its capital level up to acceptable standards in the view of the superintendent of insurance. Hancock may have been a good provider, but it wasn't a bottomless pit. Dick Crawford arrived at Maritime after 22 years with North American Life in Toronto, just in time to pick up the pieces. Says Crawford: "The Hancock had other expansion directions, so it was not as if we were the only people crying for more capital. Everybody knew that the kind of growth we had from 1979 to 1981 couldn't continue indefinitely."

A quiet-spoken actuary who likes to think of himself as a coach, rather than an autocrat, Crawford is nevertheless intent on continuing along Maritime's radical path. The company continues to refine and update its new money policies, he says, putting the needs of the consumer first. Crawford aims to expand Maritime—which ranked sixteenth in the industry by assets in 1985—at a more measured speed. "We want to grow at a pace that's faster than the industry but not as dramatically as before," he says. The old vessel is still in the race, but it's not in full sail.

### The Termites from Transamerica

The invasion came from California. In 1927, an agent of Occidental Life, later to be renamed Transamerica Occidental Life, arrived in Canada from the United States with a briefcase full of life insurance policy applications and a headful of heretical ideas. J. W. Miller was a devotee of term insurance, the product that Occidental had sold with great success to California farmers since its foundation in 1906. To Miller, term insurance was insurance as it was meant to be. In return for low premiums the customer bought straight protection for a fixed period of time. There were no bells and whistles attached, like the cash values in whole life policies which increased the cost of coverage. Miller's slogan was "Buy term and invest the difference." He reasoned that Canadian consumers, who for decades had only been offered whole life policies by insurance companies, would find his policies attractive. He was right. Today, Toronto-based Transamerica Life (which was named Occidental until 1984) sells insurance through 160 independent general agencies across the country and 12 branches located in major Canadian cities. But nearly 60 years after the company began business in Canada, its agents and executives are still a breed apart in the life insurance industry.

Miller was greeted with a hostile reaction from the entire Canadian insurance fraternity, and his successors in the field are getting the same cold shoulder today. Term insurance was really the first assault on the traditional ways of doing business in the insurance industry. The more it sold, the more other companies became upset. The problem was that customers could cash in their whole life policies, then use the cash surrender value of the policy to buy a much greater amount of term insurance. For the same premiums as a $5,000 whole life policy, a person could buy $50,000 worth of term. Term insurance eventually becomes more expensive than whole life as the policyholder advances in age, but if he invests the money saved by buying term, he won't need life insurance when he is 65 anyway. The old-line companies knew that the more popular term insurance became, the greater would be their problems as customers cashed in their whole life policies. With Miller's arrival, the first breath of real competition rustled through the Canadian insurance industry.

One of Miller's first disciples in Canada was Valeriam (Val) Taylor. In 1923, at age 14, Taylor arrived alone in Montreal on a cattle boat from his native Rumania. After working at various odd jobs, Taylor ran into Miller by sheer coincidence. In the early 1930s, the young immigrant was hitchhiking home to Toronto from Windsor, Ontario, where he had gone for an unsuccessful job interview he had obtained through a want ad. Miller gave him a ride and converted him to the insurance business. Taylor went on to open up an insurance business in Toronto in 1934 that is still thriving today under ownership of his daughter, Mary Lou Taylor. A striking blonde in her mid-forties Mary Lou recalls the travails of her late father. "He travelled all over the country preaching about term insurance," she says, "exposing what he called the thievery of the other policies." By 1969, Val Taylor's agency was servicing about 1,500 life insurance clients and had expanded into group and business insurance. But the rest of the industry treated him like a pariah for his insurance philosophy. Occidental agents came to be known as "termites."

Like father, like daughter. Mary Lou, who joined her father's agency in 1969 and took control of it in 1979 when her father retired, says she never sells whole life insurance because it is such a bad buy. Taylor concentrates on selling term, universal life and various products for business executives. The work is rewarding. In 1970, her second year in the business, she made about $75,000. She now runs an agency with a staff of five and more than 5,000 clients. "In a good year," she says, "it's easy to gross $250,000 in commissions." Her conclusion: selling good products honestly pays off, even if it makes you unpopular with agents from more traditional companies.

Sam Parsons spent 16 years selling term insurance for Transamerica before being promoted to vice-president of marketing in 1985. He still remembers the cool reception he received from competing agents when he moved to Simcoe, Ontario, in 1970 to set up an agency. "When I arrived the other agents in town got together and had a meeting," he recalls. "Then two of them came around to my house and told me I wasn't wanted in town, that there were too many agents already in Simcoe." Parson ignored the threat and went on to make a killing selling term insurance. The secret to his success, he says, was that he not only advised clients to buy term and invest the difference; he also gave them some good ideas on how they could invest their money wisely. Since Parsons also sold the products of 15 trust companies, he could simply pull out a selection of guaranteed investment certificates and place them on the kitchen table for the client to choose from.

Term insurance, of course, is now offered by most companies in Canada, although many don't push it because its low premiums make it less lucrative for the company than whole life. But Transamerica has continued its innovative ways, not only in designing new policies, but also in introducing new management techniques. The pace of change has been maintained under James Roszak, an American who was parachuted into the Canadian operation from California in 1980 and took over as president in 1982. Roszak, 44, and his vice-president of corporate services, Bob Hansen, have reorganized the 350 people who work at head office into work groups similar to the quality circles made famous by Japanese companies. "In the old days," says Hansen, "work was carried out in an assembly line fashion. If a policy application came into the company, each person would do a particular thing to it and pass it on to another department." Under the new system, each worker handles a task from start to finish. A given group of head office staff, for instance, handles all aspects of the business flowing in from one agency in the field. Likewise, a single team in the data processing department would do all the processing work for another department in the company. "Work groups increase productivity. People can relate to the whole job," says Hansen. The company even coined a new word as a slogan for the productivity campaign. Says Roszak: "We call it 'effectency,' a combination of effectiveness and efficiency."

There has also been a host of new policy offerings at Transamerica. The company was among the first to introduce non-smokers' rates and a universal life policy. Until the early 1980s, says Roszak, 90 per cent of Transamerica's sales were in term insurance. But in 1985, universal life accounted for 40 per cent of the company's annual sales. According to Hansen, universal life is not really a departure in philosophy for the company. He points out that when a customer buys universal life, part of the premium buys straight protection, just like term insurance. The rest of the premium is invested by the company for the client at current interest rates. Sales of universal life have helped boost the company's annual premium income up fourfold, from $6 million in 1980 to $22 million in 1985.

Roszak, a tightly wound business school graduate who rose up through the parent company's administrative ranks, sees his main job as keeping the company prepared for the future. "We have to know how to adapt," he says, "to anticipate what will come next in the marketplace." J. W. Miller would be pleased.

### A Two-Way Street

Foreign control of financial institutions, whether they be insurance companies or banks, trust firms or investment dealers, has always been a controversial subject in Canada. Several federal government royal commissions have addressed the subject, with differing conclusions. In 1955, the Royal Commission on Canada's Economic Prospects took a dim view of foreign investment in Canada's financial sector. Chaired by economist Walter Gordon, who subsequently became a Liberal finance minister, the Commission declared: "We believe it to be most important that Canadian control be maintained of our financial institutions—the chartered banks and life insurance companies which are incorporated in Canada."

That nationalistic stance contrasted with the recommendations of the 1961 Porter Commission on Banking and Finance.

Stated the report: "The Canadian insurance industry is more international than most sectors of our financial system...its international character brings increased competition and new techniques to the Canadian insurance market." To be sure, the operating techniques of the foreign general insurers carrying on business in Canada have left a lot to be desired, but foreign-controlled life insurers have brought welcome innovations and competition. Overall, foreign insurers have made a valuable contribution to the Canadian economy, whether through the creation of jobs or investments in bonds, shares and real estate. They are welcome guests, even if the general insurers have had bad manners at times.

Nevertheless, foreign life insurers face restrictions on their lending and investment powers in Canada, a problem not shared by Canadian companies operating in foreign jurisdictions. Federal restrictions also prevent Canada's (stock) life insurance companies from falling into the hands of foreign investors. No individual nonresident is permitted to own more than 10 per cent of a Canadian life insurance company. Likewise, a group of nonresidents cannot own more than a total of 25 per cent of a Canadian insurer. The entire Canadian life insurance industry, Canadian-controlled and foreign-controlled companies alike, opposes these discriminatory regulations, since Canadian insurers would be loath to face similar controls abroad. Their position is a valid one. As financial markets become increasingly international in nature, there is no need for the Canadian insurance industry to have special protection from foreign interlopers. After all, the Canadian insurance industry as a whole collects 55 per cent of its income from outside Canada.

# PART V

*Running around the Regulators*

# CHAPTER 11

## The General Insurance Crisis: Authors of Their Own Misfortune

LIFE, IN ANY NORMAL sense of the word, came to an end for Brian Lindal on May 18, 1975. The young man from Delta, British Columbia, was out for a car ride with his brother, Ken, on a local road when tragedy struck. Ken, who was driving the automobile, lost control of it and slammed into a telephone post. Brian was severely injured. He lay comatose in a hosptial for three months and when he eventually did regain consciousness, he faced a future that left him wondering whether he was better off alive or dead. Extensive brain damage suffered during the accident had rendered him quadraplegic, unable to control the muscles of his arms and legs, and afflicted by a severe speech impairment and uncontrollable muscle spasms. To gain compensation for his suffering and loss of income, Brian sued his brother, who was covered by insurance. The B. C. court judgement, on April 1978, was reasonably satisfying for Brian. He was awarded $135,000 for *nonpecuniary* damages (pain and suffering, and loss of the amenities of life).

But the insurance company representing Ken was dissatisfied. It appealed the $135,000 award before the B. C. Court of

Appeal, pointing to previous Supreme Court of Canada rulings that placed a $100,000 upper limit on awards for non-pecuniary damages.[1] The appeal was upheld in 1980 and the award was reduced to $100,000. Later, in 1981, the case went before the Supreme Court of Canada, which agreed with the appeal court's ruling.

The case of Brian Lindal, which reaffirmed the justice system's refusal to award more than $100,000 to accident victims for pain and suffering,[2] is rarely, if ever, cited by the insurance industry in its uproar about the impact of high court awards on insurance rates. The reason is simple. The existence of the cap undermines the industry's case that an increase in the frequency and size of awards by North American courts is largely to blame for the worldwide insurance crisis that erupted late in 1985.

In a formidable public relations campaign that expertly exploited the often poorly informed and gullible media, the industry managed to focus the public's attention on the legal system—money-hungry lawyers, naive judges, and misled juries—as the cause of the crisis, which saw premium rates soar. Clients, from day-care centres to municipalities, could no longer afford coverage, general insurance companies failed or barely staved off insolvency, and reinsurers refused to provide coverage for whole categories of risks. As evidence of their case against the legal system, the insurers cited what they called the absurd awards for *general* damages, such as loss of income and the cost of health care, which the courts have handed out to victims of accidents or medical malpractice. Jack Lyndon,

[1] The Supreme Court of Canada established the $100,000 limit in three judgements delivered on January 19, 1978. Lawyers refer to this precedent-setting group of cases, all of which involved severely injured accident victims, as the "trilogy." To the chagrin of the insurance industry, the trilogy decisions also established that a seriously injured plaintiff who will never work again is entitled to full costs for both his future care and loss of income; that is, for general damages.

[2] Since 1981, the court-imposed limit has been increased to about $184,000 to reflect inflation.

president of the Insurance Bureau of Canada, an industry lobby group, argues that the large court awards reflect an overly generous attitude on the part of society at large. "Society has been expecting too much," he says. "The womb to tomb philosophy has a very big price-tag."

The awards cited by the industry have an impressive ring to them. Many of them, if not most, are in the million-dollar range. Nevertheless, the frequency of settlements has increased marginally in recent years, and their size has increased hardly at all after inflation is taken into account. Furthermore, the awards are not determined in a fit of whimsy by judges or juries; they are based on generally reasonable calculations of the future financial losses that the victim will incur as a result of his or her injury. There is no denying that panic gripped the industry in 1985 and 1986, and the availability of insurance shrank dramatically worldwide. But when insurance companies try to lay blame for company insolvencies and soaring premium rates, they would do well to look to themselves— they are the authors of their own misfortune and of the misfortune of the insurance-buying public.

### Hoodwinking the Media

The scare began in the United States, when a flurry of large court awards in product liability, personal injury and professional malpractice suits brought cries of woe from the insurance industry. Like Henny Penny, the giant insurers ran about telling everyone who would listen that the sky was falling. A continuation of the trend toward ridiculously high court awards, they said, would bankrupt the insurance industry. The major media outlets picked up the alarmist refrain and replayed it for the public. A July 1985 article in *Forbes*, the respected business magazine, was headlined "A World without Insurance?" Warned the writer: "The open season on insurance companies in courtrooms all over the country has gone on so long that the insurers can no longer afford to play." Other major media helped whip up a crisis atmosphere. *Newsweek* proclaimed "Malpractice Insurers are Ill"; the *New York Times* warned that the insurance industry was "overwhelmed by lawsuits and huge awards."

Eventually, the Canadian media joined in. *Maclean's*, the national newsmagazine, laid the blame for the insurance crisis and soaring premiums at the door of the court system in a fall 1986 story. Stated the article: "As insurance companies struggle to cope with an increasing number of claims, escalating settlements, and decreased profits...the shortfall is being passed on to consumers." A headline in the *Toronto Star* screamed "Medical malpractice suits and awards climbing." *The Globe and Mail* joined the fray with an amusing but alarming story on seemingly nonsensical court awards in the United States entitled "Love to sue."

To be sure, some of the settlements sounded ridiculous. Many of those that sounded ludicrous were recycled in hundreds of different newspapers, magazines and televisions shows. The trouble was, the journalists didn't bother to take a closer look at the lawsuits to see if the awards were justified. The idea that court awards were rising to absurd and perilously high levels in the United States and to a lesser extent in Canada, was consumed by the media with very little proper analysis.

One of the timeless traits of journalists, of course, is that they can't resist a good tale. And over the last 24 months, insurance executives and public relations people have fed the media an endless stream of irresistible horror stories. One story making the rounds went like this: A man entered the World's Strongest Man contest in California and hurt his knees while running with a refrigerator strapped to his back. He sued everybody in sight and was eventually awarded $1 million by a jury.

Presented so simply, with little elaboration on the circumstances, the award seems absurd. A closer examination of the facts of the case presents a different picture. To begin with, the incident was already eight years old in 1985 when *Forbes* and other publications used it to illustrate the current insurance crisis. The injured party, Franco Columbo, was a world champion body builder who had won the "Mr Olympia" contest in 1976. In 1977, he agreed to participate in a television show called *The World's Strongest Man*, which was to be aired on one of the largest U.S. television networks. The event was to include ten participants, all well known, who would compete in "off-beat" contests. One event was the refrigerator race, in which each contestant would walk or run 40 yards with a 400-pound refrigerator on his back. Before the event, each contestant was given a written contract guaranteeing that all the equipment had been tested for safety.

Columbo didn't get far in the refrigerator race. As he bent his knees, then leaned forward to take the weight of the appliance on his back, he collapsed, severely dislocating his knees. His injuries required extensive surgery. At the trial, the manufacturer of the equipment for the race admitted it had never been tested by anyone who had to run with it or, for that matter, by anyone of Columbo's size. (At five feet, six inches, Columbo was by far the shortest of the contestants.) The manufacturer's spokesman also said that he had told the film company producing the race that the race and the equipment were not safe. The film company was told to pay $1,036,760 to Columbo but settled with the victim for an even $1 million. Since the film company was not insured and paid the amount out of its own coffers, the insurance industry was not affected at all by the settlement. Columbo was no death-defying crackpot looking for headlines: he was a professional body builder participating in a high-profile, organized event.

The Columbo settlement is not the only example of oversimplification by the press. Warning of soaring court awards, several major publications in both Canada and the United

States publicized another absurd-sounding case. The story went that an overweight man in Pennsylvania who had a history of heart disease suffered a heart attack while trying to start a lawnmower. He sued Sears, the manufacturer, charging that too much force was required to yank the mower's pull rope. A jury awarded him $1.75 million. Told in such simple terms, the story made it seem as if the jury was made up of nut-cases determined to soak the big bad company for all it was worth. Not true. The victim, a 32-year-old medical doctor, had pulled the starting cord of his tractor lawnmower 15 times before he had a massive heart attack. The jury found that the product was defective because the cord was excessively hard to pull and the exhaust valve had a faulty clearance that did not meet the manufacturer's own specifications. As a result, the exhaust valve could not open enough to ease the pressure inside the engine cylinder during start-up.

Sears didn't pay the full award; it settled out of court for an undisclosed sum in return for dropping its appeal of the verdict. Even if the settlement was large, it wasn't part of a current crazed trend to high court awards, as many publications implied. The incident occurred in 1977.

The above instances are instructive because they demonstrate the ease with which dis-information can be spread by the insurance industry and the media. It is a matter of telling only some of the facts to make the desired impression on the public conscience. In general terms, the press has helped propagate the idea that court awards in the United States and, increasingly, in Canada, have soared out of all sensible proportion. Commenting on the overall legal climate, Art Despard, senior vice-president of Reed Stenhouse Ltd., says: "The legal system has not treated the insurance system fairly."

There is no denying that a number of high-profile awards have grabbed headlines and shocked insurance executives. Industry sources generally cite a March 1985 award by the Ontario Supreme Court as an example of why Ontario, in particular, is becoming the "California of the North." In this case, the court awarded $6.3 million to Michael McErlean. In 1977, at age 14, McErlean had been paralyzed while riding his trail bike on vacant city-owned land in Brampton, Ontario. He rounded a blind corner and collided with another rider. The boy was left paralyzed, incontinent and unable to speak. It should also be pointed out that he was found to be partially responsible for his accident and the award he received for damages was reduced by several million dollars to reflect that fact. The case is currently under appeal; not a penny has yet been paid by insurance companies.

In its scare campaign, the industry also refers to the $920,000 award handed out to Wayne Gershon, a Michigan man whose school teacher wife was killed on an Ontario highway when another vehicle crossed the median and collided with the Gershons' car. But in making the award, the court recognized that women are now important income earners in many families and that husbands should be compensated for the loss of the wife's income.

There is some truth to insurers' arguments that court decisions are interpreting insurance policies in ways that the companies never intended. In a number of instances, courts have been applying the so-called "doctrine of reasonable expectations." Put simply, it means that if there is ambiguity in an insurance contract, or if the buyer could reasonably expect that the policy gave him broader coverage than it actually did, the courts have often been ruling in the injured policyholder's favour. Take the example of an Ontario man, Mr Wigle, who was injured when his car was struck in a hit-and-run accident. In Ontario, many auto policies have an underinsured motorist clause which stipulates that if the policyholder has a collision with another driver who has no insurance, then the policyholder's own company has to pick up the tab for its client's damages up to a total of $1 million. In the Wigle case, the court invoked the doctrine of reasonable

expectations and ruled that Wigle was covered by the underinsured motorist clause because the driver who hit him fled
the scene. Insurance companies grimaced and cried foul.

For a few years, they continued screaming because Ontario
courts did seem to be interpreting the underinsured motorist
clause to mean that everybody from the grandparents to the
bereaved cousins of injured parties were entitled to awards of
up to $1 million. But more recent court decisions have been
more to the liking of insurers. The Ontario Court of Appeal
stopped the high-awards trend in 1985 when it ruled that
only $1 million in total could be handed out to a plaintiff
and his relatives. Insurers also breathed a sigh of relief in
1986 when an Ontario appeal court overturned a lower court
decision to award $400,000 to a man who had been injured
in an inner tube race down a snow-covered slope. The appeal court pointed out that the man had been drinking and
that the perils of the race "were abundantly self-evident...." In
short, the courts have not treated the insurance companies as
bottomless pits of money, as industry spokesmen suggest.

Members of the legal profession, from judges to lawyers,
bridle at the idea that it is irresponsible to award high levels
of compensation. Says Humphrey Waldock, president of the
Trial Lawyers Association of British Columbia (TLABC): "The
insurance industry is blaming the lawyers, juries and judges.
They are attributing blame where no blame exists. But the
awards are paid for the support of the seriously injured."
Justice Allen Linden, president of the Law Reform Commission of Canada, also points out that the courts are not in the
business of handing out money needlessly; it is given to people who are paraplegics, quadraplegics or brain damaged. As
Justice Linden told Peter Gzowski, host of CBC radio's *Morn-
ingside,* "The legal system is not being fooled or bamboozled
by a bunch of fraud artists. It is money meant to compensate
people for enormously serious injuries...it is being given
away after people have proved to a court that it is necessary

to keep the victim alive and functioning."[3] Lawyers also oppose insurance industry proposals that the courts should place a cap on awards for general damages. Adrian Charter, a Vancouver lawyer and member of the TLABC says that such a ceiling would only discriminate against victims who need the money most, and favour claimants with less serious injuries.

The industry points to high court awards as the reason why premium rates on insurance are skyrocketing for everyone. The increases range anywhere from 30 per cent for auto insurance in Ontario to 800 per cent for liability insurance in all provinces.

During 1986, tales of hardship proliferated in the press as insurers closed the vice on rates. People needing liability insurance were hit the hardest. Rolly Graham, an official with the Malton, Ontario, Softball Association was unable to find liability coverage for his 500-member organization after polling five insurers. Family Day Care Services, a Metro Toronto organization providing care for about 600 infants, was refused coverage by 23 insurance companies. When it finally found insurance, the new policy provided $1 million in liability coverage at a cost of $17,000 a year. And the day-care centre was left responsible for the first $2,500 of any claim.

Liability coverage for the directors and officers of corporations, called D&O coverage, also became scarce and costly. One major food company with assets of $100 million was spending $7,500 in 1983 for $5 million worth of D&O coverage. In 1986, the bill increased to $20,000.

Still, insurers held firm to their conviction that such increases were overdue. Says Serge Lapalme, president of Gore Mutual Insurance Co. of Cambridge, Ontario: "The consumer is going to have to realize that insurance is not going

---

[3]Justice Linden, on leave from the Ontario Supreme Court, argues in fact that most injured Canadians are undercompensated in liability cases. He has proposed that Ottawa should establish a royal commission to study the possible establishment of a national, government-operated injury compensation plan.

to be cheap anymore." Explaining soaring auto insurance rates, Cliff Fraser, vice-president of Toronto-based State Farm Insurance, says: "The motoring public is going to have to pay. But they should not get mad at us [the insurers]." The problem, says Fraser, is that "the courts have gone off their rockers and we are losing our shirts."

To back up their arguments, insurance lobby groups eagerly provide the press with figures showing their enormous annual underwriting losses—the amount by which claims surpass premium income each year. From 1970 to 1983, the Canadian industry had total underwriting losses of $3.1 billion. This regularly elicits a lot of sympathetic headlines. In fact, however, the true profit picture of general insurers only emerges when their income from investments is also taken into account. In the same period, the industry also earned investment income of $7.3 billion, enough to keep its members solidly in the black. In 1985, despite dire warnings that the industry as a whole might slip into the red even after investment income, its $1.3 billion underwriting loss was more than offset by $1.6 billion in investment income.

There is additional evidence that, despite all the furor created by the industry about rising claims, they have not been all that punishing to the companies' bottom lines. In 1974, total insurance claims amounted to $2.05 billion; by 1984 that figure was up to $6.4 billion. Taking into account the annual inflation rate, which was in the double-digit range for a time during that ten-year period, the rise is not breathtaking. In the United States, the source of the so-called shocking escalation in court awards, studies have also thrown cold water on the insurance industry's cries of alarm. A 1983 Rand Corporation study entitled *Designing Safer Products*, concluded that when inflation is taken into account, court awards were no higher than they were in 1960. In addition, the Association of Trial Lawyers of America (ATLA), a group which is trying to counter some of the bad publicity directed at lawyers by the insurance industry, has compiled some tell-tale numbers of its own. ATLA cites U.S. government statistics which show that the frequency of claims in the United States has increased by an annual rate of only 3.4 per cent in recent years. ATLA also points out that awards in medical malpractice suits, for instance, have not skyrocketed as the insurers claim. In fact, between 1981 and 1984, the average award in such cases increased by only 3.9 per cent each year. Indeed, the U.S. insurance industry's own figures show that since 1976, the cost of malpractice insurance has actually declined as a percentage of total health care costs in the United States.

### The Heart of the Matter

*"In far too many cases, people are being victimized by a giant industry facing a crisis of its own making."*
Conclusion of a bipartisan Joint Study Committee on Insurance Availability and Affordability for the state government of Washington (November 1985)

The primary cause of the insurance crisis lies in the undisciplined greed displayed by many general insurance companies in the 1982-1984 period. In a binge of competitive price cutting, most companies discarded wise accounting practices and fought like a school of voracious piranha for a piece of the action. As interest rates climbed into the 20 per cent range, the companies were caught up in a scramble for premium income, which they then invested at lucrative rates. "The competition was cut-throat and insane," says Humphrey Waldock. In the frenzy, premium rates were slashed to absurdly low levels to attract business. It didn't seem to matter if the companies shaved their premium rates to unprofitable levels and failed to set proper reserves aside to meet future claims because their burgeoning investment income would surely cover all their future liabilities and produce healthy profits to boot. In insurance industry jargon, this is called cash-flow underwriting. Says David Holbrook, the superintendent of insurance in British Columbia: "All the companies were doing it. The more conservative companies did it too, but to a lesser extent."

International reinsurance companies, which shared the risk on large policies in return for a share of the premium payments, got caught up in the scramble and, by so doing, increased the potential for calamity. Since the 1970s it had been common for small insurance companies to underwrite jumbo risks backed primarily by reinsurance rather than their own assets. Small companies with, say, only $5 million in capital (shareholders' equity) and surplus (retained earnings), began taking on policies in the $50 million to $100 million range and then spread the risk around to reinsurers. There were certainly plenty of takers for the business. About 400 reinsurance companies operate internationally, doing about $50 billion in business annually. By the 1980s, however, the system began to be abused. The small insurers began placing their business with reinsurers not licensed in Canada. The financial stability and reputation of many of these unlicensed reinsurers were questionable or simply unknown, since Canadian regulators had no access to their books. More problems arose when the reinsurance companies joined in the free-for-all for premium income. They, too, were lured by the huge profits possible by investing the funds at high interest rates. Worldwide insurance capacity, meaning the industry's ability to take on new business, seemed unlimited.

### Everybody Out of the Pool

By 1985, the fragile house of cards had come crashing down. When North American interest rates dropped to more normal levels, the international insurance industry could no longer count on the profits from investment income to bail it out of the liabilities it had taken on. Some reinsurance companies failed, or reneged on their obligations to small property and casualty companies, throwing them into bankruptcy. Many of the survivors found themselves perilously close to insolvency and took drastic action to shore up their balance sheets.

Against this backdrop, reinsurers were pushed into a state of apoplexy by a series of disasters that darkened their prospects still further. Among them: the $15-billion (U.S.) class-action suit launched against Union Carbide by the victims of the 1984 toxic gas leak in Bhopal, India; a catastrophe in which at least 1,757 people died and 300,000 more were injured. Then a series of grizzly airline crashes around the world clogged up the court systems with claims. 1985 was the worst year ever for airline crashes. As a result, the insurance industry is coping with claims for almost 2,000 deaths and more than $430 million (U.S.) in equipment damage. The crash of the Air India jet off the Irish coast in June 1985 could eventually trigger up to $1 billion in claims. There has also been a rash of smaller but still substantial insurance losses, such as the $100 million paid by the industry after the Ocean Ranger oil rig sank off the coast of Newfoundland in 1982 and the $180 million (U.S.) paid for two abortive satellite launches by the United States in 1984.

The insurers have also been nonplussed by product liability claims. In August 1982, Denver-based Manville Corp. filed for protection under Chapter 11 of U.S. bankruptcy laws after it was hit with 16,500 lawsuits demanding $12 billion for individuals injured by exposure to asbestos. At time of writing the company was still trying to reorganize and devise a scheme to pay at least part of the claims. When it does, the insurance industry will have to pick up the tab. The U.S. justice department estimates that total liabilities against the asbestos-producing industry could eventually reach $40 billion, as more people discover they have asbestosis or cancer.

Roughly 8,000 claims have been made so far against A. H. Robins Company, the maker of the Dalkon Shield, by women who allege the intrauterine device caused infertility, involuntary abortions and pelvic disease. The prospect of rising payouts from disasters and product liability claims like these made the insurance industry's situation worse. But they were not the root cause of the insurance crisis—the real culprits were greed and bad management on the part of the insurers.

Whatever the cause of their misfortune, reinsurers began taking harsh measures to regain stability. Rates were increased dramatically, and companies simply refused to take on certain types of business, particularly liability policies for companies engaged in activities with a high risk of lawsuits. The effects of the belt tightening are still being felt throughout the insurance world. It is this larger scenario that lies behind the difficulties truckers, bus companies and automobile owners, to name a few, are having in obtaining insurance at all, or at reasonable rates.

Some insurance company executives concede that the industry itself must bear a good deal of the responsibility for the crisis. Roy Elms, executive vice-president of Royal Insurance Canada, agrees that problems arose because too many companies were low-balling on premium rates. "The companies had access to very liberal and cheap reinsurance coverage," he says. "Now the chickens have come home to roost." Elms adds, however, that the reinsurers are now going too far in their efforts to cut back on business and screen out risky business. "They are overreacting to the situation," he says.

By 1987, the meteoric rises in premium rates being demanded by general insurance companies should put the industry back on stable footing. Their problem then will be explaining sky-high profits to a still-numbed public. The question is, however, can a similar convulsion, with its high cost to property and casualty companies and the insurance-buying public alike, be avoided in the future? Since the general insurance industry operates in a free-market system, it will always be subject to the cyclical swings of business. In part, however, that cycle's ups and downs are accentuated by the legislation governing insurance companies.

To ensure that insurance companies remain solvent, the governments in most countries impose guidelines on their operations. One important test of financial stability is the ratio between the company's surplus and the premiums it takes in. Typically, insurers are allowed to take on new business until their premiums equal three times their surplus. Premium income can break through that limit as long as the insurance company passes on some of the risk of the additional business to reinsurers.

The business cycle in insurance, as in most industries, is profit driven. As profits increase, the companies reinvest their earnings to reap still larger profits. New capital from stock market investors is attracted to the industry. Since the surplus and capital of the companies are increasing, government regulations permit them to take in more premiums from new business. Next, as the drive for new business gains momentum, a period of increasing competition sets in and rates are driven down. Profits are reduced and some companies experience losses. Finally, premium rates are increased to return the industry to the beginning of the cycle once again.

The industry went on this roller-coaster ride every six years between World War II and 1972. But in the early 1970s, the cycle seemed to go out of whack. A bust period that began in 1972 lasted until 1976, and then boom times set in again until 1978. Insurers hope that in 1985 they hit bottom in the current cycle. But there is no guarantee of that. There is no doubt that the latest cycle showed up huge cracks in the industry's carapace of respectability. The industry lost all sense of responsible business practice in its fever to reap the easy lucre to be made from investing the proceeds from premiums and leaving reserve funds low. This time around, lax attention by provincial and federal regulators permitted the companies to behave like wild speculators in search of wealth. As of mid-1986, general insurers were not required to hire professional property and casualty actuaries to calculate whether premiums and reserves set aside to meet future claims were set at realistic levels. Unless regulators take a closer look at property and casualty company books, and legislation is changed to require the general industry to use actuaries who are answerable to the government for a company's financial practices, the industry will continue to operate by the seat of its pants. And, as the most recent crisis has shown, it is the public that suffers the most as a result.

# CHAPTER 12

## *Company Collapses:*
## *A Watchdog without Teeth*

ROBERT HAMMOND, THE federal superintendent of insurance, stretches out his lanky frame in an armchair and heaves a heavy sigh. "In the old days," he says, "the superintendent of insurance was looked on as being next to God. It was a time when gentlemen were gentlemen, if you know what I mean. But those days are gone." The fact that the superintendent's job is no longer simple is written all over the 48-year-old bureaucrat's face. His youthful good looks are obscured by heavy bags that droop under bleary eyes, the result of sleepless nights and harrowing work schedules. "We are being looked at to death," he moans. "When things don't go well everybody starts looking at you." Hammond doesn't dispute, however, that the attention of the press, federal legislators and even the auditor general on the affairs of the Department of Insurance is warranted. The department is going through a major crisis that started in 1981 and has been getting worse ever since. Seven federally registered property and casualty insurers have failed in that time, several more have been rescued from a financial abyss by takeovers and

315

another batch of foreign-owned insurers have pulled up stakes and left the country rather than face further losses.[1] Prior to 1981 there had been only four failures in the industry: two in the 1880s, one in 1920 and one in 1967. By the 1980s, something had gone drastically wrong.

Theoretically, Hammond and his 37 full-time inspectors and actuaries are responsible for ensuring the solvency of the roughly 250 federally registered property and casualty insurers in Canada. Another 36 full-time employees watch over the financial stability of the life insurance industry. The trouble hasn't been a lack of regulatory manpower. It has been that Hammond and his predecessor, Richard Humphrys, who served as superintendent from 1964 to 1982, did too much watching and took too little decisive action as companies lurched toward insolvency. Reluctant to move in and wind companies up, they watched in frustration as insurers ignored or misinterpreted department directives and continued dubious management practices that alarmed the regulators. In some cases, the companies expanded too rapidly, in other cases they relied excessively on reinsurance agreements that worried Hammond's inspectors. Hammond is certainly right that the good old days are over for the superintendent. Unfortunately, he and his colleagues came to the realization about six years too late.

Hammond has spent his career with the department. He joined its actuarial ranks in 1963 after graduating in mathematics from Queen's University in Kingston, and served as

[1] The general insurance companies put on the auction block in 1985 alone included Pilot Insurance Co. of Toronto; Wausau Insurance Co. of Toronto; The Canadian Indemnity Co. of Winnipeg; and Fireman's Fund Insurance Co. of Canada. Foreign insurers that pulled out of Canada included the Dublin-based Insurance Corp. of Ireland, which closed its Canadian unit after failing to find a buyer, and the New York-based Ideal Mutual Insurance Company. After New York regulators placed Ideal Mutual in liquidation, the company's Canadian subsidiary was taken over by Hammond's department and is in the process of being wound up.

assistant superintendent from 1977 until 1982 when he moved into the top post. So far, his tenure as superintendent has been filled with one nightmare after another. Defending the department's actions as property and casualty and trust companies collapsed around the country, he points out that its inspectors recognized quickly that trouble was brewing at each of the failed companies. Says Hammond: "We didn't have any surprises. We knew there were some problems there. But it's what to do about the problems when you identify them." The dilemma over what action to take was caused in part by the outdated and grossly inadequate powers given the department in the Canadian and British Insurance Companies Act, which hasn't been substantially updated since 1932. But, arguably, it was also caused by the department's reluctance to move forcefully in dealing with developing crises.

### The Bubble That Burst

The phones rarely ring in the Toronto headquarters of Northumberland General Insurance Company. Rows of offices sit empty in the company's nineteenth-floor quarters in the Cadillac Fairview Tower. Occasionally, a glum-faced accountant in shirtsleeves pads down the beige-carpeted hallway clutching a sheaf of papers. Northumberland is being laid to rest; its affairs are being put in order by a team of experts from the accounting firm Coopers & Lybrand. It is a painful process for Peter Reeve, the 65-year-old owner of the company. Seated behind a massive wooden desk in his executive office and wearing a grey pin-striped suit that has obviously been a favourite for years, Reeve is a tragic figure. Beside the desk stands a three-foot-high, gleaming brass engine-room telegraph, which some boat captain used long ago to set the sailing speed of his vessel. The speeds printed on its large, round face range from stop to full-speed ahead. Reeve has it set on stop. The collapse of Northumberland in June 1985 has personally cost Reeve $24.5 million. The cost in terms of broken dreams is much higher. But Reeve is more sad than bitter about the series of missteps and bad luck that abruptly ended his scramble for the big time in the insurance business.

Northumberland was the centrepiece of a network of insurance companies that Reeve began assembling in the early 1970s. The tall, grey-haired businessman had decades of experience in the industry. Since graduating with a degree in commerce from the University of Manitoba in 1942, he had held increasingly senior positions with a number of companies, from Canadian Indemnity and the Insurance Company of North America to Marsh & McLennan, the world's largest broker. In 1971, Reeve struck out on his own, setting up Ivanhoe Insurance Managers (IIM) in Toronto, and began placing reinsurance business with Lloyd's of London. It wasn't long before Reeve began implementing more ambitious plans. In February 1975, IIM bought Northumberland from Empire Company Ltd., the corporate feifdom of Nova Scotia's Sobey family. At the time, Northumberland was losing money and had only $500,000 in equity.

Northumberland then began a period of growth, specializing in property commercial lines and later in specialty lines such as satellites and oil rigs, as well as in some personal lines—mainly auto insurance in Quebec. But Reeve also wanted to expand in the United States. "The Canadian business was so competitive," he says, "we thought we would be better off doing business in the United States." To do so, he spent 13 months in Bermuda and in 1977 created Ivanhoe International Limited (IIL), a management company, responsible for developing the group's U.S. business. The Bermuda company, in turn, owned and managed two insurance companies in the island tax haven, including the Southampton Insurance Company. Initially, Southampton was not licensed to do business in the United States but Northumberland was. So the two companies worked out a deal in which

Northumberland sold policies in the United States and passed 100 per cent of the risk—and the premiums—on to Southampton, a reinsurer. Northumberland received a fronting fee of about $50,000 every three months from the Bermuda company to cover Northumberland's business expenses and leave it with a profit. Reeve then added an intermediary to the relationship. He made arrangements with a New York company, Haddon S. Fraser Associates Ltd., to sell Northumberland's policies in the United States and serve as U.S. claims manager for Northumberland, Southampton and the other companies in the fast-expanding Ivanhoe Insurance Group.[2] Reeve had the pieces of his mini-empire in place. But it was soon to fall victim to a series of mistakes, undisciplined over-expansion in the United States, a punishing rise in claims and just plain bad luck.

Reeve was by no means perceived as a shady character by the Department of Insurance. After all, he had turned Northumberland into a profitable operation despite a downturn in the insurance business. In fact, when Ottawa-based Strathcona Insurance collapsed in 1981, the regulators turned to Reeve to help sort out the ensuing mess. Between 1981 and 1983, Northumberland acted as an agent for the department, collecting about $35 million in reinsurance funds, which enabled Strathcona's policyholders and creditors to be paid in full. Still, beginning in 1982, the regulators in Ottawa became worried about certain aspects of the Ivanhoe Insurance Group's operations. Hammond's inspectors were troubled initially because Northumberland was ceding part of the business it wrote to the Southampton reinsurance company, which was

---

[2] At the time, the group included Wellington Insurance Managers Limited and Shamrock Insurance Company Limited, both of Bermuda. In 1983, Haddon S. Fraser was merged with Northumberland. Also in 1983, Northumberland acquired York Fire & Casualty Insurance Company, an Ontario personal lines insurer which, after Northumberland's collapse in 1985, was sold to Toronto-based Kempton Investments Ltd.

not registered in Canada and therefore not subject to federal
scrutiny. Hammond had no evidence that Southampton was
unsound or unreliable, but the relationship bothered him. "It
was not arm's-length," he complains, "so you don't have that
second independent look at the quality of business." Reeve
counters that Hammond's concern was unfounded. "Each company dealt with other companies within the Group on an
arm's-length basis," he says.

Nevertheless, Northumberland was asked by the Department of Insurance to hold back the reinsurance company's
share of the premiums. Explains Hammond: "We were concerned about the adequacy of its claims reserves and the security of the reinsurance provided by the reinsurer [Southamp-
ton]." According to Hammond, his officials discovered that
Northumberland wasn't following this directive. Says Hammond: "When it changed that procedure without consulting us
and contrary to our direction, we began to insist that they
[Southampton] put up letters of credit."

But the situation grew more serious as Northumberland
expanded rapidly in the United States, passing most of the risk
on to reinsurance companies. At the end of 1982, Northumberland had taken in only about $8 million in annual premiums
from its U.S. business. In 1983, it wrote $28.9 million of pre-
miums in the country and in 1984, $131 million. The Ottawa
regulators were alarmed because the company didn't seem to
have proper control over its U.S. business, which was being
carried on by Haddon S. Fraser Associates. Concedes Robert
Webber, president of Northumberland for about two years
before its collapse: "The U.S. branch reported directly to the
board of directors of the Ivanhoe Insurance Group. This is
where the problems developed." Says Hammond: "The company's accounting and record-keeping systems were inadequate... Their U.S. operation got out of control."

In March 1984, when Northumberland's licence came up
for renewal, Hammond renewed it for only a limited period so

that the department could make sure the company complied with its requests that it infuse more capital into the operation. "Our people were in and out of there on an almost weekly basis during 1984," says Hammond. In June, the regulators tried to clamp down on Northumberland's rapid growth. The company was directed to restrict its 1984 gross premiums to the same amount it had written in 1983. The directive came at an awkward time for Northumberland; by that stage it had already written 30 per cent more business than in 1983. Still, on the Canadian side, the company made an extraordinary effort to comply. Says Reeve: "By severely restricting writings in the last quarter of 1984, which was very damaging to Northumberland's reputation, we met this request."

A misunderstanding arose, however, over whether the restriction applied to the U.S. business written by Northumberland and passed on to reinsurers. According to the company, the New York manager did not understand that the restriction applied to business that was passed on to reinsurers. Indeed, in the past the regulators had always compared the net premiums of a company (minus reinsurance) against its equity to test its financial soundness. Moreover, the Ivanhoe Insurance Group as a whole had made solid profits in both 1983 and 1984—its capital and surplus totalled more than $20 million by that time—and viewed this as a solid basis to step up their U.S. business.

Still, the regulators were startled to find out that the surge in U.S. business continued. Recalls Hammond: "The company's records were chaotic in respect of the U.S. business so we sent our examiner down to their New York office. He came back and he was very concerned. He immediately got in touch with the New York authorities and it was evident at the time that they had written a considerable volume of business despite the restriction." Unimpressed by the company's explanation for the continued increase in business, Hammond put a further restriction on the company. In December 1984, he ordered it to stop writing business in the United States. In fact, Northumberland had already stopped writing new U.S. business of its own volition in November.

The regulators were also bothered by the fact that all of Northumberland's Canadian business was sold by its management company. Ivanhoe Insurance Managers (IIM) of Toronto brought in the business, collected the premiums, then passed them on to Northumberland. Hammond had no reason whatsoever to supsect that the management company was doing anything wrong with the premium funds before passing them on, but it irritated him in principle that he had no legal right to look at IIM's books. He points out, for example, that in such an arrangement, a management company could be putting the funds in short-term, high-risk investments that an insurance company is not permitted to invest in. Once again, Reeve counters that Hammond's concern was unwarranted, and points out that the relationship with IIM allowed Northumberland to raise extra capital to bolster its financial position.[3]

Northumberland's problems were increased by rising claims on its commercial business in both Canada and the United States. Accidents involving large claims seemed to come in a flurry. Testifying before the House of Commons Committee on Finance, Trade and Economic Affairs in 1985, Hammond pointed out that the claims included an explosion at a Mexican oil refinery and a fire at the Syncrude energy plant in Alberta. The company, said Hammond, had "a book of bad business," written at inadequate rates.

In fact, the Northumberland's energy business was mostly reinsured under an arrangement with a Lloyd's of London

---

[3]Reeve points out that IIM provided additional financing for Northumberland. For example, in 1982 IIM borrowed $4 million for Northumberland and purchased preferred shares in the insurance company for the same amount. The money is still in Northumberland and is part of the assets available to Northumberland's policyholders. Another advantage of the management company arrangement, says Reeve, is that it removed accounts receivable exposure on premium collections for Northumberland since IIM guaranteed the payments.

syndicate. As a result, Northumberland was left with a profit on its energy-related business, despite the large claims. The company was not so fortunate, however, when it came to other claims. Its U.S. manager had written a large book of business on satellites, which were not profitable for any company in the industry. There were also large losses on its automobile business.

The regulators continually pressed Northumberland's owners to inject more capital into the firm to put it back on sound footing. The owners complied, investing a further $2 million in 1984. But the end was looming for the company. Reeve blames the Department of Insurance for aggravating the company's problems. Says Reeve: "The arrival of insurance department personnel in both Toronto and New York meant a loss of credibility in the market and disrupted the work of accounting staff who were required to provide reams of information on past operations resulting in a loss of control of current operations." Between August 1984 and June 1985, he adds, "this loss of credibility and increasing pressure on accounting personnel finally overwhelmed them and the demise of the company became a self-fulfilling prophecy."

In March 1985, Northumberland failed to provide Hammond with annual audited financial statements for the previous year. The reason: unable to look at Southampton's books, the auditor could not be sure of the adequacy of the reserves that were maintained on business reinsured for Northumberland. Anxious to save the Northumberland from liquidation, Reeve talked to several investors who expressed interest in buying into the company. In February, one prospective partner emerged who was willing to inject about $15 million into the firm. But that deal fell through when Northumberland's auditor kept delaying the release of audited financial statements, citing problems in the New York and Bermuda operations. The same delays scared away several other investors. As the situation worsened, major brokers in the insurance community informed Reeve that they would no longer pass on business to Northumberland—a step that effectively put the company out of business. Reeve phoned Hammond to tell him the news. Then, in June 1985, Hammond recommended to the minister of state for finance, Barbara McDougall, that she direct him to take control of the company and apply for a court winding-up order. McDougall did so and Northumberland's high-wire act came to an ignominious end.

At the time of its demise, Northumberland faced about $100 million in liability claims and had assets of $123 million. The company needed an additional $15 million in capital to meet federal solvency tests. Hammond estimates that Northumberland's policyholders and claimants might eventually receive 50 cents on each dollar owed them.[4] By the end of 1985, the liquidation of Northumberland by Coopers & Lybrand, acting on Hammond's behalf, had cost $11 million, and the meter was still running in mid-1986. Most of the wind-up expenses will be paid by the general insurance industry as a group under a long-standing arrangement regarding company failures between the industry and the Department of Insurance.

Recalling the sequence of events, Hammond concedes that it might have been wise to take control of the company early in 1984. In July 1985, he told the house of Commons Standing Committee on Finance, Trade and Economic Affairs: "Maybe in hindsight, this company should have been put out of business in, say, the beginning of 1984."

For his part, Reeve has had plenty of time to consider his future. Despite his heavy losses in the Northumberland debacle, he still has a 350-acre cattle farm near Cobourg, Ontario, to repair to. But he doesn't plan to idle away the hours there in retirement. He thinks that he might put his knowledge of the business to work by investing in the new insurance exchange

---

[4]The preferred creditors in insurance company bankruptcies are claimants and policyholders who have outstanding unearned premiums (paid-up policies with coverage periods not yet used up).

planned for Toronto. In his view, the drought the entire industry experienced in recent years is over and there are big profits
to be made. At the end of the interview, he rises from behind
his desk, goes over to the engine-room telegraph and pushes it
defiantly to a forward position. "I'm mad as hell about being
out of the business," he mutters.

## A Road Well Travelled

The twists and turns on Northumberland's journey into obli-
vion were by no means new for officials at the Department of
Insurance. They had been in the same hostile terrain before—
three times in the previous five years. Two companies, Strathcona General Insurance Co. of Ottawa, and Pitts Insurance Co.
of London, Ontario, had failed in 1981. Cardinal Insurance
Co. of Toronto followed suit in 1982. Those collapses shared
common elements with the case of Northumberland: overly
rapid expansion, heavy reliance on reinsurers, soaring claims
and poor management.

The record of the regulators in dealing with the early failures is also blemished. Hammond concedes in retrospect that
the department was caught with insufficient legal powers and
inadequate expertise—and might have erred in not taking
stronger action in certain situations.

In the spring of 1981, Strathcona General Insurance Co. of
Ottawa was seized and wound up by the regulators. Strathcona
was caught up in the scramble for new business that dominated the period, and to handle the volume, it passed most of
the risk on to unlicensed reinsurers. In fact, it was retaining
only about 5 per cent of its business and ceding the rest to
reinsurers. Describing Strathcona's problems before the House
of Commons Standing Committee on Finance, Trade and Economic Affairs on June 12, 1985, Hammond testified: "...they
really did not have the incentive to write good quality business
because they were ceding most of it and making most of their

money on reinsurance commission." He added: "We believe the source of difficulties were inadequate capital and surplus, business written at inadequate rates; and the difficulty in recovering amounts due from reinsurers not licensed in Canada." Indeed, Strathcona was pushed to the brink when some of its reinsurers refused to pay up on claims. They alleged that Strathcona misrepresented certain aspects of the business when the treaties (reinsurance contracts) were drawn up. Looking back on the debacle, Hammond says that his department's solvency requirements should have included rules limiting the amount of business that a company can pass on to reinsurers that are unlicensed in Canada.

Strathcona was writing high-risk business at low rates, and some of its competitors complained to regulators about the practice. But according to Hammond, the department had difficulty cracking down on the practice. He told the committee: "A number of people complained to us that they were writing business at inadequate rates, and we did a number of checks. We would get a complaint that a rate quoted in respect of a particular commercial risk was unduly low. Then we would find out that some other company was offering the same rate. So we were in a difficult situation."

To deal with Strathcona's precarious state, the regulators put the company on a tight leash and insisted that it bolster its surplus and capital—and its shareholders complied, putting an additional $2 million into the company. But throughout the developing crisis, the department was hamstrung to a certain extent. It lacked the expertise to take a strong stand on the inadequacy of Strathcona's premium rates. When Hammond appeared before the House of Commons Committee in the summer of 1985, he was asked by Conservative MP Don Blenkarn, the Committee chairman, why department officials hadn't told Strathcona that it was impossible to make money on some of its business because of the low premium rates. In reply, Hammond pointed out that his department did not have property and casualty actuaries on staff who could have performed the duty. Said Hammond: "We do not pretend to be underwriting experts at the Department of Insurance, so it was difficult for us to say the premiums were not adequate." Fortunately, in the case of Strathcona, all outstanding claims were eventually paid off by a number of general insurers who voluntarily created a $4.5 million fund for the purpose. The policyholders and claimants in succeeding failures were not so lucky.

The uproar over Strathcona had barely subsided when the Department of Insurance found itself with another full-blown emergency on its hands. Even as Strathcona was inching its way off the precipice, Pitts Insurance Co. of London, Ontario, was being watched nervously by the regulators. Pitts was no upstart in the insurance business—it had been around since 1956 and had acquired an aura of soundness and respectability. But by 1980, that reputation had been undercut by financial difficulties. Today, its litany of troubles sounds strikingly similar to that of other failed insurers. The tragic difference in the case of Pitts was that, when it failed, the repercussions were felt especially severely by ordinary consumers with policies and claims rather than by commercial clients.

Pitts specialized in high-risk business, mainly nonstandard automobile and motorcycle policies. Like so many other insurers in the late 1970s and early 1980s, Pitts enjoyed a surge in business in the period, much of it written at highly competitive rates. In order to expand rapidly, the company relied on ceding risks to international reinsurance companies. But as investigators were to discover later, the cost to Pitts of acquiring and administering the business was greater than the reinsurance fees it received. Pitts had had a brush with insolvency in 1978, but on the direction of the Department of Insurance, Robert Trollope, the London entrepreneur who owned the company, injected the needed cash to correct the situation. By 1981, however, the situation had become much more serious. A number of circumstances had combined to deal Pitts a lethal blow. According to Hammond, the company not only had inadequate capital and reserves to support its business, which he considered poor quality, but it was also affected by the onset of an economic downturn and rising interest rates. As well, says Hammond, the company got caught in a mismatching of assets and liabilities because it had invested a high proportion of its assets in long-term, low-yielding government bonds. "They were stuck with low-rate bonds and they were having to cash them in to pay their claims," says Hammond. It did not help that First Atlantic, a Bermuda-based reinsurer also owned by Trollope, stopped making payments on liabilities it shared with Pitts.

Despite Pitts' gloomy situation, officials in Ottawa, who had been monthly visitors at Pitts since 1980, were reluctant to seize its assets. Throughout the early months of 1981, Pitts' licence was renewed on a monthly basis; the department resorted to the measure so government inspectors could keep a close watch on Pitts' finances. The company did not file an audited statement of its 1980 financial position until July, several months late. By that time, however, a white knight had appeared on the scene. John Ingle, a 41-year-old Mississauga businessman who had made himself a millionaire through real estate investments, had been looking to buy an insurance company since 1968. After months of talks with Trollope and officials from the Department of Insurance, Ingle settled on Pitts. On September 18, he struck a deal to buy the company. He put down a $500,000 deposit and agreed to invest a further $1 million. But within two weeks of taking over as owner of the company, Ingle decided he wanted his money back. In that time period, he says, he discoverd a financial mess that he considered hopeless. Costs incurred for such items as administration and agents' commissions took most of every dollar the company earned. And claims far outstripped the money left over.

Internal documents showed that the company lost $500,000 in July 1981 alone. Alarmed, Ingle alerted Ottawa on October 3 about what he had discovered. A few weeks later, on November 6, the superintendent was appointed to liquidate the firm. Ingle's deposit of $500,000 was frozen.

In an affidavit later filed in a Supreme Court of Ontario action to get his money back, Ingle alleged that for the 1980 financial year, insurance regulators allowed Pitts' management to substantially reduce the amount of reserves held for payment of claims, "with the result that the audited statement for the [1980] year-end shows the company to be insolvent." For its part, the department disputed that view and maintained that the company was solvent. Robert Trollope took the position that he never made any representations: "I made no warranty or guarantee on the position of the company."

Whether or not Ingle was misled by Department of Insurance officials about the condition of Pitts when he bought it remains a matter for the courts to decide. He said, "Pitts' problems go back at least three years and are related to ill-advised re-insurance arrangements in the overseas market that were bleeding the company to death." Ingle is suing the Department of Insurance for damages in the fiasco. Throughout, the Department has maintained that its assessment of Pitts' financial situation before its collapse was accurate and that an even closer scrutiny of Pitts' books would not have revealed a different picture. In an outstanding five-part series on Pitts in February 1982, London *Free Press* reporters Gordon Sanderson and Cheryl Hamilton quoted then-superintendent Richard Humphrys as saying: "I don't feel this...indicates our supervisory procedures are unsound or that our administration was inadequate." However, four years later, Humphrys' successor Robert Hammond conceded to the author: "I guess Pitts maybe should have been shut down in June rather than having it sold to Mr Ingle."

The effects of the Pitts collapse in terms of human suffering are difficult to measure. When the company closed, it had

80,000 policyholders across Canada, mainly with residential, automobile and motorcycle insurance policies. There were also about $20 million in unpaid claims. The claims did not merely involve bent bumpers or sprained wrists. Mark Morrison, a young man living in Englehart, Ontario, was covered by a Pitts policy when he suffered a broken back in a motorcycle accident at age 19. He was left paralysed from the chest down. When the receivers moved into Pitts, his weekly payments of $140 a week in permanent disability benefits stopped. In addition, $25,000 in rehabilitation expenses due from Pitts was put in jeopardy. Several months later, Morrison was fortunate enough to have 80 per cent of his payments reinstated by the receivers. He and nine other individuals who initially had their payments cut off were judged to be special hardship cases. All were paid out of Pitts' assets. Thousands of other people with claims for fire-destroyed homes or other accidents weren't so lucky. At the end of 1985, they had received only about 70 cents for each dollar in claims.

As if to prove the aphorism that bad luck comes in threes, another company failed amidst a flurry of newspaper headlines in 1982. Cardinal Insurance Company of Toronto followed Pitts and Strathcona into business history after it, too, became embroiled in a dispute with its reinsurers. Cardinal had been in business for only two years when it ran into problems with the Department of Insurance. It was incorporated in 1979 by Antony Mendez, a businessman who already owned insurance operations in Hong Kong and Great Britain. Mendez's new Canadian venture began writing high-risk business such as long-haul trucking, commercial fishing and municipal liability. Much of the risk was passed on to reinsurers. In 1980, for example, Cardinal reported $2.6 million in gross premium income, of which only $711,000 was retained on its own account. The rest was ceded to reinsurance companies. Such an arrangement is fine when business is booming and claims are reasonable. But Cardinal's arrangement with its re-insurers became strained when claims began to mount and the reinsurance companies found themselves saddled with them. Said Hammond: "There was a poor quality of business result-ing in heavy claims against the reinsurers, which I think had a significant impact on the reinsurers' decision to deny liability." (Reinsurers can deny claims on the basis that the insurance company they are doing business with failed to properly esti-mate the extent of future claims at the time that a treaty was signed.)

The morass that Cardinal found itself in involved a Quebec City-based reinsurer, Canadian Union, which was part of a 20-company reinsurance syndicate formed by the London-based brokerage firm of Stetzel Thomson and Co. Confusion developed over Canadian Union's responsibility for the risks that Cardinal ceded to the syndicate. Canadian Union was supposed to be responsible for only 4.2 per cent of the busi-ness taken on by the syndicate. But it was also operating as a representative company for the syndicate's Canadian business. As a result, the Department of Insurance ruled that Canadian Union was 100 per cent responsible for the Cardinal reinsur-ance. Because of this change in Canadian Union's solvency position, the department also rescinded its status as an approved reinsurer and requested that it create a $2.1 million trust fund to cover Cardinal's liabilities.

The situation deteriorated after Canadian Union, through Stetzel Thomson, asked the other syndicate members to pay their share, amounting to 95 per cent, of the $2.1 million payment. Stetzel demurred on the grounds that Canadian Union had represented itself as a licensed Canadian reinsurer.

Cardinal's fate was all but sealed when Canadian Union took the position that its reinsurance treaties with Cardinal were null and void because they allegedly contained irregu-larities and misleading information when they were written in early 1981. From the point of view of the regulators, the

reinsurance dispute made Cardinal's financial position untenable. Without the reinsurance, concluded the Department of
Insurance, Cardinal would be insolvent, with liabilities of
about $6.2 million and assets of only $4.7 million. In February
1982, the regulators took control of Cardinal's assets, stopped
the company from writing new business and applied for a
court winding-up order. After a bitter, five-month court battle
which went through the Federal Court of Appeals and the
Ontario Supreme Court, the winding-up order was granted. It
remains unclear whether Cardinal's claimants and policyholders
will recover the losses they suffered as a result of the company's collapse. That will depend on the outcome of ongoing
court actions in which the Department of Insurance, as Cardinal's liquidator, is trying to prove that the disputed reinsurance contracts are valid and, therefore, the reinsurers should
share in Cardinal's liabilities.

Once again, the Cardinal catastrophe underlined shortcomings in the way the Department of Insurance tried to do its
job. Testifying before the House of Commons Standing Committee on Finance, Trade and Economic Affairs on June 13,
1985, Hammond talked about the major lessons learned in the
Cardinal collapse. "In the past we used to concentrate on the
net position of the company, the net claims experience...the
Cardinal Insurance Company was doing reasonably well, net
of reinsurance. The problem was that the nature of the treaties
was such that the losses were being dumped on the reinsurers.
We realize now that we must pay attention to the gross experience of the company because the reinsurers—and this is
obvious—are not going to stand by and absorb those losses
...without limit."

Hammond was serving as deputy superintendant of insurance in 1979 when the department gave Cardinal a licence. He
now concedes that the department didn't dig deeply enough
into Mendez's background before it gave him the green light

to open the company. When Hammond appeared before the Commons Committee on Finance, Trade and Economic Affairs on June 13, 1985, MP Norman Warner, a former insurance man, put the following question to him: "When the Cardinal Insurance Company started operating in Canada, my Lloyd's of London broker, Robert Baril, advised me that the principal [Antony Mendez] had a very bad reputation and that it was quite possible I would be approached by Cardinal to represent them. He suggested quite strongly that I avoid doing business with them...At the time they [Cardinal] came to you, did you have any questions in the back of your mind about Mendez and his previous reputation?" In reply, Hammond pointed out that the department had originally turned down Mendez's overtures to have his Hong Kong and U.K.-based companies registered in Canada because they were judged to be too small. Undeterred, the persistent Mr Mendez became a Canadian citizen and lobbied hard with the department for permission to open a Canadian incorporated company. Then, after Mendez developed a proper business plan for the new company at the request of the department, it gave him the go-ahead. The department was reassured about Mendez's credentials by the major Canadian auditing firm that helped him develop the business plan. "To the best of my knowledge," testified Hammond, "we did not get these negative reports [about Mendez] until after the company was incorporated. Now, with hindsight, we are taking more precautions. If we were doing this today I would insist that we check with the U.K. authorities, the Hong Kong authorities. We would have asked for a police report. Often, unfortunately, people in the industry know something about companies or people but they are not usually willing to come forward. If they do come forward it is usually on the basis of some sort of rumour, nothing in writing." Ah, the benefit of hindsight.

## *Closing the Barn Door...*

In the wake of the failures of Strathcona, Pitts and Cardinal, officials at the Department of Insurance hurriedly reassessed their inspection techniques and the powers granted them by legislation. The collapses had made the inability of the department to perform its major task—overseeing the financial stability of the companies under its supervision—glaringly apparent. Always cautious about coming to conclusions without the advice of the companies it regulated, the department worked with representatives of the industry to arrive at a consensus on what changes should be made.

The record was pathetic. Companies had courted disaster by writing business at unprofitable rates and passed most of the risk on to reinsurance companies. In some cases the insurance companies had simply become fronting operations for the reinsurance market. Inspectors lacked the expertise to state categorically that the premiums charged by the companies were inadequate. Owners had misunderstood or blithely ignored department directives, arguably because the inspectors lacked penalties to give their orders weight. By law, the fines the department could impose on wrongdoers were limited to a meaningless level: from $20 to $5,000. In most cases, the department had allowed the debacles to drag on, ever hopeful that somehow the insurers would be able to stave off bankruptcy.

In 1982, Hammond put forward several proposals for change. They included raising the minimum capital and surplus requirements for a new property and casualty company from $1.5 million to $5 million; requiring that companies not cede more than 50 per cent of their business to reinsurers that are unregistered in Canada and therefore not supervised by the Department of Insurance; and establishing a guarantee fund for policyholders. Hammond put the package of proposals forward urging that the insurance legislation be amended accordingly as soon as possible. The Liberal government apparently did not share his sense of urgency. "For one reason or another," says Hammond, "the government didn't see fit to press the matter. We didn't get our so-called urgent amendments done and we didn't get the compensation plan done." Giving a half-hearted explanation for the government's dallying, Hammond points out that after the three failures, all seemed quiet on the insurance front and the government was preoccupied with other concerns. "There were a lot of other things going on," he says. "Remember, too, that we had this rash of failures…within a year and then we didn't have any others until Northumberland this past year at the federal level."

Since taking power in 1984, the Conservative party has pressed ahead with plans for major amendments to the legislation governing insurance companies—the Canadian and British Insurance Companies Act—as part of a wider overhaul of the country's financial laws. In the spring of 1986, Barbara McDougall, then the minister of state for finance, tabled legislation to beef up the solvency requirements for property and casualty insurers along the lines that Hammond proposed. More sweeping changes were put off until the fall of 1986 for inclusion in the wide-ranging reform package for financial services. At that time, the powers of federal regulators, whether they be wielded by a separate Department of Insurance or a new super-ministry with control over all sectors of the financial services industry (as proposed by the Blenkarn Committee), will be considerably strengthened. The regulators, says Hammond, will be given the power to issue cease and desist orders against a company to stop it from engaging in questionable practices. The financial penalties available to him will be increased. He will also have the power to prevent companies from doing business with unlicensed reinsurers of which he doesn't approve. Says Hammond: "I don't think we'd be enthusiastic about a company ceding business to some little two-bit Bermuda company that happened to be owned by the same owner."

According to Hammond, general insurance companies will be required, within a certain time period, to hire property and casualty actuaries. In each case, the actuary will be responsible for submitting reports to Ottawa endorsing the adequacy of the company's claims reserves. There are two types of claims reserves, both of which count as liabilities on a company's balance sheet. The first type is for claims that have already occurred. The second type, reserves for unearned premiums, is more ephemeral and subject to abuse. For example, a company might have a policy with six months of coverage left as of December 31. The policyholder has paid his premiums for the full coverage but the company has not "earned" half of them because it still "owes" the policyholder six months of coverage. The company therefore sets up a reserve equal to 50 per cent of the unearned premiums. This reserve is supposed to cover future claims. "That is fine," says Hammond, "as long as the premium is adequate. But if the premium isn't adequate there is a problem." Indeed there is. In the cost-cutting fever of the early 1980s most companies in the industry cut premium levels far too low in order to gain business, confident that they could remain afloat by investing premiums at the high returns then prevailing. When interest rates fell the gambit backfired.

The actuary's job will be to ensure that sufficient reserves for unearned premiums have been stored away. If they aren't, the company will be required to increase them, and that, in turn, says Hammond, will force the company to raise premium rates. Since there are only a few dozen property and casualty actuaries in Canada, Hammond will give the companies a transition period before they must have hired one as a full-time employee or on a consulting basis. Eventually, the presence of the actuaries should help to reduce pricing abuses and moderate the severity of the business cycles which periodically convulse the industry. Says Hammond: "It should have some impact, we *hope*."

## Signs of Danger in the Life Industry

The superintendent of insurance has traditionally not run into the same sort of troubles with the life insurance companies it oversees. Life insurance has always been a comfortable calling, cushioned by reserve estimates that have been overly conservative and profit margins that have been too high, from the consumer's point of view at least. Superintendents of insurance like to see fat profit margins in the industry. The regulators' mandate has been primarily to ensure the solvency of companies, rather than to protect consumer interests. (Insurance *policies* fall under the aegis of provincial regulators.) In short, while the property and casualty business has been guilty of suicidal price cutting, the life insurers have usually been guilty of just the opposite: charging consumers too much for outdated products.

The life industry never tires of pointing out that no federally registered life insurer has ever failed, although several provincially registered life insurers have failed in the past decade, including Paramount Life and Rocky Mountain Life, both of Alberta. Other companies, such as L'Économie and Les Prévoyants, have been rescued only through mergers with larger insurers in years past. Still, Hammond is pleased with the life insurance industry's record: "The Canadian companies have been well run," he says, "but partially it's the nature of the business, too. It has always had very large margins and it's been a long-term business. But the nature of the business is changing."

Hammond is referring, of course, to the new product mix offered by some life insurance companies. Old policies like whole life insurance provided a steady income stream to the company, and the money is then put into conservative, long-term investments. But policies like universal life, which pay current interest rates, require short-term investments with high yields. Hammond believes that the industry has to pay more attention to matching liabilities (policy obligations) and assets (investments). He has proposed that legislation be changed to reduce the amount of assets companies can invest in real estate, a long-term, high-risk field.

Occasionally, real competition and price cutting has even crept into the life industry. In 1985, Hammond became concerned because several companies were cutting premium rates on term insurance to levels that were too low. He told the House of Commons Standing Committee on Finance, Trade and Economic Affairs in June 1985: "…the rates were getting to a level that we became concerned about. We had some doubts about whether the moneys some of the companies were getting would be adequate to cover claims costs." Hammond directed the life insurance company actuaries to calculate the reserves set aside for the policies in question on a more conservative basis. (Life insurers, unlike general insurers, have been required to employ valuation actuaries since 1977, under an amendment to the Insurance Act.) Despite Hammond's January 1985 directive, however, many companies failed to comply when they filed their 1984 year-end statements early in March. Some companies complained that Hammond had not allowed them enough time to make the necessary adjustments to their statements. Others contended that his request was too drastic. Always ready to consult, Hammond referred the matter to the Canadian Institute of Actuaries for consideration.

Don Blenkarn, the chairman of the House of Commons Committee, was appalled. Said Blenkarn: "You made certain regulations and rules, and people who have licences did not comply with your requirements. It would seem to me they told you they could not be bothered replying. I do not think I would be very pleased about that if I were you." Replied Hammond: "Well, I am not particularly pleased, but I think in fairness to the profession, there are some people who may question our judgement as to whether or not we are going too far." To that, Blenkarn remarked: "It would seem to me that when they become the superintendent they can question the superintendent's judgement. But right now you are the super-intendent..."

Enhanced regulatory powers alone will not clean up the Augean stables of the insurance industry. That will require a new, tougher attitude toward rule benders and sleight-of-hand artists on the part of Ottawa. Legislative powers are meaningless without the will to wield them. For his part, Hammond appears to have modified his once-lenient attitude toward the industry he supervises. Says Hammond: "There is one thing that I've learned in this business. If you have doubts about a company and you think there is a problem, you are usually right. Things just don't click together and you're usually right. My conclusion is we should trust our gut reactions." As Hammond points out, gentlemen are no longer gentlemen in the insurance industry, and the players no longer look on the superintendent as God. But by the same token, the superintendent should act less like a patient gentleman, and more like a hard-nosed regulator.

# PART VI

*The Winds of Change*

# CHAPTER 13

## *Weeding an Overgrown Garden*

*"Power, like lightning, injures before its warning."*
Calderón: a 17th century Spanish dramatist

CANADA'S INSURANCE COMPANIES are key participants in the vast transformation of the nation's financial services industry that is currently taking place. More and more, marketing muscle and financial power are coalescing into a handful of conglomerates, most of which have life and general insurance companies as their central building blocks. The names of some of these emerging financial behemoths—Trilon, Power Financial and Crown Financial—are already household words to most Canadians and have made frequent appearances in this book. Lesser stars in the financial galaxy, like E-L Financial, Traders Group and The Laurentian Group have not entered the popular lexicon. Hardly a week goes by without a newspaper report that at least one of these conglomerates has added another life insurance company, general insurance company, trust company, real estate firm or mutual fund dealer to its stable of subsidiaries.

In seemingly ineluctable fashion, these new aggregates of economic power are taking their place beside the major chartered banks as powerbrokers in the financial arena. The large mutual insurance companies, such as Sun Life and Manufacturers Life, are itching to join the fray once federal laws that limit their ability to diversify are revised. Many shrewd observers of, and participants in, this process predict that within ten years, four or five major financial institutions will emerge as the dominant players in the marketplace—resulting in a sort of oligarchy of the most acquisitive.

Aware of the stakes involved, the four major types of financial institutions—the banks, trusts, investment dealers and insurance companies—have been poaching on each other's business territory, breaking down the barriers that once restricted them to specific categories of financial service. The immediate impact of all this jostling for position in the corporate sweepstakes has been an increase in competition among the so-called Four Pillars of finance. (Some observers call them, more appropriately, the Four Pastures.) But the danger in the long term is that this growing concentration of power will result in decreased competition and that the financial conglomerates will abuse their growing power in various ways. They could, for instance, carry out transactions between subsidiary companies that benefit their majority owners but are not in the best interest of minority shareholders. As Bernard Ghert, president of Cadillac Fairview Corporation, a Toronto-based real estate developer, warned in a 1986 speech to the Vancouver Board of Trade: "The greater the concentration of power...the greater the risk of abuse, either directly or through networks and spheres of influence in the business community."

That is the rather sobering scenario the federal Parliament must take into account in the fall of 1986 as it begins its overhaul of key legislation governing the financial system in Canada—specifically, the Canadian and British Insurance Companies Act and the separate laws governing trust and loan companies. In the case of insurers, the government must decide how far it should go in conceding to the companies' demands for greater powers to diversify into other financial services and product lines; it also has to determine what legislative and regulatory curbs should be in place to prevent abuses of corporate power. Festering problems in the insurance industry also need to be addressed—among them the shoddy business practices of general insurers that precipitated a string of company collapses and a nationwide insurance crisis. But not all of the insurance industry's flaws are fair game for federal legislators. Control over the design and marketing of policies and the regulation of agents fall within provincial jurisdiction. Arguably, however, the industry should act on its own initiative to improve the quality of both its products and its agents. The playing field is changing for insurance companies. This chapter will look at the new developments and put forward proposals for changes in the way the industry is regulated and the way it conducts its affairs.

### An International Phenomenon

The transformation of Canada's financial industry is by no means occurring in isolation. Financial conglomerates north of the 49th parallel are taking their cue from their much larger counterparts in the United States, such as American Express, Sears, Roebuck, BankAmerica and Prudential Insurance, which for years have chased the dream of achieving synergy by building multifaceted financial empires. In 1981 alone, these four companies swooped in to buy four of the biggest investment dealers on Wall Street. American Express acquired Shearson Lehman, Prudential bought the Bache Group, BankAmerica bought Charles Schwab & Co., the largest U.S. discount broker, and Sears, Roebuck bought Dean Witter. So far, the large U.S. conglomerates have experienced more growing pains and red ink than synergy in their attempts to build financial supermarkets. For example, American Express sold off control of Fireman's Fund, its money-losing general insurance subsidiary, in 1985; BankAmerica and Schwab are locked in management in-fighting; and Sears has yet to make a profit through its one-stop financial shopping centres. But that hasn't deterred some Canadian companies from following their lead.

What is more, the blurring of traditional divisions between the major types of financial institution is well advanced in several of the countries that are currently Canada's major trading partners. For example, in the United States, banks were allowed to engage in securities brokerage services for the first time in 1983. In the same year, South Dakota set a precedent by allowing state-chartered banks to engage in out-of-state insurance underwriting. Other states may follow suit. In Japan, banks have steadily encroached on the territory of investment dealers. Since 1983 banks in that country have been allowed to sell long-term bonds; soon they will be give the right to deal in short-term securities as well. And already they provide advice to firms that float new share issues, although investment dealers still do the actual underwriting (selling). In West Germany, there has never been any division between commercial banking and corporate securities underwriting. And there are no restrictions on the ownership of banks by non-bank firms. Since the early 1970s in the United Kingdom, banks have been allowed to underwrite securities and manage investment funds.

### The Rise and Fall of Canada's Four Pillars

In Canada, the distinctions between the activities of banks, insurance companies, trust firms and investment dealers evolved in a very random way over 100 years, and they have disintegrated in an equally haphazard fashion in the last decade.

When they first appeared in the early 1800s, Canada's chartered banks confined their activities to issuing notes (paper currency) and making short-term loans to businesses. When

the Bank of Canada was created in 1934, it took over the power
to issue currency from the chartered banks. But in succeeding
years, revisions to the Bank Act opened up other avenues of
business to those institutions. In 1954, the banks began making
consumer loans (an overdue concession to modern realities by
generally elitist bankers). And in 1967, they began offering
conventional mortgages. Until the 1980 revisions to the Bank
Act, the chartered banks also had the legal power to underwrite securities, although they usually left this activity to investment dealers. Ironically, the banks have been trying to get into
the securities business ever since they lost the right to do so in
1980. Both the Toronto-Dominion Bank and the Royal Bank of
Canada have created discount brokerage service subsidiaries
in co-operation with investment dealers. Staff at the banks'
discount operations take the clients' orders but, by law, the
actual trade must be carried out by licensed brokers at the
co-operating investment dealer.

But if the banks are encroaching on what is legally the
terrain of investment dealers, other institutions have also been
making raids on the banks' territory. In the late 1800s, Canada's
first trust companies were restricted to offering trustee services
and making mortgage loans. Laws were passed to prevent trust
companies from taking deposits in an attempt to separate the
trusts' activities from those of the banks. The attempt failed.
The fiduciary powers granted trust companies permitted them
to take in funds in the form of guaranteed investment certificates and trust accounts. So eventually legislators gave up trying
to keep trust companies out of the deposit-taking business.

Investment dealers have also spread their wings somewhat
since the early 1900s when they specialized in issuing government and corporate securities. In recent years, some investment dealers have begun offering cheque-writing privileges
and daily interest on their customers' accounts.

Life insurers, too, have forayed into the traditional deposit-
taking business of the banks. Insurers were originally confined

to selling life insurance at the time the first General Insurance Act was passed in the early 1900s (previously, insurers were governed individually by special Acts for each company), but they now do a booming business in deferred annuities, which pay interest and include withdrawal privileges.

Over the decades, then, the spheres of power carved out by the Four Pillars began to overlap, sometimes with the blessing of legislative change, sometimes without. Federal banking legislation has been updated to reflect those changes more often than has the legislation governing loan and trust companies. The federal Bank Act has been revised and adapted to new realities every 10 years; the latest revisions were made in 1980. But federal loan and trust comany legislation has existed for 54 years without revision. Provincial laws for trusts (two-thirds of all trust companies are provincially registered) are equally antiquated. Ontario's trust company legislation hasn't been overhauled since 1912. The laws in most provinces are modelled on Ontario legislation and are also outdated. Similarly, the provincial regulations that govern investment dealers, which are enforced by provincial security commissions, are in various states of disrepair.

But insurance legislation has suffered from unsurpassed neglect. The federal Canadian and British Insurance Companies Act has had only minor revisions since it was passed in 1932. In 1948, insurers were allowed to invest in real estate under a so-called "basket clause"; in the 1960s another revision was made to permit life insurers to sell mutual funds; in 1970, life insurers were given the power to own some types of subsidiaries under certain restrictions.

Since 1980, federal and provincial lawmakers have undertaken a flurry of studies and made various proposals for legislative change in an appallingly belated attempt to catch up with the new realities of finance.[1] In the meantime, the

[1]The various federal committees and reports included: (1) A discussion paper on revision of the Trust Companies Act and the Loan Companies Act released by the

members of the Four Pillars have been engaged in an unseemly scramble to steal business from each another.

## What the Insurers Want from the Regulators

No members of the financial industry have cried foul louder
about the need for new rules than the life insurers. For the
past five years, they have mounted a well co-ordinated campaign to persuade federal and provincial legislators. Much of
the work has been done by the industry lobby group, the
Canadian Life and Health Insurance Association (CLHIA),
which has issued various position papers in the past three
years. The individual efforts of insurance executives, some of
whom, such as Sun Life chairman Tom Galt, have considerable influence in Ottawa, have also helped.

In a nutshell, the life insurers want to be freed to better
compete with other types of financial institutions for consumer

federal Department of Insurance in July 1982; (2) a discussion group on financial
institutions formed in 1984 by then minister of state for finance Roy Maclaren; (3) a
study by the federal Finance Department entitled "The Regulation of Canadian
Financial Institutions: Proposals for Discussion" (otherwise known as the Green
Paper), which was issued in April 1985 by then minister of state for finance Barbara
McDougall; (4) a June 1985 report by a committee (chaired by investment firm
executive Robert Wyman) called "The Final Report of the Working Committee on
the Canada Deposit Insurance Corporation (CDIC)"; (5) a study issued in November 1985 by the House of Commons Committee on Finance, Trade and Economic
Affairs (chaired by Conservative MP Donald Blenkarn) on the proposals contained
in the Green Paper and the CDIC report; (6) a May 1986 report by the federal
Senate Committee on Banking, Trade and Commerce on the Green Paper and the
Blenkarn committee's recommendations; and, finally (7) the 1986 report of an
inquiry headed by Mr Justice Willard Estey into the collapse in September 1985 of
the Canadian Commercial and Northland banks.

There have also been several provincial efforts, including the following: the
Ontario Securities Commission Report on the investment industry in February
1985, and the Ontario Task Force on Financial Institutions headed by University of
Toronto professor Stefan Dupré, which reported in December 1985. Quebec
passed a new Insurance Act (Bill 75) expanding the powers of Quebec-registered
insurance companies in June 1984, and new Quebec legislation for trust companies is pending. The Ontario legislature, for its part, is considering a new Loan
and Trust Corporations Act. The other provinces are, for the most part, sitting on
the sidelines.

dollars. They crave a world where they can lend money to, and take deposits from, consumers—or at least a world where they can control trust or banking subsidiaries to do the same thing. Visions of automated teller machines (ATMs) bearing the logo of, say, Sun Life or Mutual Life are dancing through their heads. The insurers also want to be able to branch out into a host of other previously forbidden areas. They have petitioned the federal government for the right to act as trustees empowered to hold and administer death benefit proceeds and the funds of pension plans and savings plans (non-annuity and non-life RRSPs). If they had their druthers, the mutual insurers would also have the power to issue preferred shares and bonds to raise capital (stock companies already have this power). Insurers of both types also want to be able to sell Canada Savings Bonds and other federal, provincial and municipal bonds. To complete the picture, they want broad powers to sell services and products—such as GICs—on behalf of other financial institutions in return for fat fees.

Apparently reasoning that they might as well ask for the moon and see what happens, life insurers have also asked Ottawa for the power to create or acquire subsidiaries in *any* lawful business activity, providing that such investments in total do not surpass 15 per cent of an insurer's assets. Quebec-based insurers already have such broad diversification powers, as do insurance companies in New York State. In case the federal legislators prove more cautious than their Quebec or New York counterparts, the CLHIA has proposed a fall-back position. It has suggested that if the government doesn't agree that insurers should be able to set up subsidiaries in any line of business, then the current restrictions which limit insurers' holdings in other corporations to 30 per cent and forbid insurers from owning life insurance subsidiaries should be amended to permit insurers to have subsidiaries in any area of the financial services industry. That would make trust companies fair game for takeovers by insurers. They would also be able to acquire a stake in investment dealers, although provincial laws in all jurisdictions but Quebec place limits on outside ownership in the investment industry. When it comes to powers of diversification, the mutual companies have the biggest beefs. Stock life insurers are allowed to have a parent, an upstream holding company. These parent holding companies—such as Lonvest in the case of London Life, Power Financial in the case of Great-West and Crown Financial in the case of Crown Life—have been able to buy up trust, real estate, and property and casualty companies while mutual insurers have looked on in envy. At the very least, mutual insurers want to be able to set up holding companies to enable them to diversify as well. The CLHIA has proposed that both stock and mutual companies should be able to create either an upstream or a downstream holding company. On an ownership chart, the upstream holding company would appear as the parent of the life insurer; the downstream holding company would appear below the life insurer, which would be the parent company.

### What the Insurance Industry Will Get

In the main, the life insurers will get what they want. If the recommendations of the Finance Department's Green Paper of 1985 and the subsequent proposals of the House of Commons Committee on Finance, Trade and Economics are any indication, the industry will be giving itself a collective slap on the back when the federal government finally gets around to revising the laws governing financial institutions in the fall of 1986. To the delight of the industry, both federal studies endorsed the idea that insurers should have—in legal jargon—"the powers and capacity of a natural person". That means that they should have the right to sell a bouquet of financial products hitherto forbidden to them. It is possible that insurance companies will be empowered to administer estate proceeds (a change proposed by the Blenkarn committee) or offer business loans (perhaps through an affiliated Schedule C bank as recommended in the Green Paper). Both federal reports also endorsed the idea that insurance companies should be legally empowered to network products, which was described as a means of increasing consumer choice and enhancing competition in the marketplace. In the future, insurance companies, backed by multimillion dollar advertising campaigns, will be in the front lines of the race to lure consumer savings.

The Green Paper suggested that mutual insurance companies should be able to diversify through downstream holding companies into any Canadian-regulated financial institution. (Laurentian Mutual, a Quebec-based insurer, has already formed a downstream holding company according to the provisions of Quebec's insurance regulations.) Stock companies would be legally empowered to form upstream holding companies which would have similar diversification powers. (This would simply legitimize the existence of Trilon Financial and Power Financial.)

The Blenkarn committee was even more generous. It recommended that both stock and mutual insurance companies be free to diversify through either downstream or upstream holding companies into any lawful business (with certain quantitative restrictions).[2] In this regard, the Blenkarn committee's

---

[2]The committee concluded that it is often advantageous for small and medium-sized financial firms to be owned by only one or a few shareholders who are willing to put up the capital to fund the company's growth. In the case of larger financial institutions, however, the committee concluded that concentration of ownership should be limited. It therefore proposed ownership limits for financial institutions depending on their asset size:
• companies with less than $10 billion in domestic assets could be 100 per cent owned by a single shareholder
• companies with between $10 billion and $20 billion in domestic assets could be 75 per cent owned
• companies with between $20 billion and $30 billion in domestic assets could be 50 per cent owned
• companies with between $30 and $40 billion in domestic assets could be 25 per cent owned
• companies with more than $40 billion in domestic assets could be only 10 per cent owned

suggestions echoed the provisions of the Quebec Insurance Act passed in 1984.

However the diversification rules emerge from the legislative process, they will at least recognize the corporate structures already in place in the case of financial conglomerates and probably give insurance companies further freedom to engage in a number of lines of business through subsidiaries.

For anyone familiar with the poor track record of life insurance companies in giving the consumer a good deal, the prospect of their gaining added powers to offer a larger array of services and products or to diversify into a broader range of businesses is at first a sobering thought. These are the same companies that for years offered poor rates of return on badly dated products (many companies still do). But then, perhaps the more the insurance companies get involved in the real world of marketing, the vicissitudes of competition will force more of them to place a greater priority on the interests of consumers, rather than on those of agents who want products that will make them the most in commissions, and actuaries whose conservatism when it comes to product pricing has been excessive.

### A Breeding Ground for Abuse

Throughout the process of formulating its new laws, the federal government has insisted that it is not *deregulating* the financial industry—that is a nasty word, considering the recent failures of trust companies, banks and property and casualty insurers. Consumer protection and solvency are the watchwords of edgy politicians on Parliament Hill. Indeed, the major thrust of the various proposals for reform of the system is the need to reduce to a minimum the potential for abuse of power by financial service companies and their owners, management or boards. The insurance fraternity has to accept the idea that increased freedom in some areas will come hand in hand with beefed up regulatory powers for Ottawa.

By introducing new measures to keep corporate power-brokers in check in the financial industry, the federal government sees itself as cleaning out the Augean stables of finance, which are already littered with past abuses—a Herculean task to be sure. On the other hand, in reacting negatively to some of the government's proposals, the insurance industry portrays itself as a sort of modern-day Prometheus, the poor fellow in Greek myth who was chained to a rock while a vulture (read "government") pecked at his body.

## Self-Dealing

In the list of major threats to the solvency of a financial institution, self-dealing is at the top. With the emergence of financial conglomerates and the trend toward giving institutions broader powers of diversification, self-dealing is becoming increasingly commonplace. Some forms of self-dealing are quite harmless. For example, many companies can achieve significant cost savings by sharing administration, data processing or policy-design services with subsidiaries or with other members of the same financial conglomerate. As well as increasing profits, these shared services, theoretically, can help lower the cost of products and services to the public. Then, too, conglomerates like Trilon are encouraging subsidiary companies to purchase the services of sister firms. As pointed out in Chapter 7, London Life, for example, can hire the real estate management or appraisal services of Royal LePage for its commercial real estate investments. This is a pretty grey area. At present, London Life's shareholders and policyholders must rely on the judgement of business conduct review committees in the Trilon group to ensure that such transactions are fair. (The Blenkarn committee recommended that these review committees be established in all companies, provided that they be made up of outside directors.)

In the case of property and casualty companies, a lot of squeaky-clean self-dealing goes on. The industry is dominated by foreign-owned firms, and these insurers regularly place part of their reinsurance with their foreign parents in a completely safe and above-board fashion. But when a Canadian-based general insurer enters into reinsurance agreements with off-shore affiliates which are not licensed or regulated by Canadian authorities, Ottawa's regulators have not been able to check whether the funds are being used properly or whether the offshore reinsurer is even financially solvent. Ottawa's new laws will circumscribe this sort of activity by limiting the amount of insurance general companies can cede to unregistered, offshore reinsurers (see Chapter 12).

But past abuses concerning self-dealing in the insurance and trust businesses have the regulators most alarmed. In the distant past, the insurance industry was a prime offender in the area. Take, for example, the case of Sun Life in the late 1800s, when the company suffered because of the disastrous investments it made in two companies in which Sun Life's president and some directors had a personal interest. In recent decades, the insurance industry's record has been relatively clean in this regard because of federal laws which provide that an insurer cannot invest in or lend money to a shareholder who has more than a 10 per cent interest in the insurer. Likewise, the insurer cannot invest in or lend to a company in which a common owner has more than a 10 per cent interest. (This rule does not sit well with London Life, which has complained that it cannot invest in other companies in the Brascan fold, that is to say, 5 per cent of the companies in the TSE 300 index.)

But there is nothing in current law to prevent the owner of an insurance company from forcing it to buy assets of questionable value from another company which he owns. In recent years, for example, the owner of a western-based life insurance company saddled it with a slew of oil and gas properties which another of his companies was trying to get rid of. Robert Hammond, the federal superintendent of insurance was not amused. But there was nothing he could do about it. Ottawa should close this loophole in the law by giving federal regulators the power to review such deals and block them.

It is the trust industry, however, that can take the blame for current concerns over self-dealing. Recent failures in Ontario have been rife with instances of the problem. Astra Trust Co. of Niagara Falls failed in 1980 after customer funds were funnelled into high-risk real estate and mining operations, some of which were partly owned by Astra officers. Astra president Carlo Montemurro was convicted, along with three other Astra officials, of defrauding about 320 depositors of $12 million. After the failure of the Argosy Financial Group of Canada Ltd. in the same year, company president David Carnie and three other Argosy officers were given prison terms for, among other things, investing depositors' money in ventures in which Argosy officers had an interest.

The trust company debacles created public fear about self-dealing abuses. But that fear turned into outright paranoia early in 1986 amid a blaze of publicity over a controversial trust company takeover. In April, Imasco Ltd., a Montreal-based tobacco and retailing conglomerate, launched a $2.5 billion takeover bid for Genstar Corp., a Vancouver-based financial services, real estate and building materials company, which owned 99 per cent of Canada Trustco. Immediately, opposition politicians, government backbenchers and banking industry spokesmen decried the deal, pointing out that it raised the possibility that a large, non-financial company like Imasco could direct a subsidiary trust company like Canada Trust to make investments that might not be in the interests of its depositors. This, they justifiably pointed out, would be self-dealing in one of its worst forms. (Long-standing federal laws prevent a trust company from making loans to its parent or other subsidiaries of the parent.)

One of the most outspoken critics of the deal was Robert MacIntosh, president of the Canadian Bankers' Association. He warned that depositors' funds are placed at greater risk when trust and insurance companies are owned by non-financial institutions because "these conglomerates provide a fertile breeding ground for self-dealing."[3] MacIntosh, although hardly an impartial observer, was right. The greatest danger is that the parent industrial company could use a trust or life insurance subsidiary as a cash cow to fund its operations.

But the most potent opposition to the Imasco deal came from a group of Tory backbenchers, particularly the members of the Commons Committee on Finance, including MPs Don Blenkarn and Paul McCrossan. They urged Barbara McDougall, the minister of state for finance, to block the take-over using powers contained in new trust and loan company legislation, which, coincidentally, was tabled just after Imasco announced its bid. That legislation gives Ottawa the right to review and roll back any transactions involving more than 10 per cent of a trust company. Even Robert Hammond, the superintendent of insurance, entered the fray, stating before the Commons Committee on Finance: "If I had my druthers, I'd prefer that financial institutions be completely independent of non-financial institutions."

In the end, a compromise of sorts was arranged by McDougall before she permitted the takeover to proceed. McDougall managed to quiet dissident Tory backbenchers by obtaining a pledge from Imasco that it would not engage in any self-dealing with Canada Trust and would not place any Imasco directors

---

[3]Federal law stipulates that no single shareholder can own more than 10 per cent of a chartered bank; the bankers have long held that the same limit should be placed on other financial institutions.

on the board of Canada Trust. Imasco, she also told the Commons, understands that it might be required to sell off all or part of its holdings in Canada Trust under financial legislation to be introduced in the fall of 1986. McDougall did not go so far as to suggest that the new legislation would indeed impose ownership restrictions on trust and other financial companies. In an interview she said she was "keeping her options open" on the matter of ownership rules. Of course, any unguarded comments on McDougall's part would have sent the stock of Imasco and other conglomerates with control of both non-financial and financial subisidiaries—such as Brascan and Power Corp.—into a tailspin. McDougall did suggest, however, that the agreement Imasco made regarding self-dealing could serve as a model for provisions in the fall legislative overhaul.

Before the Imasco/Canada Trustco furor had died down, several controversial examples of self-dealing became public. In April 1986, Canada Trustco chairman Mervyn Lahn disclosed that Genstar Corp. had engaged in some non-arm's-length transactions with Canada Permanent, a trust subsidiary, between 1981 and 1982. (Genstar bought Canada Trustco in the fall of 1985 and then merged Canada Permanent's operations into Canada Trustco's.) In a press interview, Lahn said he had learned that nine months after Genstar had bought Canada Permanent in 1981 for $288 million, three transactions took place, in which Genstar sold $211 million in property and equipment to Canada Permanent. Critics immediately suggested that Genstar used the deals to recoup the money it paid for Canada Permanent. The revelation sparked the House of Commons Committee on Finance to take the unprecedented step of issuing formal summonses, like a court of law, requesting appearances by two Genstar executives; by chief executives of Brascan and two other companies controlled by Peter and Edward Bronfman, Trilon and Great Lakes Group; as well as by executives of Olympia & York Developments. Explained committee member Paul McCrossan: "We want to examine the extent, size and implications of self-dealing."

Before the Commons committee, Genstar chairman Angus MacNaughton and president Ross Turner denied suggestions that the transactions were somehow designed to finance the purchase of Canada Permanent.

The executives of Brascan and its sister companies also came in for some grilling before the committee. The MPs were particularly interested in a 1986 share transaction in which Great Lakes Group, which acts as a merchant banker for Bronfman-controlled companies, collected a $2 million fee for helping to sell a $102 million Trilon share issue to major Trilon shareholders. Since the shares were to be bought by the major shareholders Brascan and Olympia & York (after approval by their boards), Commons committee members thought Great Lakes undertook very little risk in the transaction. "I think the fee was unwarranted," said Commons committee member Bill Attewell. "I really fail to see any risk in this deal at all." Trilon president Melvin Hawkrigg countered the criticisms, however, by pointing out that the other investment dealers who formed a group with Great Lakes to sell the Trilon shares would not agree to the proposed $30-a-share price until Great Lakes agreed to buy 1.7 million of the total 3.4 million shares. The shares would have sold for less than $30 without Great Lakes' involvement, said Hawkrigg. He also pointed out that Great Lakes would have been at risk if the market rate for Trilon shares had dropped.

In a similar transaction in April 1986, Brascan issued $10 million worth of shares at $25 each, with half of the shares being taken up by Great Lakes for resale to Brascan's parent company, Brascan Holdings Ltd. Great Lakes collected a commission of $5 million on the sale. Once again, Brascan officials defended the transaction on the grounds that the participation of Great Lakes in the deal ensured a higher share price. But Brascan minority shareholders were not greatly appeased by the explanations. At the company's annual meeting in late April, several of them complained that paying fees to one Bronfman-owned company for placing the stock with a third Bronfman-owned company reduced the potential dividend income available to minority shareholders of the companies issuing the shares.

Self-dealing is like a case of eczema that won't go away. In its most innocuous forms it is nothing more than a slight itch that causes few problems. In its more virulent form it threatens to spread perniciously. Some medical attention is required.

Financial executives, of course, hope that the medicine contained in new federal legislation will be relatively weak. Says Hawkrigg: "It would be a tragedy if self-dealing or inter-company dealings are absolutely prohibited, particularly when transactions are done at a market rate." Those views are echoed by Michael Burns, chairman of Crown Life and president of its parent, Crownx. "I sincerely believe there has to be a method for self-dealing," he says. For instance, Burns points out that if Crown Life's real estate division makes an investment in a nursing home, there is no reason why Extendi-care, Crownx's nursing home subsidiary, should not be hired by Crown Life to manage that facility. Burns adds the proviso that any such transactions should be scrutinized by a corporate conduct committee made up of independent company directors.

To prevent self-dealing abuses the Green Paper recommended a complete ban on self-dealing, except in a few minor exceptions. That action, the Blenkarn committee concluded, would be a case of overkill. For one thing, it would deprive financial holding companies from achieving any useful degree of efficiency and integration within their subsidiaries. For example, sister companies would not be allowed to cut costs by sharing common data processing facilities.

There is no simple, practical way of coping with the problem of self-dealing. In general, a complete legislative ban, backed by fines, would involve a too heavy-handed interference by the government in the affairs of business. But the government should pass laws which impose a selective ban on self-dealing. Subsidiary companies should not be permitted to buy the shares of other companies with the same ultimate owner. Whether or not the shares were exchanged at a fair market price would be a continual source of controversy. The government should also ban self-dealing where a financial institution is being exploited by an owner intent on using it as a cash reservoir to buy up low-quality assets from another company he owns; and especially where the solvency of the financial institution is threatened by a non-arm's-length transaction. Violations of these legislative provisions should be dealt with by the courts and subject to heavy fines. The courts should be empowered to roll back the offending transactions and order restitution to affected parties.

For the free market system in Canada to function well, there has to be a certain degree of trust between the government and business—trust that in most cases, business executives will act honestly. In some cases, the scrutiny of business conduct review committees made up of independent directors will have to be the main watchdogs charged with ensuring that the interests of minority shareholders or policyholders are not abused. By law, however, *all* transactions between related companies or between companies and their principals should be subject to review by these boards, not just the transactions that the managers or owners of the companies selected for vetting.

### Conflicts of Interest

Conflicts of interest arise every day in the running of financial institutions. They occur every time a company must choose between its own interests and those of a client on whose behalf it is acting or whom it is advising. The client doesn't necessarily suffer. A trust company, for instance, is in a conflict-of-interest situation when it decides to invest trust funds it administers into its own guaranteed investment certificates. Normally, that should not be a problem. But if the trust company finds itself with liquidity problems caused, say, by a run on its deposits, it might pump trust funds into its own securities or into deposit instruments like GICs. Ultimately the client who owns the trust funds could suffer serious losses.

Another example of a potentially dangerous situation is when a financial institution has made loans to a company and has also invested trust funds in it. If that other company ran into trouble, the financial institution would have to decide whether to invest more trust funds in the company to protect its loans or, conversely, to make further loans to the company to protect its investment.

Conflicts of interest form a snakepit full of problems for regulators. The most they can do is keep a close watch on the actions of companies that are either in trouble themselves or are involved with other companies that are in danger of failing. Probably the most naive stand the insurance industry has taken is its opposition to government proposals for consumer protection in cases of conflicts of interest. The Green Paper proposed the creation of a Financial Conflicts of Interest Office to investigate complaints from consumers and, where warranted, bring actions to court on the complainant's behalf. The CLHIA dismisses this idea brusquely. States the CLHIA: "The current remedies available to consumers for redress in cases of abuses of conflicts of interest [the legal system] are totally adequate and need not be expanded." Further, warns the insurance lobby group: "A Financial Conflicts of Interest Office could try conflict of interest cases in the media before they reached the court and, as a result, unnecessarily damage a financial institution's reputation." That risk is not one to be lightly dismissed, since consumers tend to act like frightened sheep, fleeing from a financial institution at the slightest suggestion that it is in trouble with regulators. But given the fact that regulators have few means of detecting conflict-of-interest situations where consumer interests are trampled on, establishing a body to hear and act on consumers' complaints is the least that should be done to protect the public interest.

### Interlocking Directorships

Since 1967, banks have not been permitted by law to have directors who also sit on the boards of trust companies, and vice versa. This law was imposed, of course, to separate the business activities of banks and trusts and to help prevent conflict-of-interest situations from arising. Insurance companies have no such rules. In 1985, 10 of Sun Life's 17 directors served as directors of banks and 2 sat on the boards of trusts. Sun Life and other major insurers argue that to rule out interlocking directorships would be a needless and disruptive measure. But, surely, the dangers of too-cozy relationships between banks and trusts now exists between life insurance companies and their financial sisters. Insurers, after all, are effectively in the deposit-taking business through annuities and are clamouring for the right to sell still more products. In addition, the interests of banks and insurance companies are often interlinked. Many insurers have historic relationships with banks, such as Sun Life with the Bank of Montreal and Laurentian Mutual with the National Bank of Canada. These ties have been forged by common investment activities. Then, too, insurers often have deals with bankers under which the insurers automatically provide insurance on the lives of consumers who take out bank loans. The consumer has no choice in the matter. The bank manager simply informs him that the terms of the loan include insurance on his life. The costs, of course, are included in the interest on the loan. This is a form of tied selling.

It should be stopped. Eliminating interlocking directorships between insurance companies and other institutions would serve to throw a little cold water on the clubby fraternity of the powerful sitting atop some of Canada's most important financial institutions and help to assuage justified consumer worries about excessive concentration of power in corporate Canada.

## Concentration of Power in Financial Services

Whatever measures are passed into law to combat abusive self-dealing and conflicts of interest, they will only amount to fingers in the dike if corporate concentration in Canada's financial service industry is allowed to proceed unchecked. The degree of power placed in the hands of a few is already considerable in each of the financial sectors. At the end of 1984, according to the federal Finance Department, the five largest chartered banks controlled 80 per cent of Canada's banking assets; the five biggest trust companies controlled 40 per cent of the assets held by all trust companies; the top five life insurers controlled 50 per cent of the life insurance industry's assets; and the five largest property and casualty companies had 20 per cent of that industry's assets. In the investment industry, the top five investment dealers accounted for 66 per cent of the industry's total capital.

But in all five types of financial service, competition is alive—if not always well. In each case, it is relatively easy for new firms to enter the business, a crucial test which economists use to measure the amount of competition in an industry. Only in the case of the banks is it plainly evident to any consumer that a more competitive attitude is needed; and it is coming. Trust companies offering deposit, mortgage and other lending services on a 12-hour-a-day, six-day-a-week basis have the staid old bankers sitting up and taking notice. Indeed, as the different types of financial service companies encroach on each other's territory, competition will only be increased.

There is a danger, however, that as takeovers and mergers accelerate in the future, power in the financial services industry will be even more concentrated among a few of the huge conglomerates and banks with the financial resources to force newcomers out of business and a penchant for engaging in other uncompetitive behaviour. Evidence suggests that acquisition-hungry financial conglomerates are playing a crucial role in the rationalization process. In May 1985, Lawson Hunter, the former director of investigation and research for the federal Combines Investigation Act released the results of a pertinent study in a speech to the Faculty of Law at the University of Toronto. Hunter measured the growing power of seven financial conglomerates between 1980 and 1983. The companies were Crownx, E-L Financial, First City, Investors Group, The Laurentian Group, Traders Group and Trilon. Hunter found that the total assets of these seven sisters of finance grew by 50 per cent between 1980 and 1983—that is, from $31 billion in 1980 to about $48 billion three years later. Canada's GNP grew by only 36 per cent (after inflation) in the same period. For the most part, noted Hunter, the conglomerates expanded by means of acquisitions, not through internal growth.

What are the likely effects of increased corporate concentration? The financial heavyweights could, for instance, restrict output and force up prices for their products and services. Without sufficient competition, these large players would likely become increasingly inefficient and wasteful, and that in turn would keep prices high for consumers. Dominant firms might also play hardball with other, smaller companies. For example, a parent company could instruct a financial subsidiary not to make a loan to a competitor of the parent. According to Bernard Ghert, president of Cadillac Fairview Corp. Ltd., who has publicly expressed fears about the prospect of increasing concentration of power in financial services, this sort of abuse has already happened. In 1986 he told the Vancouver Board of

Trade that he knew of one instance where a financial institution was instructed by executives of a parent non-financial company to refuse a loan to one of its competitors. Cadillac Fairview Corp. is a $3 billion company 50 per cent owned by Charles, Edgar, Minda and Phyllis Bronfman—cousins of Edward and Peter, who control Brascan—and 20 per cent owned by the Olympia & York Developments Limited. It is therefore ironic that Cadillac Fairview warned vehemently about the dangers of corporate concentration in financial services in its submission to the House of Commons Committee on Finance, Trade and Economic Affairs. Declared the August 1985 report: "In our view, Canadians have been insufficiently concerned about the "darker side" of the concentration of economic power. They appear to have been more concerned about the putative benefits of large-scale enterprise, particularly where such firms are believed necessary to compete in international markets."

If this were a perfect world, no single shareholder would be allowed to own more than 10 per cent of a financial institution such as a (stock) life insurance company or trust company, just as current laws impose a 10 per cent ceiling on any single investor's holdings in a bank. That would be the surest way to prevent unwanted forms of self-dealing, conflict of interest abuses and other unsavoury manipulations of power by financial powerhouses. Unfortunately, this is not a perfect world.

Apart from the banks, widely held financial institutions are a thing of the past in Canada. Men like Mervyn Lahn, the outspoken chairman of Canada Trustco, who has long called for a 10 per cent ownership limit on trust companies, might as well be shouting into the wind. What is more, the public alarm over Imasco's takeover of Canada Trustco came several years too late. It would hardly be fair if one company with industrial or manufacturing interests were barred from owning a financial institution when the government has turned a blind eye to similar holdings by the likes of Brascan and Power Corp.

Various journalists, the Consumers' Association of Canada and the federal New Democratic Party have called for the imposition of 10 per cent ownership limits for all financial institutions. They propose that the existing majority owners of financial institutions should be ordered to divest their holdings over a certain number of years. As well, in June 1986, the Blenkarn committee proposed that the financial conglomerates be required to divest all but 30 per cent of the holdings in individual finanical holdings. But this would be a Draconian measure, unjustified because it would be changing the rules of the game after it was already underway. As federal NDP finance critic Nelson Riis put it, trying to roll back existing ownership positions, which he favours, "is like trying to put toothpaste back in the tube." That route would also fail to recognize the fact that the present ownership pattern has evolved because federal and provincial legislators have been asleep at the switch. Should private enterprise be penalized for government neglect?

The solution lies elsewhere. As well as passing laws to crack down on managements that abuse their power, the federal government must use effective competition legislation to prevent mergers and acquisitions that will increase corporate concentration and decrease competition in the financial marketplace. The horses may be out of the barn, but they needn't be given the freedom to forage wherever they like. A competition bill passed in mid-1986 might serve the purpose. A replacement for a law passed in 1912, the new law created a competition tribunal composed of federal court judges and laypeople. Modelled after a similar system in the United Kingdom, the tribunal will report to Parliament on cases referred to it. More control of corporate concentration should also be possible because mergers and monopolies, formerly dealt with under criminal law, have been shifted to civil law. This should make convictions easier to obtain because the burden of proof is less onerous in civil than in criminal cases.

With an effective competition law to keep the excesses of acquisition-hungry corporations in check and with rigorous laws to deter harmful self-dealing and other abuses, Canada's financial system needn't become an arena where only the mighty prosper and the interests of consumers are ignored.

### Cures for the Insurance Industry's Ailments

To understand the major flaws in the way the insurance industry operates at present, one has to look beyond the issues of corporate concentration and competition policy. Those matters are germane to the industry's future evolution, but they shed little light on the insurers' poor record in the past. Many of the misdeeds of the property and casualty insurers relate to feverish over-competition rather than a lack of it. And the life industry's historical habit of proffering unattractive policies is mainly attributable to consumer naivety and outright confusion that has made the public easy marks for zealous salespeople.

### Potent Pills for the Property and Casualty Insurers

As Chapter 12 demonstrated, the property and casualty companies have regularly acted more like a school of cannibalistic piranhas than bloated whales. Reforms are necessary that would improve the way insurance companies do business with the public and prevent a recurrence of the insurance crisis that reached its apex in 1986.

*Financial Safeguards:* The general insurance industry's cyclical bouts of excessive cost cutting, combined with a flouting of sound reserve calculations—as well as the resultant high rate of company failures—can best be dealt with by tougher solvency regulations, the introduction of valuation actuaries, and higher capital start-up requirements. According to superintendent of insurance Robert Hammond, all of these measures will be contained in the upcoming amendments to the Canadian and British Insurance Companies Act.

*Policyholder Compensation Plans:* Commendably, one province at least has taken steps to set up a policyholder compensation plan to protect clients who hold policies with, or have claims owning from, failed general insurers. In February 1986, Monte Kwinter, Ontario's minister of consumer and commercial relations, introduced amendments to the provincial Insurance Act requiring general insurers to contribute to a common $10 million policyholder compensation fund that will provide consumers with a up to $200,000 in the event that they are left with outstanding claims after a general insurance company collapses. To obtain a licence to do business in Ontario, insurers will have to participate in the plan. Other provinces should either join the Ontario-created plan, as Kwinter has suggested, or form similar funds of their own with the participation of insurance companies active in their jursidictions.

*No-Fault Insurance:* As noted earlier, insurers have grossly exaggerated the increasing size and frequency of court claims in Canada and the United States and the role these factors played in precipitating the insurance crisis. In a well-orchestrated publicity campaign, Canadian insurance companies have cited large court awards in Canada such as the $6.3 million award for a Brampton youth rendered quadraplegic in a motorcycle accident, as evidence that Ontario in particular is becoming a "California of the North." The publicity campaign had considerable impact on public opinion. A Gallup Poll released in March 1986 showed that 33 per cent of those polled blamed escalating court awards for the insurance crisis. That is an unfortunate misconception. The insurers usually neglect to mention that not a penny has been paid in the Brampton case, since it is currently under appeal. Because of such appeal processes, compensation is often not paid for anywhere from 2 to 13 years. As the 1986 Ontario Task Force on Insurance concluded, Ontario is not becoming the California of the North. There are crucial differences between the Canadian and American court systems which guard against this development. They include the fact that Canadian tort cases are usually determined by a judge alone and not by juries, which arguably grant larger compensation awards to accident victims, as is the case in the United States. Furthermore, awards for pain and suffering, which comprise a large portion of personal injury awards in the United States, are limited by law in Canada to $184,000.

Despite the fact that the legal system has been unjustly blamed for the insurance crisis, there are strong arguments for taking the responsibility for awarding compensation to accident victims out of the hands of the courts and placing it in the hands of either government- or industry-run no-fault insurance plans. Under no-fault insurance, it does not matter who is to blame for an accident; victims are automatically compensated based on the extent of their injuries. Already, three provinces with government-run auto insurance—Manitoba, Saskatchewan and British Columbia—have no-fault auto insurance schemes in place. In Quebec, a government corporation handles personal injury auto insurance but not vehicle damage insurance. Quebec has a no-fault plan for personal injury compensation which does not permit victims to sue under any circumstances. The other provinces allow lawsuits under restricted conditions. The Ontario Insurance Task Force recommended that that province also implement a no-fault plan in which the private companies would compensate their policyholders for personal injuries regardless of whether they were at fault in an accident or not.

No-fault insurance makes sense. In the court system, victims must prove that the other party was at fault before they can receive an award. If the victim is unsuccessful, or if the victim is successful but the guilty party carries inadequate insurance, the victim will receive either no compensation or an inadequate award, even in spite of permanent disablement. The

Ontario Task Force on Insurance also reported that in provinces where the courts determine awards, more than 50 cents of every premium dollar paid to insurers can go to the administrative and legal costs of running the system. Only about 50 cents of each premium dollar collected by insurers is actually paid out in compensation, compared with 80 to 90 cents in no-fault systems. No-fault insurance, in short, should mean cheaper insurance for consumers. And there is no reason why no-fault insurance should apply only to automobiles. The optimal situation would be one in which victims of all accidents could be covered by no-fault insurance schemes.

*A Canadian Insurance Exchange:* The 1986 insurance crisis demonstrated just how vulnerable Canadian consumers and businesses are to the whims of international reinsurers. The crisis struck after a binge of competitive rate slashing in the early 1980s, in which general insurance companies and reinsurers ignored proper accounting methods and failed to set aside sufficient reserves to cover future claims. They were over-eager to take in as much money in premiums as possible in order to invest it at double-digit rates of return. But the fall in interest rates ruined their scheme. By 1986, insurance companies were running scared, raising rates and declining most risky types of liability insurance—even if the individual clients involved had never made a claim. Behind the scenes, reinsurance companies were also pulling in their horns, refusing to take many kinds of business from primary insurers. There was a sudden scarcity of insurance in Canada. The cost to clients for many types of insurance became exorbitant; some types of insurance were not available at all.

By January 1, 1987, the Ontario government hopes to have a new insurance exchange in place that should reduce the risk of a similar scarcity of insurance recurring in the future. Based in Toronto, the exchange would be an insurance market much like Lloyd's of London, in which investors would form syndicates (groups) to underwrite insurance risks. According to

Robert Hillborn, chairman of the exchange's implementation committee, the market should be able to start with about 20 syndicates of Canadian and foreign investors, with a total of $100 million in capital. Initially, the exchange will deal only in reinsurance, but the syndicates will later underwrite all types of general insurance. If successful, the exchange will increase the amount of capital available for insurance in Canada and help ensure that Canadians will not suddenly find themselves unable to find insurance at reasonable rates in the future.

*A Better Rating System for Auto Insurance:* There is no doubt that the discriminating rate classification system of insurance companies, which includes the policyholder's age, sex and marital status as criteria for setting premium rates, will soon go the way of the dodo bird. Already, in the provinces where government-run auto insurance is in place, these factors have been eliminated with no related increase in premiums for the majority of drivers. The private insurance industry is also currently improving its entirely inadequate system of keeping track of the driving records of individual drivers. In the past, it has been common for drivers with poor records simply to switch companies and lie about their records to receive better rates. If a central, computerized pool of information on the driving records of drivers was created, insurers could confidently base rates on the records of drivers rather than on whether they happen to be young or old, male or female, single or married. The computer pool would probably have to be run by each provincial government, as is the case in British Columbia.

The rating system could be further refined by introducing a *bonus-malus* system similar to that used by several European countries. Under this sytem, a driver is awarded points for each year he is not involved in an accident and, accordingly, receives discounts on his insurance premiums. He loses points for each accident, and these are deducted from his merit points. Once he has passed the break-even mark on the point scale, he begins paying a surcharge for his insurance. British Columbia has a variation of this rating system in place. Other provinces should follow suit.

*Unbundled Homeowner Policies:* There is too little flexibility in the standard homeowner insurance policies offered by general insurers. Either the provincial regulators, who are responsible for approving the content and form of these policies, or the insurers themselves should take steps to redesign policies so that the client has more choice as to the type and quantity of insurance he or she can buy. Consumers should be able to choose whether or not they want third-party liability coverage—for their swimming pool for instance. The automatic coverage for outbuildings like toolsheds or barns, which do not exist in most urban settings, should not be automatically included in policies. Straight fire insurance should be made more readily available to those who desire it. In the cases where the homeowner has a high-ratio mortgage, he should not have to obtain insurance equal to value of the mortgage, since this means that his backyard, which cannot be burned down or stolen, will be covered, along with his home. At present, as Helen Anderson of the Consumers' Association of Canada has pointed out, homeowners' policies are "indigestible lumps" from the point of view of the consumer. They should be separated into bite-size pieces. (The same can be said for the standard liability policies offered to small businesses. Often these policies have a totally unnecessary robbery and hold-up coverage built in. That may be useful for some small business people, like storeowners, but it is unnecessary for many types of businesses such as consultants or freelance journalists.)

## Coping with Life's Shortcomings

There is a joke in insurance circles that goes like this: "What's the definition of an actuary?" Answer: "An actuary is someone who didn't have enough personality to make it as an accountant." Part of the explanation for the conservative, risk-averse character of the life insurance industry can be traced to the pre-eminent role that Canada's more than 1,200 life actuaries have played in every aspect of the insurance companies' affairs. Actuaries are cerebral, low-key, often likeable people who like to get lost in mathematical mind-games, not bruise themselves in the cut and thrust of the business world. Yet, remarkably, they have long dominated the executive ranks of the life insurance industry. Marketing types rarely make it to the top. Critics such as Rod McQueen, author of *Risky Business*, a book on Canada's insurance industry, are right when they say that actuaries should be ushered out of the boardrooms and into the backrooms where they belong. The companies that seem to be making the most progress in updating their operating practices have all, to a greater or lesser degree, brought in new management blood from outside the industry's ranks or relied on executives with a background in marketing to introduce change. But it is an oversimplification to suggest that banishing actuaries to the stage wings will somehow rejuvenate the life industry. Instead, its flaws must be dealt with on a systematic basis, both through the regulatory process and through decisive action by the insurers themselves.

*Putting the Consumer First instead of Last:* The failure of life insurance companies to respond adequately to consumer needs from time immemorial is a puzzling problem. One might expect that the life insurance companies' record of offering highly priced products with uncompetitive rates of return is due to some sort of near-monopoly power—such pricing practices often are.

There is no denying that the life insurers are a close-knit fraternity that has adopted a fortress mentality to fend off criticisms. Only a leading few, particularly those profiled in this book, are making an attempt to adapt to the modern realities of commerce by paying more attention to consumer needs than to actuaries' mumblings. But various academic

studies in Canada (as well as in the United States) have concluded that there is not an overconcentration of power in the life
insurance industry, since there is a multitude of large and small
companies in the business. Why, then, the appalling record?

A 1983 study by the federal Ministry of Consumer and Corporate Affairs, entitled *Regulation of the Canadian Life Insurance
Market: Some Issues Affecting Consumers*, offers some insights into
the issue. The scholarly study reported some devastating findings about the prices and rates of return offered by life insurance policies in Canada. Between 1960 and 1980, the researchers
found that nominal (after accounting for inflation) long-term
interest rates in Canada rose from about 5 per cent to more
than 10 per cent. In the same time period, the rates of return
offered on the savings portion, or cash value, of participating
life insurance policies (in which the policyholder is paid yearly
dividends) rose to a meagre 3.2 per cent. The rate of return on
non-participating policies stayed in the 2 per cent range. The
study's findings are a scathing indictment of the insurers' habits
over two decades. In fact, using an economic model, the researchers found that in 1980, premiums on non-participating
policies were about 40 per cent above what could have been
expected in a competitive market.

The study placed part of the blame for the low rates of
return and high premium charges on federal regulators who
stipulated that only certain interest rates and mortality tables
could be used by insurers to compute their policy reserves.
Those requirements were so conservative that the insurers
built up reserves far in excess of what was needed to meet
future policyholder claims. (It should be noted that the insurance industry didn't complain about this lucrative state of affairs, and that several upstart companies, including Maritime
Life, offered current interest rates on new money policies despite the federal regulations.)

But the researchers also observed that after 1977, when
Ottawa freed companies to set rates of return and mortality

rates based on their own experience, premiums did not fall as might have been expected. This led the researchers to conclude that prices in the life insurance industry were as high as they might be in a monopoly situation, where a handful of firms controls the market, because consumers were so confused about life insurance policies that they couldn't comparison shop. Therefore, there was no pressure on insurers to price their policies competitively.

Since the Consumer and Corporate Affairs study was completed, some insurers have raised their rates of return on traditional whole life policies by a few percentage points. Many have also introduced interest-senstive new money or universal life products that pay close attention to market rates in order to staunch the flow of consumer dollars to more competitive investment products. But there are still wide discrepancies in the cost of similar policies offered by different insurers. As economists have pointed out, such gaps should not exist in a competitive market, where insurers fear losing business to more aggressive competitors. Evidently, innovations such as non-smokers' rates, new money and universal life policies, that have been introduced by small, usually foreign-owned companies, have not been enough to shake the industry out of its state of torpor. Insurance company executives like to say that there is little or no difference in policy costs, but that is simply not true. (See Appendix D.) Many executives and agents also told the author, in the course of his research, that they are not interested in selling to consumers who are worried about price comparisons rather than the quality of the product. These comments only reflected the extent to which many insurance people are removed from the real world of commerce.

Traditionally, life insurance company managers have placed more emphasis on what agents want than on what consumers want. Says John Gardner, senior vice-president of Sun Life: "Competition in this business is a very funny thing. When you say competition you immediately think of the customer looking at a half a dozen companies and comparing the products to see which ones he likes.... In life insurance it doesn't work that way. The competition is felt at the level of the agent or broker." According to Gardner, life insurance sales pitches succeed or fail primarily as a result of the agent's ability to establish a relationship of trust with the prospective customer. Says Gardner: "The client is usually much more tuned into the relationship with the agent and is saying, 'What this man is telling me makes sense.'" As Gardner sees it, the role of the company is to make sure that the agent has a range of products in his briefcase so that he doesn't get caught off base if a customer requests a policy he hasn't got. Put more bluntly, Gardner's explanation underlines the fact that consumers lack sufficient knowledge to shop for life insurance policies the way they do for a stove or car.

The onus is on the industry to start putting the consumer's needs first, just as any healthy business does. Some companies— Crown Life, for example—have adopted a new so-called "market driven" approach to selling insurance which stresses the desires of the buying public, rather than the latest whims of agents. More companies should follow suit. But the onus is also on the public to buy insurance more wisely.

*How to Buy Life Insurance:* There is little likelihood that, in the future, life insurers will suddenly be gripped by a competitive urge and start slashing insurance costs to consumers. True, many companies now offer interest-sensitive products. But at present the only intense competition within the insurance world is taking place in annuity products, where margins have truly been cut to the bone. As long as consumers leave their fates in the hands of an agent intent on selling one company's products, there will be no real pressure on insurance companies to price their life products more competitively.

To correct this state of affairs, consumers should be more ambitious when it comes to buying insurance. At the very least, they should become familiar with the different types of policies available. Apart from this book, there are very few objective sources in Canada that describe the flaws and merits of different policies. But a comprehensive listing of Canada's life insurance companies and the prices of the products they offer is available in a handbook entitled *Life Insurance Tables*, which costs less than $20 and is published annually by Stone & Cox Limited, a Toronto-based publisher. The more technical parts of this handbook can be ignored. The most important information is the premium rates that companies charge for their policies.

The number one rule for buying insurance, of course, is: Don't talk to only one agent. Countless consumers have been sweet-talked into buying policies that are either too expensive or inappropriate for their needs by charming agents who often happen to be the friend of a friend. (At one point in his life, the author fell victim to an agent who was a brother of a close acquaintance. The agent was pushing one and only one product that his company had just brought out—a 20-year endowment plan for children. Not knowing much about insurance at the time, the author was talked into buying the policy for his new-born daughter. Later in life, when he realized he was paying very high premiums for very little insurance, the author promptly cashed in the policy and vowed never to be duped again.)

Before buying insurance, consumers should shop around. The first question to ask is how much has to be paid in premiums each month for how much insurance. Agents might try to explain away high premium levels by saying that the cash surrender value of the policy builds up faster than it does in a competitor's product that has lower premiums. Ignore this argument. The purpose of insurance is protection, not savings. At any rate, the policyholder never receives the cash value unless he cashes the policy in.

Using this criterion, term insurance is the most attractive product. The old battle-cry of buy term and invest the difference still holds merit. But for those Canadians who don't think they can salt enough cash away in investments to obviate the need for insurance protection later in life (over age 50) when term becomes prohibitively expensive, another course of action might be advisable. It is important that young married couples with dependents and a mortgage or rent to pay buy enough term insurance to save the family from destitution should one of the household's wage-earners die. If they want to, they can prepare for old age by buying a much smaller whole life, new money, variable life or universal life product that will stay in force at a reasonable cost after term becomes too expensive. One caution, however: Stay away from participating whole life policies, which are still the mainstay of insurance companies' product life insurance lines but, as explained in Chapter 1, overcharge customers for insurance and then pay the money back in dividends at the discretion of the company. Never buy endowment policies or similar products that are "paid-up," that is, no further premiums are necessary after 10, 20, or even 30 years. In these policies, the company simply gets more of your money faster by charging high premium rates. Children and single people with no dependents arguably do not need insurance. The money could be more profitably invested elsewhere.

*Cleaning Up the Agents' Act:* The love of money—in the form of commission rates—is the root of most of the evil in the ranks of insurance agents. Being human, agents have found it to their advantage to push products, such as participating whole life insurance, which pay them the highest commission levels, and downplay products like term insurance that pay lower commissions. The higher remuneration for certain policies, however, is no accident. The companies use higher commission payments to encourage their field forces to stress policies that are more lucrative for the company because they bring in more premium income. The provincial governments, which are the watchdogs over the design, marketing and pricing of insurance policies, should amend their Insurance Acts to make it mandatory that agents reveal the commissions they earn on different policies to their prospective clients. Despite protestations from the industry, the Ontario government, in mid-1986, was taking steps to introduce such a provision.

Action must also be taken by either the industry itself or, if necessary, by provincial regulators, to stop the spread of rebating scams. As long as first-year commission rates can range anywhere from 150 to 500 per cent of first-year premium payments, the system will be ripe for abuse. Agents will continue devising schemes in which they simply give the client a cheque for the first-year premiums, mail in the policy application, then wait a couple of weeks for a hefty commission cheque from the company. Instead, so-called level commission rates, in which commission payments are spread more evenly over at least the first ten years of the policy's life, should be introduced universally. First-year commission rates plus production bonuses should not exceed 100 per cent of the first-year premium payments on a policy. New York State insurance law stipulates that commissions plus bonuses cannot exceed 95 per cent of premiums in the first year of the policy. That law, which has all but wiped out rebating scams in the state, should be emulated in Canada.

*The Role of the Regulators:* There have been glaring inadequacies in the way the supposed watchdogs of the insurance industry have carried out their duties. At the federal level, the insurance department, which is responsible for the financial solvency of federally regulated companies, has been partially hindered from taking decisive action in the case of failing general insurers by inadequate legislative powers. That should be remedied late in 1986 when the government adds muscle to the long arm of the law by strengthening the power of regulators to crack down on misbehaving companies. The new supervisory powers will include: the right to issue cease and desist orders to stop questionable practices; the power to appoint a curator to run a financially troubled insurance company pending the outcome of court actions by the company's management to prevent federal seizure of the operation; the authority to deem certain transactions as not arm's length; and the power to force the divestiture of prohibited investments or loans. But these additional regulatory powers must also be backed up by a more aggressive, adversarial approach on the part of federal regulators. As the Senate Committee on Banking, Trade and Commerce noted in its May 1986 report: "To a considerable degree, the recent problems in the financial sector appear to reflect not so much an inadequate range of regulatory powers as an inadequate exercise of existing powers. To the extent that this is the case, it is important that legislators do not react to recent events by endowing regulators with unnecessary and unwarranted powers."

The answer at the federal level, then, is not to make more and more power available to insurance regulators. The main problem has not been a question of legal authority or, for that matter, of person power: the insurance department currently has 36 full-time investigators and actuaries keeping watch over the life industry and 37 more to keep an eye on property and casualty insurers. The real need is for Insurance Department officials to take hold of the reins and start steering.

At the provincial level, government ministries are responsible for regulating the business practices of agents, the design of policies and the financial solvency of companies that are provincially, rather than federally, registered. Yet most provincial regulators—with the exception of those in Ontario and Quebec—have lacked either the will or the resources to police the insurance industry properly. British Columbia, for example, gets by with only about a dozen investigators to watch over the insurance, trust and investment industries. Manitoba watches over the dealings of about 4,000 insurance agents with a total staff of six. Earl McGill, Manitoba's superintendent of insurance, does not see his department as being an antagonist of the industry. "The essence of regulation," he says, " is that it should be effective without being overbearing." He prefers to use moral suasion and the power of suggestion to keep the industry in check rather than threatening wrongdoers with legal action when they misbehave. McGill realizes that he differs from his tough-minded counterparts in Ontario and Quebec in this regard. Arguably, however, abuse is so prevalent in the insurance industry that such a gentlemanly approach is outdated. Regulators should actively seek out illegal activities, not just react to them when they happen to come to their attention.

As far as regulation goes, there is also a need for a harmonization of the federal and provincial laws governing financial solvency in the insurance industry. Currently, the various federal and provincial superintendents of insurance are making an effort in this regard. Yet, government regulations alone cannot provide all the solutions to the insurance industry's woes.

### The Need for Greater Industry Self-Regulation

As the experience of the Registered Insurance Brokers of Ontario (RIBO) has shown, former insurance brokers are unsurpassed in their ability to ferret out illegal manoeuvrings in the property and casualty business. Having experience in the industry themselves, they are familiar with the sort of financial legerdemain and fradulent activities that can occur in the industry. RIBO has been a litmus test for self-regulation in the insurance industry—a test watched with interest in other provinces as well as in various U.S. states. In one regard, RIBO has had difficulties. Responsible for the financial solvency of Ontario brokers, it has had trouble with too many overdue financial reports from brokers. Yet, in its most important function— tracking down fraudulent and other illegal practices—RIBO has been an outstanding success. It is a model that should be followed in other provinces, not only in the general insurance field, but also in the life industry.

As already noted, CLHIA-sponsored surveys have revealed that insurance agents are held in low esteem by the public. The image of agents, in fact, remains mired somewhere between Willy Loman types and snake-oil salesmen. Based on RIBO's experience, a good way of cutting down on the illegal activities that have given agents a bad name would be to create self-regulatory bodies in each province that would be reponsible for the licensing, supervision and disciplining of agents. Created with legislative approval, each organization would have a board of directors made up of industry representatives and qualified lay people. They would oversee the affairs of the corporation, which would be funded by the industry, and they would sit on disciplinary committees to consider complaints against agents and conduct hearings. They would also have the power to revoke licences or levy fines. Criminal breaches of the law would be referred to the appropriate police authorities. Several hundred life insurance agents, who have already joined together in a group called the Life Insurance Agents and Brokers Association National (LIABAN), are studying the possibility of setting up a RIBO-type organization for life agents in Canada. Their main immediate goal is to eliminate the practice currently going on in all provinces, by which a life agent or broker must have his or her licence sponsored by a life insurance company. This step, they argue, would give them greater freedom to offer consumers a wide range of products and obviate the need for a salesperson to push the products of the company that sponsored his licence.

Already, there are industry-appointed bodies in British Columbia and Saskatchewan which handle the licensing of agents. (In most provinces, however, licences are still issued by the government.) These organizations could serve as a starting point for full-fledged self-regulatory bodies that would oversee the disciplining as well as the licensing of agents.

In the future, the insurance industry will play a more prominent role in the financial services marketplace and likely in the public's awareness. The general industry has already had experience with intense media attention because of the recent liability crisis. Deftly, it managed to unfairly deflect most of the blame for the crisis onto the court system. Soon, life insurance companies will share the media spotlight as they diversify through acqusitions and broaden their product lines. The mutual companies will find the change most dramatic. With acquisition-minded executives at their helm and vast pools of capital in their vaults, they will no longer be brushed off as impotent adversaries by other financial institutions. Some of the companies profiled in this book will be on the leading edge of the transformation of the industry's role. But as the insurers are subjected to increased media attention, their flaws will be exposed as never before. The challenge for insurance companies is to move quickly to cure the industry's ills and, in so doing, rid themselves of old stigmas. Fear of misfortune will always be an integral part of buying and selling insurance. But with a well-regulated, competitive industry and a well-informed public, it need not be a source of exploitation.

# APPENDICES

## APPENDIX A

### *The 15 Largest Life Insurers in Canada (1985)*

| Rank by Assets | Assets ($'000) | Premium Income ($'000) | Company (head office) |
|---|---|---|---|
| 1 | 16,425,715 | 2,602,996 | Manufacturers Life Insurance Co. (Toronto) |
| 2 | 15,959,527 | 2,983,333 | Sun Life Assurance Co. of Canada (Toronto) |
| 3 | 10,801,022 | 2,319,703 | Great-West Life Assurance Co. (Winnipeg) |
| 4 | 7,148,828 | 1,329,386 | Mutual Life Assurance Co. (Waterloo, Ont.) |
| 5 | 6,914,602 | 1,231,526 | Canada Life Insurance (Toronto) |
| 6 | 6,751,510 | 1,670,724 | Confederation Life Insurance Co. (Toronto) |
| 7 | 6,390,300 | 1,045,000 | London Life Insurance Co. (London, Ont.) |
| 8 | 5,936,742 | 1,734,978 | Crown Life Insurance Co. (Toronto) |
| 9 | 4,127,872 | 493,690 | Standard Life Assurance Co. (Montreal) |
| 10 | 3,709,522 | 569,328 | Metropolitan Life Insurance Co. (Ottawa) |
| 11 | 3,443,640 | 508,497 | Imperial Life Assurance Co. (Toronto) |
| 12 | 3,246,607 | 483,792 | North American Life Assurance Co. (Toronto) |
| 13 | 2,285,576 | 379,160 | Prudential Insurance Co. of America (Toronto) |
| 14 | 2,178,792 | 453,886 | Prudential Assurance Co. (Montreal) |
| 15 | 1,657,149 | 363,286 | Excelsior Life Insurance Co. (Toronto) |

## APPENDIX B

### The 15 Largest General Insurers in Canada (1985)

| Rank by Net Premiums Written | Net Premiums Written* ($'000) | Underwriting Profit (loss)† ($'000) | Company (head office) |
|---|---|---|---|
| 1 | 493,412 | (115,914) | Royal Insurance Canada (Toronto) |
| 2 | 483,877 | (73,397) | The Co-operators General Insurance Co. (Guelph, Ont.) |
| 3 | 368,168 | (23,018) | Lloyd's, Non-Marine Underwriters (Montreal) |
| 4 | 288,747 | (54,702) | General Accident Assurance Co. of Canada (Toronto) |
| 5 | 280,991 | (52,315) | Travelers Canada (Toronto) |
| 6 | 277,765 | (37,028) | Economical Group (Kitchener, Ont.) |
| 7 | 259,949 | (38,088) | Phoenix Continental (Toronto) |
| 8 | 259,090 | (31,060) | Wawanesa Mutual Insurance Co. (Winnipeg) |
| 9 | 259,074 | (46,533) | Zurich Insurance (Toronto) |
| 10 | 247,370 | (30,199) | Allstate Insurance Co. of Canada (Toronto) |
| 11 | 242,319 | (36,217) | Commercial Union Assurance Group (Toronto) |
| 12 | 233,832 | (50,565) | State Farm Group (Toronto) |
| 13 | 230,932 | (53,329) | Dominion of Canada Group (Toronto) |
| 14 | 225,779 | (46,694) | Prudential Assurance Group (Montreal) |
| 15 | 201,397 | (32,835) | Guardian Insurance Co. of Canada (Toronto) |

*Source: Stone & Cox Limited*

*Net premiums written refers to premiums on insurance sold minus those on business ceded to reinsurers.

†Despite the underwriting losses, all of the companies except Travelers, Zurich, State Farm and Dominion of Canada made a profit after income from investments and other sources was taken into account.

## APPENDIX C

### The 10 Largest Reinsurers in Canada (1985)
*(All lines of reinsurance except life)*

| Rank by Net Premiums Written | Net Premiums Written* ($'000) | Underwriting Profit (Loss) in Canada ($'000) | Company (head office) |
|---|---|---|---|
| 1 | 122,459 | (3,437) | Munich Reinsurance Group (Toronto) |
| 2 | 64,219 | (259) | Canadian Reinsurance Group (Toronto) |
| 3 | 57,549 | (6,159) | Universal Reinsurance Group (Toronto) |
| 4 | 51,756 | (6,621) | Adriatic Insurance of Canada (Toronto) |
| 5 | 49,699 | (10,352) | General Reinsurance Corp. (Toronto) |
| 6 | 45,906 | (7,719) | American Re-insurance Co. (Toronto) |
| 7 | 35,961 | (8,265) | Mercantile & General Reinsurance Group (Toronto) |
| 8 | 34,398 | 297 | Gerling Global Reinsurance Co. (Toronto) |
| 9 | 34,274 | 1,523 | Quebec Mutual Reinsurance Association (Ste-Foy, Que.) |
| 10 | 33,593 | (5,971) | SCOR Reinsurance Co. of Canada (Toronto) |

*In the case of reinsurers, net premiums written refers to premiums on reinsurance sold minus those on reinsurance ceded to other reinsurers.

# APPENDIX D

## *A Comparison of Life Insurance Premiums*
*(Cost per $1,000 worth of insurance for males and females aged 35)*

### *Whole Life:*

| Company | Plan | Cost per $1,000*<br>Male nonsmoker<br>(smoker) | Female nonsmoker<br>(smoker) |
|---------|------|---------|---------|
| Canada Life | Executive Security (participating; rates for $10,000-$49,999 policies; add a $50.00 annual policy fee) | $19.67 ($21.69) | $19.37 ($20.37) |
| Crown Life | Select Ordinary Life (participating; rates for $25,000-$99,999 policies; add a $50.00 annual policy fee) | 18.73 (20.58) | 18.04 (18.94) |
| Laurentian Mutual | Whole Life (participating; rates for $5,000-$149,999 policies; add a $50.00 annual policy fee) | 11.75 (14.25) | 11.08 (12.48) |
| Metropolitan Life | Whole Life (participating; rates for $25,000 policy; for higher coverages deduct $1.00 for every $1,000 of insurance) | 15.12 (20.65) | 13.35 (18.35) |

*The reader should note that participating policies usually charge higher premiums than non-participating policies. That cost discrepancy is reduced over the life of the policy because participating policies pay annual dividends to the policyholder which can be taken as cash or used to buy more insurance. Also, some policies pay higher dividends than others. Then, too, the cash surrender value, which goes to the policyholder if he cancels or cashes in his policy, builds up faster in some policies than others. Still, the most important aspect of any insurance transaction is the cost per thousand dollars of insurance.

**Whole Life:** *(continued)*

| Company | Plan | Cost per $1,000 Male nonsmoker (smoker) | Female nonsmoker (smoker) |
|---|---|---|---|
| National Life | Ultralife (non-participating; cash value accumulates at new money interest rates; add a $75.00 annual policy fee) | $10.99 (14.93) | $ 8.98 (11.63) |
| New York Life | Whole Life (participating; rates for policies greater than $50,000) | 14.57 (15.53) | 12.78 (13.49) |
| Standard Life | Participator (participating; add a $40.00 annual policy fee) | 22.46 (25.01) | 21.58 (23.33) |
| Sun Life | Whole Life (participating; add a $42.50 annual policy fee) | 14.69 (16.05) | 13.91 (15.20) |

**Term Insurance:**

| Company | Plan | Cost per $1,000 Male nonsmoker (smoker) | Female nonsmoker (smoker) |
|---|---|---|---|
| Crown Life | Term 10 (10-year renewable convertible term; rates for policies of $100,000 or more; add a $50.00 annual policy fee) | $1.48 ($2.34) | $1.12 ($1.65) |
| Maritime Life | 5-Year Term (renewable and convertible; rates for policies from $25,000 to $499,999; add a $75.00 annual policy fee) | 1.36 (2.45) | 1.13 (1.98) |

**Term Insurance:** *(continued)*

| Company | Plan | Cost per $1,000 Male nonsmoker (smoker) | Female nonsmoker (smoker) |
|---------|------|-----------------------------------------|---------------------------|
| North West Life | Term 5 (5-year renewable and convertible; rates for policies from $100,000 to $249,999; add a $40.00 annual policy fee) | $1.50 (2.83) | $1.33 (2.44) |
| Norwich Union | 5-Year Term (renewable and convertible; rates for first $100,000 coverage; add a $60.00 annual policy fee) | 1.60 (3.01) | 1.39 (2.57) |
| Prudential Insurance | 5-Year Term (participating; renewable and convertible; minimum policy size $100,000; add a $15.00 annual policy fee) | 2.27 (3.25) | 2.13 (2.46) |
| Standard Life | 5-Year Term (renewable and convertible; minimum policy size $50,000; add a $65 annual policy fee) | 1.19 (2.44) | 1.06 (1.63) |
| Sun Life | 5-Year Term (renewable and convertible; add a $55.00 annual policy fee) | 1.38 (2.29) | 1.17 (2.23) |
| Transamerica Life | 6-Year Term (renewable and convertible; rates for policies from $100,000 to $499,999; add a $50.00 annual policy fee) | 1.25 (2.50) | 1.10 (1.95) |

*Source: Stone & Cox Limited,* Life Tables (1986)

# Index